SOCIAL INEQUALITY

Classical and Contemporary Theorists

SOCIAL INEQUALITY
Classical and Contemporary Theorists

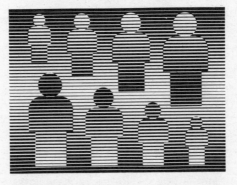

Edward G. Grabb

Holt, Rinehart and Winston of Canada, Limited Toronto

Canadian Cataloguing in Publication Data

Grabb, Edward G.
  Social inequality

Includes bibliographical references and index.
ISBN 0-03-921194-0

1. Equality.   2. Social classes.   3. Power (Social
sciences).   I. Title.

HT609.G72   305.5   C83-098533-6

Acquisitions Editor: Anthony Luengo
Developmental Editor: Brian Henderson
Illustrations: Mark Summers
Design and Graphics: Pronk & Associates

Printed in the United States of America

1 2 3 4 5   88 87 86 85 84

For Denise

PREFACE

This book has been something of a surprise for me. What began as a brief theoretical introduction for another project—an empirical account of inequality in Canadian society–has gradually evolved into a separate volume all its own. For, in retracing the ideas of early thinkers, and in examining the thoughts of more recent writers, I became increasingly convinced that students could benefit from a more thorough analysis and comparison of the central theorists in the field of social inequality. Hence, the present volume is a relatively detailed attempt to document, clarify, and evaluate the major perspectives on inequality that have emerged from classical and contemporary social theory.

One truth I have learned anew in writing this book is that it is impossible to please everyone. It seems inevitable, for example, that certain readers will argue too much has been attempted, while others will contend far more should have been done. Nevertheless, at the outset I should like at least to make my *intentions* clear. On the one hand, the book is meant to be more than a series of unconnected reports, summarizing who said what on the topic of social inequality; instead, I hope to show that many of the influential writers in this area, in addition to their important differences, sometimes reveal surprising parallels that point us in a broadly similar direction on the question of how to conceive of or understand social inequality. On the other hand, the book makes no pretensions to being a new synthesis of previous viewpoints, a completely novel outlook that will somehow revolutionize our thinking in this field; rather than break fresh ground, I have raked through the existing terrain and uncovered a limited set of themes and issues that most of the principal theorists, in varying degrees, have already emphasized. The end product is meant to be a summary picture of how structured inequalities may be conceived in modern societies, one that sets these themes and issues alongside one another in a more or less consistent fashion. I suggest that this is a useful strategy of presentation to adopt, one that may be especially helpful for new students of the topic, who need some coherent overview to keep in mind if they are subsequently to deal with the complexities and exceptions that invariably present themselves in any examination of sociological theory.

There are some additional points about the presentation that also require comment. It will be plain very early in the book that I have devoted considerable space to outlining and clarifying the ideas of Marx and Weber. Clearly, I disagree completely with those colleagues who claim that the views of these two men are by now too well known to justify more than a cursory review. On the contrary, it seems to me that a full appreciation of their perspectives is absolutely essential if we are to understand not only their own enormous contributions but their continuing influence on recent theorists as well. In order to underscore the pivotal importance of Marx and Weber, as well as to give students some sense of the origins of their ideas, I have also provided brief biographical sketches of both writers.

The claim that the thoughts of Marx and Weber have become common knowledge relates to another matter of concern to me in preparing this volume. One of the reasons I am skeptical of this claim is that Marx and Weber never used or espoused many of the ideas and concepts attributed to them by some of their subsequent interpreters. This is apparent from even a moderately close inspection of their original writings. Thus, to minimize wrongful attributions and other problems of this sort, I have relied heavily on the use of direct quotations and page references, not only from Marx and Weber, but from all the theorists examined in the text. Although some may see this as overdocumentation, I make no apologies for it. Such information on sources is useful for the interested reader and also reduces the frustration students sometimes feel from not knowing, for example, if it is Marx's own words or someone else's version of those words that is being expressed.

If there is an unexpected intruder among the writers reviewed here, it is probably Durkheim. While Durkheim is normally grouped with Marx and Weber as one of the three most important theorists in sociology, most reviewers do not consider his work relevant to the specific topic of inequality. Certainly, Durkheim's role is secondary in this regard, at least in comparison with the other two thinkers; nevertheless, Durkheim has rather more to say about social inequality than is commonly recognized and, furthermore, he provides a useful bridge between the early perspectives and the more recent structural-functionalist treatment of inequality in society. These reasons make it important that Durkheim be included.

The structural-functionalist perspective, of course, is itself of some significance, and I have tried to give it a fair hearing in the text. While it was once thought to be the principal alternative to a Marxist view of social inequality, it has increasingly fallen into disrepute and become a target for criticism by virtually all other camps. Still, this critical reaction is illuminating to review, especially since it was the start of the movement back toward Weber and Marx and to a revival of interest in debating and reworking the ideas of these two central figures.

This debate over the views of Marx and Weber continues even now and is a principal focus for the material presented in the latter part of the text. As one final point of clarification, I should note that, for obvious reasons, it is not possible to assess all the current theorists involved in this exchange. While most major writers are referred to, six have been selected for detailed discussion: Dahrendorf, Lenski, Poulantzas, Wright, Parkin, and Giddens. This choice may seem somewhat arbitrary; however, in what follows I shall endeavor to convince the reader that these six theorists capture the essential flavor and direction of current views on how social inequality is to be conceived and understood.

Perhaps the most pleasant task connected with writing is thanking those who have helped make the final product possible. First of all, I am grateful to several organizations for their financial and administrative assistance. The University of Western Ontario generously granted me sabbatical leave in 1982-1983, during which time part of the book was written. I also thank the Social Sciences and Humanities Research Council of Canada for supplementary funding of my leave, and the Anthropology and Sociology Department at the University of British Columbia for giving me a congenial place to work.

The support staff, both at Western and at UBC, have been extremely helpful as well. In particular, Veronica D'Souza, Athena Economopoulos, Grace McIntyre, and Denise Statham provided special assistance in preparing the manuscript.

The people at Holt, Rinehart, and Winston of Canada have lent their consistent support and editorial advice. Beth Burgess and Joe McKeon were mainly responsible for getting me started, while Brian Henderson and Tony Luengo offered most of the later guidance that has brought the book to fruition. I heartily thank them for it.

I owe an intellectual debt to many more people than I can name. In varying ways and degrees, my conversations with Jim Curtis, Leo Driedger, Dick Henshel, Alf Hunter, Ron Lambert, Martin Meissner, Jim Rinehart, and Stuart Whitney have been of much help. There are three additional people for whom I reserve special mention. I am indebted to Jim Teevan, whose encouragement convinced me to do the project and whose sense of humor kept me on track at crucial times. I am also grateful to Kevin McQuillan, for his receptive ear and his thoughtful reactions to much of the first half of the manuscript. And I owe a great deal to Neil Guppy, who throughout the writing has been an invaluable source of information, advice, and friendship.

Finally, I thank Denise Thompson, who continues to sustain me in all things. It is to her that this book is dedicated.

Edward G. Grabb

CONTENTS

Chapter Three: Max Weber and the Multiple Bases for Inequality   37

Chapter Four: Durkheim, Structural Functionalism, and Inequality   69

Chapter Five: Recent Perspectives on Social Inequality 111

CHAPTER ONE

Theories of Social Inequality an Introduction

It is a paradox of life that its familiar features are often the most difficult to comprehend. This poses a special problem for sociologists, who are expected to explain these familiar things but who are commonly accused of doing so in unduly complicated ways. And yet, while such accusations are sometimes justified, it is also true, as Randall Collins notes, that obvious social questions may not have obvious or simple answers. Sociology's great strength, in fact, is precisely its potential for penetrating the superficial observation of everyday life and finding the fundamental social processes hidden beneath (Collins, 1982).

These remarks have a particular relevance for the topic of concern in this book—the problem of social inequality. For inequality is one of the most familiar facts of social life, a pervasive element in social relationships that is well-known, even to the most casual observer. At the same time, however, social inequality has not been an easy problem to solve or explain. Instead, it has provoked protracted and perplexing arguments over whether it is good or bad, natural or contrived, permanent or transitory in social settings. It has involved many of the most prominent social thinkers in debates about its origins, causes, and what, if anything, should be done to eliminate it. The central purpose of this volume is to review and assess the major elements in these debates, both past and present. In carrying out this purpose, the analysis will highlight the important differences and similarities in the approaches that have been developed, in an effort to trace the main direction that these theoretical exchanges seem to be taking us in understanding the problem of social inequality.

But what is social inequality, exactly? Even this most basic question is unlikely to produce a universally acceptable answer, though most would agree it involves such concerns as the gap between the rich and the poor, or the advantaged and the disadvantaged, in society. More generally, however, social inequality can refer to any of the differences between people (or the socially defined positions they occupy) that are *consequential* for the lives they lead, most particularly for the rights or opportunities they exercise and the rewards or privileges they enjoy. Of greatest importance here are those consequential differences that become *structured*, in the social sense of the term, that are built into the ways that people interact with one another on a recurring basis. Thus, people differ from one another in an infinite number of respects—in everything from height or weight to eye color or shoe size—but only a finite subset of these differences will be consequential for establishing unequal relations between people, and fewer still will generate structured patterns that are more or less sustained over time and place.

This leads us to a second very basic question: what are the main bases for inequality in society, the key differences between people that affect their rights, opportunities, rewards, and privileges? Once again, a universal answer is far from clear. Complications arise around this question for a variety of reasons.

First of all, some observers argue that the central bases for inequality are *individual differences*, in natural abilities, motivation, willingness to work hard, and so on. In contrast, other analysts contend that inequality is primarily based on the differential treatment people are accorded because of *socially defined characteristics*, such as economic class, race, ethnicity, gender, or religion.

A second difficulty in trying to list the main bases for social inequality is the great discrepancy in the importance attached to some criteria across different places and historical periods. Thus, for example, religion was once a major determinant of people's rights and rewards in countries like Canada or the United States but now is of relatively minor significance. In other nations, however, such as Iran or Northern Ireland, religious affiliation is still a key factor affecting the differences in economic well-being and political influence among the population and continues to provoke grave conflicts between factions.

A third complication to consider is the disagreement that exists over how many bases for inequality are truly important, and which of these are the most consequential in any general portrayal of inequality in society. Opinions on this issue vary; some theorists see a whole spectrum of cross-cutting, individual and socially defined, inequalities, while others stress only one or two key bases as predominant over the rest. (For discussion, see Curtis and Scott, 1979; Jeffries and Ransford, 1980.)

Finally, the issue of what bases for inequality are most crucial in society is clouded further by the related issue of why some human differences are viewed as significant but not others. As an extreme case, we might wonder, for instance, why eye color has virtually no impact in creating unequal social relations, when something almost as superficial, color of skin, has been used throughout history as a basis for granting or denying rights and rewards, thereby establishing persistent inequalities between people.

This list of issues provides us with some indication of the challenges involved in attempting to deal with the questions of what social inequality is about and where its major origins and bases should be traced. In subsequent chapters, we shall examine the ways in which leading social theorists have addressed such questions. Although a variety of themes and ideas will be considered, it is helpful at the beginning to be alert to certain topics that will be of particular concern. Hence, in the rest of this opening chapter, we shall briefly introduce four topics around which much of the later discussion revolves. These include the concept of class and its significance for the analysis of social inequality, the part played by the concept of power in theories of inequality, the role of the state in discussions of inequality in modern times, and the outlook for reducing or ending social inequalities in future societies.

Class and Social Inequality

While controversies abound in much of the literature on social inequality, one point that most observers accept is the central importance of the concept of *class* for the original development of theory and research in this area. Some have suggested that sociology itself, not just the analysis of inequality, really began with studies of class, especially in the work of Karl Marx (cf. Dahrendorf, 1969; Giddens, 1973; Hunter, 1981). The term class, of course, is now part of the everyday vocabulary of many people, and there is even some vague agreement in much of the population on how classes are perceived: as social groupings that differ mainly in their command of *economic* or *material resources*, such as money, wealth, or property (e.g., Coleman and Rainwater, 1978; Bell and Robinson, 1980; Grabb and Lambert, 1982).

Thus, it is no surprise that class has been central to most discussions of social inequality, since it pertains to that most basic of life's inequalities: the differential access of people to the material means of existence. However, although most social thinkers can agree on the importance of the concept, numerous disputes and questions persist over the more precise meaning of class, how it should best be defined and what its real significance is in the general analysis of inequality. Among the many issues that have been raised, the following should be kept in mind in our review of the major theorists.

First of all, are classes simply *categories* of people in similar economic circumstances, or should the concept of class be reserved solely for those situations in which such categories are also real *groups*, with a common consciousness of membership and some basis for sustained interaction among the people involved? A somewhat related question is whether classes are equivalent to *strata*, to statistical aggregates of people ranked according to criteria such as income, or whether such delineations miss the essential significance of the term class (cf. Stolzman and Gamberg, 1974). Another issue of this sort concerns the distinction between *relational* and *distributive* studies of inequality: are classes most important or interesting for the uneven distribution of income and other rewards among them, or for the relationships of control and subordination that are established in their interactions with one another? (See, for example, Goldthorpe, 1972; Curtis and Scott, 1979.) Fourth, are classes best understood concretely, as sets of real people, or abstractly, as sets of economic *places* or *positions*, filled by people and yet distinct from them, in much the same way that boxes are distinct from their contents? And finally, of course, there is the longstanding dispute over the number of classes that exist in modern societies: are there just two, a small dominant one and a large subordinate one? Or are there instead some intermediate classes between top and bottom, and if so, how many? Or is it more accurate to say that there are *no* discernible classes, just a finely graded hierarchy without clear breaks?

Power and Social Inequality

Along with class, *power* has emerged as the other key concept in most major theories of social inequality. Like class, power is recognized as an important idea but at the same time has generated considerable debate over its exact meaning or significance. Largely through the early work of Max Weber, many theorists accept that power occurs where some people are able to control social situations as they see fit, whether other people accept or oppose this control. But many questions continue to arise around the concept. Can power differences between people be dispensed with under the appropriate social conditions, or are relations of control and subordination inherently necessary in society? Is power unjust and oppressive by definition, or can it be a means for preventing or reducing injustice and oppression? Does power always flow downward from those who command to those who obey, or is there some reciprocal influence back up the chain of command? Such questions of power, of the ability to control social situations, obviously bear on the problem of social inequality, for such control normally has a direct effect in generating and sustaining unequal rights, opportunities, rewards, and privileges among people.

Yet, of all the important questions that have been asked about power, perhaps the most crucial one in recent years has been: from what and how many sources does power stem? In other words, does power ultimately originate in a single source or collectivity? Does it lie with a few principal factions or interest groups, or is it widely dispersed to a multitude of individuals in society? While there is still a range of opinion on this question among social theorists, many now seem to believe that power is considerably more concentrated than was once thought. Within this narrower range, the central debate which currently exists is one which pits those, on the one hand, who see power as primarily (even completely) a consequence of class differences against those, on the other hand, who see class as one basis (or the key basis) among a limited but nonetheless multiple set of power differences in society.

As shall be argued later, it is misleading to overstate the disagreements between these two competing viewpoints, since they share more elements in common than is sometimes acknowledged. Still, there are some fundamental distinctions between them that have crucial implications for how we are to think about or conceive of inequality in society. The key difference is mainly in their emphases: the first view contends that social inequality is principally about class inequality and, though it acknowledges nonclass inequalities between races or between genders, for example, treats other inequalities as secondary to and largely explicable by class differences; the second view contends that inequality is about class, perhaps first and foremost, but is also about other socially defined differences like race or gender which are used to assign people unequal power, power that is not reducible to class differences and that operates whether or not classes exist in society.

The State and Social Inequality

The choice of placing primary emphasis on class or on power when analyzing social inequality is roughly paralleled by a second debate that has taken on great significance in recent discussions. This is the question of whether the economic structure is the key mechanism through which inequalities develop and are sustained in society, or whether instead it is the political structure, or *state*, that is the central arena for determining the nature of social inequality in modern times.

On the one hand, the economic structure, the system of material production, is the main engine for creating the necessities (and the luxuries) of social life; because of this essential activity, and because control over what is produced and how it is distributed is so closely tied to class differences, there is a case to be made for the view that the economic system and the class relations emerging from it form the crux of any analysis of social inequality. On the other hand, the state is supposed to be the official representative of the general will, at least in nominally democratic societies; hence, it has the responsibility for creating and implementing, by force if necessary, those laws and policies that can either entrench or reduce inequalities in society. This right to legislate and enforce gives to the state leadership ultimate *formal* control, not only over class inequality but over racial, sexual, and other forms of inequality as well. Moreover, the recent trend toward increased political intervention in economic affairs has prompted some observers to suggest that the state is also beginning to usurp the essential activities of the economic structure. Such arguments provide the main basis for the view that the state has become the principal player in the modern power struggle and thus the predominant factor to consider in any analysis of social inequality.

The Future of Social Inequality

Probably the main reason why social theorists have devoted so much effort to the problem of social inequality has been their desire to answer one fundamental question: is inequality among people a natural and inevitable feature of society, something that might be reduced but never abolished in social settings, or, on the contrary, is inequality an unnatural and imposed social arrangement, an injustice that can and should be eliminated through social change?

The extensive discussions that have developed around this difficult question have given rise to several important controversies. Some theorists argue, for example, that inequality must be natural, since it is found in all societies. Others counter that its universal existence is no proof that inequality is natural; after all, slavery too was once a universal phenomenon but it is now judged to be an unnatural social arrangement, subject to complete abolition throughout the world. A somewhat related issue is whether people should receive unequal rewards because they contribute different degrees of talent or effort to society, or whether it is possible to develop a social system where such inequality is virtually unnecessary, since people will have subordinated these self-interested motivations to a greater concern with serving the collective good. Still another question along these lines is the problem of the organizational necessity of social inequality: is it possible or not, in any complex society, to establish differences in tasks and administrative responsibilities that do not also promote persistent inequalities in the rights, opportunities, rewards, and privileges of people?

These are just some of the more prominent issues that underlie the general problem of social inequality. Although this introduction is not meant to be exhaustive, it should offer the reader an initial sense of the major topics and questions that theorists in this field have addressed. The points noted here will serve to guide and to structure most of the review and analysis that follow.

We begin in Chapter 2 with the work of Karl Marx, whose original thesis on class structure in capitalist society is an essential backdrop for virtually all of the theories that follow. In Chapter 3, Max Weber's attempt at a constructive critique and extension of Marx's views is the main concern. In Chapter 4, the work of Emile Durkheim is briefly examined, his role in the transition from Marx and Weber to the so-called structural-functionalist school is considered, and the ideas that structural function-alists have put forth about inequality are assessed. Chapter 5 focuses on more recent theories, most of which involve a critical reaction to, or rejection of, structural functionalism and a resurgence of interest in build-ing from the ideas of Marx and Weber. Six writers have been singled out for discussion in Chapter 5: Dahrendorf, Lenski, Poulantzas, Wright, Par-kin, and Giddens. Last, Chapter 6 provides a brief summary and evaluation of the major elements in both the classical and contemporary perspec-tives, and concludes with some speculative observations on the contri-butions of existing theories to a more unified overview of social inequality in advanced societies.

CHAPTER TWO

Karl Marx
and the Theory of Class

*"Follow your own course and
let people talk."* Karl Marx,
Introduction to Volume 1 of
Capital, 1867

Introduction

We begin our consideration of the major theories of social inequality with the work of Karl Marx. To some, this choice may seem inappropriate, for in a sense Marx was not a theorist of general social inequality at all (cf. Benson, 1978:1.) Thus, for example, Marx showed no sustained interest in examining the numerous ways in which people are ranked in societies at any one time. Nevertheless, several aspects of Marx's work do provide the crucial basis from which to build an analysis of social inequality in advanced societies.

First of all, Marx has been characterized by certain analysts as the father of modern sociology itself (e.g., Berlin, 1963:158; Singer, 1980:1), although Comte usually gets credit for this role and others, most notably Saint-Simon, may have an equal claim (Durkheim, 1896:104; Giddens, 1973:23). Because of Marx's central position in the general development of sociology, any of his work that is relevant to the study of social inequality necessarily should be examined and assessed.

A second reason why an examination of Marx's work is essential is that he, more than any other thinker, is responsible for bringing to the forefront of sociology the concept of class. Some have claimed that this concept is now an obsolete one in social theory (e.g., Nisbet, 1959). Others argue on the contrary that class continues to be the principal explanatory variable to consider when trying to understand the workings of society (e.g., Giddens, 1973:19; Wright, 1979:3). In either event, it is true that the idea of class has had a significant influence on the way people think about society and their own positions in it. Academics routinely employ the term in their research into the operation of the social structure, while people regularly allude to class or related ideas in their everyday conversation. It is the use, and frequent misuse, of the concept of class that forms the bulk of what until now has constituted the study of social inequality. Thus, Marx's original formulation of the theory of classes and class structure is a critical starting point for our discussion.

A third reason for Marx's importance is that his analysis of class structure, coupled with his conclusion that future societies will see an end to class-based inequality, has helped to stimulate, or provoke, virtually all of the attempts by subsequent social thinkers to explain social inequality and its transformation over time. Marx shared with later thinkers such as Weber and Durkheim a keen interest in the process by which earlier forms of society, particularly feudalism, eventually gave rise to the contemporary form of society known as advanced capitalism. Marx's view was that the capitalist stage of social development would itself ultimately be superseded by the final and highest form of society, alternately labeled *socialism* or *communism*. It is on the questions of why societies change, and what their ultimate form will be, that many later theorists seem to take issue with Marx.

In fact, what has been called "the debate with Marx's ghost" (Salomon, 1945:596; Zeitlin, 1968:109; cf. Giddens, 1971:185) frequently amounts to a debate with certain *Marxists*—individuals who have adopted Marx's ideas as their own and have interpreted or modified his original work in a variety of ways. As is the case with other schools of social thought, too often these many versions of Marxism have proven internally inconsistent, even contradictory, leading Marx himself to utter his famous remark "What is certain is that I am no Marxist" (quoted by Engels, 1882:388). The confusion surrounding what Marx really said, or at least really meant, inevitably makes the understanding of his work more difficult. Nevertheless, it will be argued here that the central features of Marx's theory, particularly as they pertain to the study of social inequality, are not as obscure as certain analysts suggest. If anything, the fact that Marx's work has produced such a wide range of reactions, for and against, says as much about the power of his ideas as it does about their complexity. That nearly four of every ten people in the world currently live under governments that at least claim to follow Marx's principles is perhaps the most telling evidence of his influence (Singer, 1980:1).

Of course, Marx himself did not live to see the birth of any society governed by socialist or communist precepts. He was a nineteenth-century man who devoted his intellectual efforts toward understanding the workings of capitalist society, with the hope that this advanced but flawed form of social organization could be radically transformed to suit the needs of all people. His special concern was European, especially English, capitalism in the 1800s. Hence, some have alleged that his analysis is not totally applicable to present-day societies, societies that have been variously labeled "monopoly capitalist," "state capitalist," or "postcapital-ist" (e.g., Dahrendorf, 1959; Baran and Sweezy, 1966). Yet, although the capitalism Marx knew may in some respects no longer exist, in other respects it seems, like the poor and the exploited, to be very much with us still. Capitalism, in its many current guises, continues to be the pre-dominant mode of economic and social organization in the world, though it seems more and more to be rivaled by the numerous varieties of so-cialism alluded to earlier. The disagreements between proponents of these two types of society, capitalist and socialist, remain fundamental. Marx is such an important figure precisely because his analysis of capitalism and his prognosis that socialism is what the future holds for all of us situate his work at the very center of this most momentous of global struggles.

For all these reasons, then, Marx's theory of class and class structure in capitalist society is our first concern in this investigation. In order to grasp more fully the origins of Marx's principal ideas, it is instructive to begin with a brief examination of some of the major events and intellec-tual influences in his life.

Biographical and Intellectual Sketch

Karl Marx was born in Trier, Prussia, in the German Rhineland, in 1818. He died in London, England, in 1883. These sixty-five years were turbulent ones in Europe, marked by considerable social change, economic devel-opment, political upheaval, and intellectual debate. It is not possible here to trace all the numerous people and events that helped shape Marx's ideas; nevertheless, several major influences should be identified for their persistent and deep-seated impact on his thought.

Early Years

Perhaps the first major influence on Marx's ideas occurred during his adolescence. Marx's father was a moderately prosperous lawyer, well-educated and a believer in the liberal ideals of the French Revolution of 1789—individual freedom and equality in particular. Within his father's circle of intellectual middle-class friends, Marx was exposed to these egalitarian views of humanity and society. As a result, Marx developed a particularly optimistic philosophy about the nature of humanity and the potential of civilization to progress. Later in life, his father would reverse himself and embrace the conservative and reactionary ideas of the Prussian government under which he lived. But Marx himself retained throughout his life the belief, learned in these early years, that people are by nature both good and rational. People have, to Marx, the potential to produce a nearly perfect society if only unnatural obstacles, especially oppression by those in economic and political control, are removed from their path (Berlin, 1963:29; McLellan, 1973:87; Singer, 1980:22). As we shall see, Marx's belief in human progress and perfectibility had a significant impact on his expectations for the transformation of the capitalist society in which he lived and for the socialist society of the future that he envisioned.

University Experiences

The second important intellectual influence on Marx comes into play during his university education. Initially Marx enrolled as a law student at the University of Bonn in 1835. Accounts suggest that the seventeen-year-old Marx started out living the "dissipated life of the ordinary German student"—drinking, writing poetry, getting slightly wounded in a duel, and being arrested occasionally for "riotous behaviour" (Berlin, 1963:33; Singer, 1980:2). After a year of this, Marx's father convinced him to transfer to the University of Berlin; however, this radically changed the course of Marx's life and ended his father's hopes that Marx would become a lawyer.

At Berlin, Marx became absorbed in the ideas of the philosopher Georg Hegel. Hegel had died in 1831, but his thought still dominated the intellectual life of German universities at the time. This was particularly true at Berlin, where Hegel had taught for many years. Marx soon switched from law to the study of Hegelian philosophy. He eventually rejected the *content* of Hegel's theories because of their preoccupation with the abstract world of the mind or the spirit and their tendency to treat ideas as mere mental constructs divorced from the real, concrete world of people and society. Yet Marx was to the end of his life strongly influenced by the *form* or *method* of Hegel's thought. First of all, he accepted completely Hegel's emphasis on the importance of understanding the past, of studying history in order to comprehend the present and project the future (cf. Giddens, 1971:4). Second, Marx employed for his own more concrete purposes the famous and often misunderstood Hegelian notion that change occurs in a *dialectical* fashion. Put simply, to say that change is dialectical indicates that it is by nature a process of struggle or tension between opposing, incompatible forces. Moreover, in the clash of these forces neither side comes out in the end unchanged or unscathed. When the struggle is resolved, the resulting victorious force is, in a sense, different from either of the original adversaries, more highly developed and advanced than each predecessor. This dynamic conflict of forces is continual, with newly emerging forces eventually entering the arena to battle the latest victor (cf. Berlin, 1963:55-56).

The problem with this notion, in Marx's view, is that Hegel makes the error of applying it only in the airy realm of ideas—a fact that is consistent with Hegel's general disregard for material, concrete phenomena. Marx's great task at this stage in his life becomes to "turn Hegel on his head," to take this dialectical method for thinking of change out of the clouds and to apply it to the understanding of how real societies, real human groups, arise, develop, and become transformed over time. Hence, for Marx the key opposing forces to examine are groups, not ideas. Ideas are important social forces, no doubt, but cannot be divorced from the social context in which they emerge or from the people who think them. Marx's application of Hegel's historical and dialectical view of change will become evident later when we consider Marx's analysis of class and class struggle in capitalist society.

Political Activist and Refugee

Marx completed a doctoral degree in philosophy at Berlin in 1841. He hoped to obtain a university teaching post; however, his political views were already known and unpopular with the conservative Prussian government, so the ministry of education ensured that no teaching position was forthcoming. Marx then found alternative employment as a journalist, an occupation that he held on several occasions throughout his life. His first such job, like virtually all the others, was short-lived. As writer and eventual editor of the *Rhenish Gazette* (*Rheinische Zeitung*), he published articles which criticized the Prussian government, especially for its treatment of the poor and working classes. This criticism led to the censorship of the paper in 1843. By this time Marx had become convinced that the same working class he was writing about was destined to be the prime mover in the progress toward a new universal society, where true freedom and full human potential would be realized for all. He now saw himself as playing a key role in awakening the largely unaware laboring masses to their revolutionary task.

In order to express his ideas and fulfill this role more freely, Marx left Germany for France. Initially he attempted to publish a joint French-German journal in Paris, but it met with indifference in France and quick suppression in Germany. Marx lived the years between 1843 and 1849 as a political refugee, first in France, then in Belgium, and briefly in Germany. During this period Marx was exposed to several crucial influences on his own thought. Out of Feuerbach's critique of religion as an alienating force for humanity, Marx developed the concept of alienation, and, as we shall see, he eventually applied this idea to his analysis of the plight of workers in capitalist society. Marx also read the works of several French socialists. These confirmed in his mind the important role of the working class in transforming capitalism, even though Marx disagreed with most of these writers on specific issues.

Probably the strongest influence on Marx in this period was Saint-Simon, a French social thinker of the late eighteenth and early nineteenth centuries whose views on social change corresponded closely with those evolving in Marx's own mind. It was largely from Saint-Simon that Marx came to see economic relationships as the key to explaining historical social change. Marx's emphasis on the role of conflict, especially between economic classes, is also in part adopted from Saint-Simon, as is the view that social change occurs because each society bears within it, and generates through its own development, the "germ of its own destruction" (Giddens, 1973:22; cf. Berlin, 1963:90-91). The parallels between this latter idea and Hegel's dialectical view of change were apparent to Marx and served to solidify further his views on this issue.

The most exciting political activities and events of Marx's life also occurred in this turbulent period. By this time Marx had met his lifelong friend and collaborator, Friedrich Engels, and together they composed a short pamphlet laying out the doctrines of the Communist League, newly formed in 1847. This work was published in 1848 as the now famous *Communist Manifesto*. In that same year popular revolts against established monarchies occurred in parts of France, Italy, Germany, Austria, and Hungary. Much of Europe was astir with the desire for liberal reform, if not radical change. However, none of these uprisings had a lasting effect, and any hopes that Marx and others may have had that these events were the forerunners of a socialist revolution were soon quashed. By the middle of 1849 Marx was once again on the move, this time to London, England. Despite occasional glimmers of political upheaval on the continent, the revolution that Marx awaited never took place, and he was to remain in England for the rest of his life.

England and *Capital*

In the more than thirty years during which Marx lived in England, his principal achievements were those of a scholar. His activities as a radical journalist, political agitator, and organizer of the working class were greatly reduced, although he did take a leading hand in the operation of the first International Workingmen's Association, between 1864 and 1872. What consumed most of Marx's energy was his monumental analysis of contemporary capitalism.

Marx, in fact, had contracted to do such a work as early as 1845, but it was repeatedly set aside for his political activities and other writing (Singer, 1980:4). It was both appropriate and somewhat ironic that Marx found himself in England during the writing of this work. England was the most advanced capitalist society in the world at the time and hence served as the most appropriate example or archetype for Marx's analysis. It was ironic, however, that Marx, a radical opponent of capitalism, should find tolerance and refuge within which to express his ideas only in England, the prime example of what he most despised (Berlin, 1963:181).

What Marx found particularly disturbing about capitalism, both in England and elsewhere, was that so much surplus wealth could be produced by this system and yet be distributed to such a small group of people. While the capitalists, the owners of large factories and agricultural lands, were themselves living in splendor and affluence, the workers, who labored to produce this great wealth, subsisted for the most part in miserable poverty. The contrast between rich and poor was particularly acute in Marx's time, with laborers sometimes working eighteen hours daily. Six-day work weeks were typical, and child labor—employment of children as young as six or seven—was not uncommon. Working conditions themselves were often of the most appalling kind, dirty, cramped, and extremely hazardous (cf. Marx, 1867:Chapters 10 and 15).

Marx's condemnation of the capitalist system in his work *Capital* (*Das Kapital*) was based on the statistical and other evidence made available to him in his laborious daily readings in the British Museum and on his own observations and first-hand experience with poverty. Marx and his family lived in squalor throughout most of this final stage of his life, although Engels and other friends lightened the burden somewhat with occasional financial aid.

One important consequence of Marx's economic plight was that it slowed his progress on the analysis of the capitalist system in England. His emotional strength and resolve to finish the work were also sapped by illness and personal tragedy, including the premature death of his wife and several of his children. Thus, while *Capital* was intended to be the crowning work of his life, only the first volume was really completed, with the second and third volumes compiled and edited by Engels from rough drafts and notes. It would appear that Marx was on the verge of outlining explicitly his most crucial concern, a detailed treatment of the class structure in capitalism, when he died in his study on March 14, 1883.

The incomplete nature of Marx's analysis of capitalism is indeed unfortunate and obviously has only added to the uncertainty and controversy surrounding his work. As noted earlier, however, it is possible to piece together from the existing material, including the *Communist Manifesto* and his numerous other writings, a more or less consistent and comprehensible theory of class, class structure, and social change. A discussion of this theory is our main concern in the remainder of this chapter.

Marx's Theory: Class, Class Struggle, and Historical Change

"The history of all hitherto existing society is the history of class struggles" (Marx and Engels, 1848:57). In this straightforward statement at the beginning of the *Communist Manifesto*, Marx provides a key to understanding the essence of his theory. While a massive and complex literature has been generated by both critics and disciples in reaction to Marx, this single assertion captures the crux of his conception of social structure and social change.

In Marx's view, historical epochs are distinguishable from one another primarily by the system of economic organization, or mode of production, that dominates in each era. Thus, the slave-based economies of ancient Greece and Rome are different in key respects from the feudalism of medieval Europe and the capitalist system of Marx's own time. What is similar about all these historical examples of social and economic systems, however, is that according to Marx each one is marked by a basic distinction between classes, between groupings of people who differ in the roles they play in the productive system. In all cases, the most important difference is between those who own and control property and those who do not. Here *property* refers not to simple personal possessions but to resources that can be used to produce things of value and to generate wealth: land, rental housing, machinery, factories, and the like (Marx and Engels, 1846:230).

The basic split between the owning, propertied class and the nonowning, propertyless class is always present, though it has taken different forms historically: masters versus slaves in ancient times, serfs versus lords in feudalism, the *bourgeoisie* versus the *proletariat* in capitalism. Certainly, more detailed divisions and distinctions might be drawn in each form; nevertheless, the two-class model is for Marx the crucial one to apply in understanding how societies are structured and how they change (Marx and Engels, 1848:58).

Why is the two-class view the key to understanding society? Primarily because, according to Marx, all societies are born of struggle, of the underlying tension or open conflict between the two major economic classes. In fact, social change or development historically has never occurred without it: "No antagonism, no progress. This is the law that civilization has followed up to our days" (Marx, 1847:132). To Marx, owners and nonowners have interests that are naturally opposed to one another. Whenever there is a situation where one group controls the property, the productive apparatus of society, the remaining population is by definition excluded from such control. Non-owners necessarily enter into an exchange relationship with the owning class, giving their labor power to the owners in return for sufficient income to survive and to continue working in the employ of the owning class. The coercive and exploitative aspects of such an arrangement are obvious in the slavery of ancient times and the serfdom of feudalism, since slaves and serfs were legally bound to labor for their masters or manor lords and had virtually no choice in the matter. Coercion and exploitation may seem absent in capitalism, since the exchange of labor for wages between workers and owners occurs between people who are legally free to choose whether or not to accept such a contract. For Marx, however, the propertyless worker in capitalism is no more at liberty to withhold his or her labor from the owner than was the slave or the serf, for the alternative to wage labor is starvation if one possesses no productive property with which to provide food, clothing, and shelter—the simple means of survival.

It is apparent, then, that Marx's theory portrays all societies up to and including his own as arenas for an elemental struggle between "haves" and "have nots," between "oppressor and oppressed" (Marx and Engels, 1848:58, 92). Societies are based on this inherent dichotomy in the productive sphere, and the major force for change in society necessarily involves a conflict of interests between these two groups. We will examine more closely just how Marx envisions the role of conflict in social change. Before doing this, however, we should consider Marx's views on the work process, especially in the capitalist system that was his principal focus. The operation of the capitalist mode of production and its consequences for the people involved in it will be of special concern in the section that follows.

Work in Capitalist Society

In our discussion of Marx's background at the beginning of this chapter, we noted his belief in the potential that humans possess for building increasingly better forms of society. Marx sees the best evidence for this in humanity's increasing mastery over nature and the material world throughout history. Human improvement is especially apparent in our ability to produce the means of life for a growing population. Compared to primitive tribal societies, for example, modern nations, with their advanced tools and technical knowledge, are far more capable of providing for the needs of people. In fact, modern societies are increasingly able to generate enough goods to accumulate a large surplus of wealth over and above basic needs.

To Marx, it is productive work, not leisure, that under the right conditions is the ideal human activity (cf. Avineri, 1968:104, 107). In fact, it is this creative capacity, this ability to produce things of value, that is essential to human nature and that mainly distinguishes humans from other life forms (Marx and Engels, 1846:31; Marx, 1867:177-178). The ability of modern societies, then, to accumulate a vast surplus of produced wealth is itself a grand accomplishment and a tribute to human potential. That capitalism is the system of economic organization that has been most successful in generating wealth is acknowledged and even applauded by Marx (Marx and Engels, 1848:65-66). The problem with capitalism, however, is that it distorts the structure and meaning of the work process, with negative consequences for society as a whole and for workers in particular. The distortion comes from several characteristics basic to the capitalist mode of economic organization: private property, surplus expropriation, the division of labor, and the alienation of work.

Private Property

Economic production is by definition a social activity, requiring groups of people working together to create things. To Marx, the social character of work is wholly consistent with the general communal nature or "communist essence" of people and belies any claim that each of us is an isolated individual in society (Marx, 1858:84). But the capitalist mode of economic organization artificially creates a situation in which people are individualized and separated in their work, even though, paradoxically, they may be working side by side.

The first factor at the root of the fragmentation of work in capitalism is the existence of private property. As was mentioned earlier, private property is mainly responsible for creating the two-class system in capitalism, the distinction between the owners of property, or bourgeoisie, and those who work for the owners, the proletariat. This initial split immediately erodes the naturally social character of production to the extent that those involved are not working as a united group toward some common goal but rather are pursuing their own special interests. The principal interest of the bourgeois owners in this context is to maximize their own wealth, rather than the general wealth or that of their workers. The workers themselves also act in their own individual interests in capitalist society and not for the general good (Marx, 1844:238).

In Marx's time, workers lacked bargaining power through unions or legal strikes. As a result, they could not form a united front against employers and their interests were rarely served. Typically, the supply of available laborers exceeded the demand, especially with the development of mechanized production methods. Hence, employers had a ready supply of unemployed workers willing to take any position left vacant by any worker who was fired for making trouble or because of illness or injury. This idle "reserve army of labour," as Marx called it (Marx, 1867:487, 632), ensured that each worker acted primarily as an isolated person, in competition with other workers for a job and unlikely to want to band together with others to see better pay or working conditions. This isolation of workers from one another obviously worked to the advantage of the capitalist, since it assured him of a docile, though frequently discontented, pool of cheap labor.

Expropriation of Surplus Wealth

A second aspect of capitalism that Marx believed distorts the natural work process is the expropriation of surplus wealth by the capitalist at the expense of the worker. One of the great ironies and injustices of capitalism, in Marx's view, is that working people are, through their labor, primarily responsible for the wealth that is generated; yet workers receive only a small portion of this wealth. To Marx, the value that a produced object has is the value of the labor used in its creation. This value should rightly belong to the workers whose labor is expended in making the object. But under capitalism, workers exchange their labor power for wages that amount to less than the value of the object when it is exchanged or sold in the marketplace. The difference between the wages and the value of the object when it is sold represents a surplus amount that goes to the capitalists as a profit, after their expenses are deducted. The capitalists treat this excess as their own and think of the wages paid out to workers as one of the costs of production.

To Marx, this perception of the process is completely incorrect. It is the workers who have incurred a cost in the exchange of labor for wages, not the capitalists. The workers lose part of the value of their own labor in the surplus the capitalists usurp. This surplus, which is often reinvested by the capitalists, is in fact the accumulated "dead labor" of past workers. *Capital* is really this accumulated past labor, which, in the purchase of new machinery and so on, is used by the capitalist to expand control over and exploitation of "living labor"—that is, the current crop of employed workers (Marx and Engels, 1848:84).

The Division of Labor

To this point we have discussed two characteristics of capitalism that according to Marx have distorted the essentially social nature of people and of work: the role of private property in fragmenting both capitalists and workers into self-interested individuals, and the unjust expropriation of wealth by capitalists at the expense of workers. A third feature of the capitalist mode of production, and one that intensifies these problems still further, is the division of labor.

In its simplest form, the division of labor arises as soon as private property is instituted and the class of owners is separated from the class of workers. Immediately there is a splitting up of the productive process into those who own the means of production and oversee its operation, on the one hand, and those who labor within the production process, on the other hand. As capitalism evolves and develops as a mode of economic organization, this simple division becomes more and more elaborate. It is soon apparent that goods can be produced more quickly and efficiently if all the tasks that go into creating an object are divided into special jobs, each of which is done by a particular worker on a continual basis.

The modern automobile assembly line is perhaps the epitome of how capitalism subdivides the production of an object into a series of small tasks. Capitalist production, based on a complex division of labor, is highly efficient, with far fewer hours of labor required to create the same volume of goods. However, this efficiency benefits the few capitalists at the expense of the many workers, in Marx's view. Workers produce more in the same working time, but are paid the same wages. In effect, then, workers have exchanged their labor power for a smaller proportion of the wealth produced. The surplus wealth generated is larger and hence so are the profits of the capitalist.

Not only does the division of labor increase the profits of the capitalist, and thus the rate of exploitation of the workers by the capitalist, but the division of labor also has severe negative effects on the worker's whole orientation to work. We have already noted that Marx believed humanity's essential ability resides in creative labor. Work is an inherently enjoyable activity under natural conditions, since it is the means by which human beings create and shape their own world. But the division of labor into a series of repetitive and routine tasks is destructive of this enjoyable quality of labor. The pleasure of making things is lost to the worker, who finds it virtually impossible to identify his or her productive power in an object to which so little of the creative self has been applied. Hence, for example, putting the same bolts on a series of automobiles all day, every day, provides none of the pride in workmanship and sense of creating something that go into the making of a custom car by one or a few people.

Alienated Labor

Thus it is that, in the operation of the capitalist mode of production, work becomes something grotesque. Each person's special capability as a creating and producing being is turned into something that divides and separates people from one another, that is used by some people to exploit others, and that, as an activity, is hateful drudgery to be avoided whenever possible.

Marx uses the concept of alienation or alienated labor to signify these negative aspects of work in capitalist society. *Alienation*, unfortunately, is a widely misused term, employed by social scientists to label every imaginable variety of psychological malaise or personal dissatisfaction. In fact, what Marx means by alienation is something quite different. At its most general level, alienation denotes the separation of something from something else (cf. Schacht, 1970). Whenever something which is an attribute or a creation of people is somehow taken away from them or made external to them, in a sense we have a situation of alienation. Marx first encountered this idea in his early studies of Hegel. In particular, Marx was influenced by a critique of Hegel's religious views by the philosopher Feuerbach. Religion, to Feuerbach, involves the attribution of special qualities and powers to a supreme being or god: mercy and compassion, knowledge, the power to create, and so on. In fact, Feuerbach claims, these qualities are humanity's own highest traits and powers, falsely separated or alienated from humans and projected onto this mythical god (cf. Giddens, 1971:3-4).

Marx sees a comparable process of alienation in the field of human labor under capitalism. We have so far discussed three features of capitalist economic organization: the existence of private property, the expropriation of surplus by the capitalist class, and the division of labor. All of these contribute in part to alienation. Following Giddens, Marx's view on alienated labor may be summarized in four main points (Giddens, 1971:12-13).

Alienation is apparent, first, in the separation of workers from control over the products they create. These products are the physical embodiment of human labor given by the worker to the capitalist in exchange for wages. This exchange means that labor has itself been alienated from the workers and sold as a *commodity*, no different from the commodities or goods that are created (Marx, 1844:272; 1867:170; Marx and Engels, 1848:68). In addition, most of the wealth that these products can garner in the market is also taken away from the worker, expropriated by the capitalist and turned into profit.

A second feature of alienation involves the actual work task, which loses its intrinsically enjoyable and rewarding character in capitalism. The division of labor into specialized, repetitive tasks and the lack of control over the work process in such a setting deny the worker the opportunity to "develop freely his mental and physical energy" (Marx, 1844:274). Work does not satisfy the human need to create but becomes an alienated, external means to satisfy other needs. Leisure time and the "animal functions" of "eating, drinking, and procreating" become most important to alienated people, while work, the essential human activity, "is shunned like the plague" (Marx, 1844:274-275).

A third aspect of capitalist production that promotes alienation is also related to the division of labor, especially to the increasing technological complexity that the division of labor entails. Machine technology, for example, is itself an important illustration of how people can harness natural forces and materials to perform useful tasks. Active human mastery of the world is apparent in this mechanization; yet, ironically, the requirement by capitalism that workers must operate this mechanized apparatus on a continual, routine, and repetitive basis means that people are subordinated to the machines they have created (Marx, 1844:273;

1867:645; Marx and Engels, 1848:69). Once again, then, people's labor takes on a separate, alienated form in the machines that dominate their own creators.

Finally, a fourth sense in which Marx identifies alienation in capitalism concerns money and its power literally to buy anything, even people and human relationships. Marx states: "I am ugly, but I can buy for myself the most beautiful of women, therefore, I am not ugly"—if, that is, I have the power money brings (Marx, 1844:324). The power of money is itself evidence of how human qualities, such as beauty in this example, are externalized from humans, converted into fluid, quantifiable assets like any other commodity. Money is "the alienated *ability of mankind*" (Marx, 1844:325), set apart from people themselves. Here again the idea of externalization or separation is basic to the idea of alienation.

Marx believes alienation in all these forms is inherent in the capitalist mode of economic organization and can be ended only by the overthrow of the capitalist system. Marx is convinced that certain conditions necessary for such a revolutionary overthrow will emerge naturally from the internal logic of capitalist development. In the next section, the major points Marx raises in this regard will be considered.

Capitalist Development and Change

We have already discussed the importance that Marx places on the struggle between opposing classes throughout history. This emphasis on the conflict between opposites is consistent with the Hegelian dialectical perspective that influenced Marx's early thinking about change. Marx combines this dialectical method with a similar conception borrowed partly from Saint-Simon: the idea that every societal form holds within itself "the germ of its own destruction"—some force or group that eventually arises out of the system which currently exists, opposes the present ruling regime, and thereby changes society in some fundamental way.

Marx applies these two conceptions to his analysis of how capitalism will develop and ultimately be transformed into socialism. Marx begins, however, by examining feudalism, the societal form that preceded capitalism in Europe. In his view, an understanding of how capitalism came to emerge from the ruins of feudalism helps to clarify just how socialist society can develop out of capitalism.

Feudalism and Capitalism

Feudal society in medieval Europe was a highly localized and community-oriented social structure, based on a rural, agricultural economy. Each serf was bonded to a manor lord and worked the lord's land in return for being permitted to live as a tenant on the lord's estate. This system was relatively stable for centuries but gradually evolved and ultimately disintegrated because of a combination of factors.

The voyages of discovery during this period opened up international trade, expanding markets beyond the local communities and feudal estates and creating demands for new goods. The new markets and new demands stimulated the development of new technology and efficient production to meet these requirements. The growth of large-scale manufacturing thus began and with it a demand for labor to work in these settings.

At the same time, the feudal economy was unable to compete in these new markets, and feudal lords saw their resources depleted by wars and civil strife. The impoverished aristocracy became less and less able to afford to retain serfs on their lands. Many serfs were therefore thrown off the land or else, intrigued by the broadening horizons of this new age, sought their own fortunes voluntarily as free people. These freed serfs migrated to the growing urban centers, where they took up employment as workers for the growing manufacturing interests located in these centers. Such workers were the beginnings of the proletariat, while the merchants, traders, and financiers involved in the manufacturing ventures were the basis for the capitalist bourgeoisie (e.g., Marx and Engels, 1846:33-35, 65-70; Marx and Engels, 1848:59-60; cf. Avineri, 1968:151-156; Giddens, 1971:29-34).

It is apparent in these historical developments how capitalism emerged within the feudal society it was to replace. The transformation, of course, occurred over several centuries and did not happen everywhere at the same pace. Ultimately, however, it occurred throughout Europe. The opposition of interests between the developing class of capitalists and the existing feudal aristocracy became increasingly evident over this time. The capitalist class in this era was a dynamic force for social and economic change, creating new ideas, new production methods, and new wealth. The feudal lords were more and more superfluous to the productive system, yet continued to reap wealth from it because of the political and other privileges they enjoyed under monarchical governments. Eventually the capitalist class threw off the feudal yoke that was hindering its progress, sometimes through a combination of confrontation and political accommodation, as in seventeenth-century England, and sometimes through violent revolution, as in eighteenth-century France (Marx and Engels, 1846:72-73).

Marx contends that the process by which the capitalist bourgeoisie emerged from feudalism will be repeated again in the future. In this same conflict-oriented, dialectical fashion, capitalism will be transformed by a new opposing force growing within itself: the proletariat. Marx's view is that the dynamic and progressive nature of the capitalist class—qualities that played such an important part in overthrowing feudalism—will gradually dissipate as capitalism matures as a system. The entrepreneurial

spirit, speculative daring, technical knowledge, and administrative skill
displayed by the capitalists will have served their purpose at this point.
According to Marx, these qualities will be replaced by increasing en-
trenchment and resistance to change among the bourgeoisie, who, having
taken power, will cling tenaciously to it. During the same period of bourgeois rule, the mass of the population, the working class, will become
aware that they themselves, not the bourgeoisie, are the force primarily
responsible for the wealth generated in capitalism.

Marx believes it is the destiny of the workers and the producers of
society to take the ascendancy and thereby transform the entire economic
and social structure. This change will signal the beginning of the final
stage of human development, socialist or communist society. This will
be a unique achievement in history, for it will be the first successful
revolution in which the victors are the majority of the people and not
some select minority. It will also mean an end to class divisions and class
struggle, since only one class, the universal proletarian class, will remain
(Marx and Engels, 1848:77; cf. Avineri, 1968:60-62).

The Factors in Capitalist Transformation

We have not yet specified those processes Marx perceives in capitalism
that will promote its demise. Though there are numerous factors that
could be noted, seven in particular seem crucial.

First of all, the rise of capitalism as noted earlier is closely tied to the
growth of large urban centers, which develop as propertyless rural in-
habitants flow to the cities in search of employment. This growing concentration of urban laborers is a key initial step toward the development
of working-class awareness, since masses of workers are housed in the
same neighborhoods and experience similar living conditions.

A second, related process is the increasing expansion of production
into large-scale factories employing many workers. This process makes
apparent the basically *social* nature of human production. It also means
concentration of workers in close proximity to one another and a further
basis for awareness of their common class position and their common
plight (Marx and Engels, 1848:69-70).

Marx suggests a third factor by which workers are made more aware
of their shared fate and their separateness from the capitalist class. This
factor is the greater suffering that workers face during economic crises.
Marx's view is that capitalism is primarily concerned with a rational and
efficient, but relentless and self-interested, pursuit of *profits* by the owning class. The drive for more and more profits has frequent and unfortunate consequences for society as a whole, but especially for workers.
The bourgeoisie's desire for greater gain often means that it produces
more goods than it can sell. This imbalance leads to a loss of money by
capitalists, since they must sell their products in order to realize any

profit and pay their costs. A common reaction by the capitalist class is to lay off workers in order to reduce costs and save money. But the workers of society are also the main purchasers of goods. Hence, laying off workers means that there are fewer people able to buy products, so that there is an even lower demand for goods and a further loss of money for the capitalists. In this spiral fashion, economic crises tend to occur regularly in the capitalist system and in fact are basic to its operation. Overproduction, followed by higher unemployment, reduced demand, slow economic growth, and depression is the typical pattern. After each crisis there is a period in which the economy stabilizes and the proletariat may once again find work (Marx, 1844:241, 258-259). Nevertheless, the greater deprivations endured by workers during crises become increasingly apparent to them and underline the basic differences between themselves and the owning class.

Of course, some capitalists also suffer greatly in hard economic times. This brings us to the fourth process in capitalist development that acts to bring about its transformation. It is mainly the small-scale capitalists—what Marx calls the *petty bourgeoisie*—and not the larger-scale owners who are most vulnerable in economic crises. Small owners have fewer reserves of wealth for absorbing losses and less influence for getting bank credit or government subsidies than do large owners. Thus, in economic crises small capitalists increasingly are forced to sell their businesses or else go bankrupt and are taken over by larger capitalists. It is in this way that the economy stabilizes because the overproduction problem lessens as the number of capitalist producers shrinks. In addition, however, the decline of the petty bourgeoisie means a concentration and centralization of ownership in the hands of an ever smaller pool of large-scale capitalists. The dispossessed petty bourgeoisie and their descendants eventually join the propertyless working class, and the ranks of the proletariat increase (Marx and Engels, 1848:70-71, 75; Marx, 1867:625-628). At the same time, the disappearance of this middle class of small owners makes it more and more apparent that workers and big capital are the only two classes of consequence in the social structure. This realization promotes the awareness among workers of the clear disparity between the two classes, of the separation between bourgeoisie and proletariat. The process whereby this separation emerges and widens is referred to as *class polarization*.

The fifth feature of capitalism to consider here is its alleged tendency to homogenize the working class as time goes on. In the early stages of capitalism, the proletariat is a varied and divided collection of people with different skill levels. These divisions—between skilled artisans and unskilled manual laborers, for example—are obstacles in the way of proletarian solidarity, since the common interests of workers are less apparent when they perform different tasks and receive different wages. Because of the continual technological advances and mechanization of production as capitalism matures, these distinctions become blurred. Increasingly, all proletarians become the same type of worker: semiskilled minders of machines. This common position is an added impetus toward proletarian class awareness (Marx, 1844:237; Marx and Engels, 1848:71).

A sixth process—one that stimulates class polarization still further—concerns the gap in material well-being and living standards between capitalists and workers. As capitalism matures, *absolute* living standards for workers may improve, or at least not worsen, because of the huge productive capacity of capitalism and the surplus wealth this production generates. However, the *relative* difference in economic rewards between owners and workers continues to widen, in Marx's view, because a larger share of the surplus always goes to the capitalist (Marx, 1867:645). Because of this widening gap and the relative impoverishment of the workers, class polarization once again is promoted.

A seventh and final factor in capitalist development that spurs its overthrow is the rise of stock ownership and the joint stock company. As noted earlier, the capitalist class begins by playing a progressive role in social change. Its innovations and leadership are essential in the push towards the higher stages of society Marx envisions, and its members play an active part in managing the productive process and making administrative decisions. However, under advanced capitalism, businesses increasingly are owned only on paper, with individuals buying stocks in companies. To Marx, such a system makes it patently obvious to the workers that mere ownership of property is entirely superfluous to productive activity. Owners, as stockholders, control the means of production and accumulate rewards from it, yet offer little in return. They may not even be involved in administration, since they can hire managers to perform this task for them. Once again, then, the distinction between proletarian and capitalist is magnified and the dispensability of the bourgeoisie underscored (Marx, 1894:427-429; cf. Giddens, 1971:52-60; 1973:34-37).

Obstacles to Revolution: Ideology and Superstructure

All of these processes and developments in the capitalist system promote the emergence of the fundamental division between bourgeoisie and proletariat. The objective differences in living conditions and the basic opposition of interests are there. Nevertheless, they must be recognized as such by the proletariat before revolutionary change can occur. The proletariat must then organize, mobilize, and act as a class-conscious group to transform society.

Although one might expect Marx to consider both the recognition of the situation and subsequent action to be inevitable occurrences, in fact he sees several important obstacles blocking the path to revolution. These obstacles are sometimes classified under the general term *superstructure*. Superstructure is frequently a confusing concept because it can refer to two separate but related phenomena. First, the superstructure is bound up with the concept of *ideology*, which is essentially the set of ideas or beliefs that govern people's lives. But superstructure also designates the social structures or organizations people erect to implement these ideas. Thus, for example, religion is a system of beliefs about the world, and the church is the structural embodiment of these religious ideas. The state or political structure is likewise the structural manifestation of the laws, political enactments, rules, and regulations by which society is governed. In many ways, the superstructure concept is like the familiar sociological concept of *institution*, which has a similar dual meaning (cf. Williams, 1960:30-35; 515-520).

Marx uses the concept of superstructure in both these senses and rarely distinguishes between them. The state and religion are the major components of the superstructure in Marx's conception, but all "ideological forms," including "the legal, political, religious, aesthetic, or philosophic," are involved (Marx, 1859:52; 1867:82). Thus, any structure that serves as an embodiment of the ideas that govern us, and moreover is used as a creator and sender of these ideas, is presumably part of this ideological apparatus or superstructure. Hence, the educational system and media of mass communication would be included here, for they play an increasingly important role in modern society as means by which people learn ideas and acquire information (cf. Marx and Engels, 1848:88).

The term *superstructure* implies that some substructure, or *infra-structure*, also exists. To Marx, this underlying basis to social life is of course the economic system, the "mode of production of material life" (Marx, 1859:52; 1867:82). What Marx means to convey in the distinction between superstructure and infrastructure is not that the two types of phenomena are entirely unrelated. On the contrary, he is strongly critical of Hegelian philosophy for setting up this artificial separation. Even worse, in Marx's view, is that Hegel then assigns causal priority to ideas over material life, implying that ideas somehow exist before the human reality in which they take shape and are implemented. Marx takes such pains to reject this view that he sometimes seems to make the opposite, and equally tenuous, argument that ideas are totally secondary results of social conditions and have no part in shaping these conditions (e.g., Marx, 1867:19). In fact, Marx's position is for the most part a middle one between the *materialist* and the *idealist* view (Avineri, 1968:69). Ideas and the social conditions in which they operate clearly interact with one another in a continual process of change, and the existence of one is not possible without the other. To argue that ideas in themselves can have no causal impact on material reality is to contradict the great influence of Marx's own ideas on the course of historical social change (Berlin, 1963:284).

The distinction between ideas and material reality is relevant to our discussion because both the ideological and the structural aspects of the superstructure are useful to the capitalist class for maintaining the existing economic system, or infrastructure. To Marx it is clear that the dominant ideas in any historical epoch are the ideas that the dominant class in that epoch generates (Marx and Engels, 1846:59). While dissenting ideas may find the occasional outlet, as in Marx's own radical journalism, the values, beliefs, and styles of thought that predominate are those created by the ruling class. In capitalism, then, it is the bourgeoisie's values and ideas that are most widely heard and accepted by the population— not only by the members of the bourgeoisie but also by large portions of the working class. This is one of the subtler and more insidious ways in which the path to revolution is obstructed. The bourgeois overthrow of feudalism was for some time impeded by the fact that the bourgeoisie itself accepted or believed in loyalty to higher authority, the divine right of kings, and other tenets of feudal society. In the same way, workers learn through the ideological apparatus of capitalist society that freedom, individualism, and equality are the guiding beliefs of the modern age. The power of ideas is evidenced by the belief among so many workers that these ideas really operate in capitalist society, even though to Marx they only serve the interests of the privileged class. To Marx the workers are free only to sell their labor power to the bourgeoisie and hence are equal only in their universal exploitation (cf. Marx and Engels, 1846:39-41; 1848:84-85; Berlin, 1963:149).

All the segments of the superstructure—the political, legal, religious, educational, and communication systems—disseminate these views. In addition, certain branches of the political or state apparatus, namely the military and the police, play a key part as enforcers of the ideas, especially the laws, enacted and administered in capitalist society. Marx asserts in the *Communist Manifesto* that the state is a mere "committee for managing the common affairs of the whole bourgeoisie" (Marx and Engels, 1848:61). This is partly a polemical exaggeration; nevertheless, Marx does believe that the prime purposes of the political system in capitalism are to administer and implement the legal relations of the society and to use force if necessary against those who disobey these laws. At the same time, to the extent that laws are consistent with bourgeois interests for the most part, then the actions of the state are ultimately in the interests of the bourgeoisie. Thus it is that the state leadership can appear to be acting for the general good and enforcing the law in the public interest. State leaders may even believe sincerely that they are doing so, since politicians are equally subject to the seductive appeal of the dominant ideology. Yet, in seeming to serve the general good, the state ultimately works in the overall interest of those who control the economic structure—the bourgeoisie.

Capitalism's End and Future Society

With all these resources at the disposal of the capitalist class, one may wonder that Marx expected a proletarian revolution to occur at all. Indeed, some critics would point to the absence of any current worldwide socialist movement as evidence that Marx's expectations will go unfulfilled. At the same time, however, many of the problems and developments Marx foresaw in the capitalist system have occurred, especially the regular economic crises. This suggests that his views have been at least partly confirmed.

As we have noted, Marx sees the end of capitalism coming about because of the internal problems it generates for itself. He expects the class polarization resulting from these difficulties to override gradually the ideological obstacles standing in the way of complete working-class awareness of their common position and their revolutionary potential. Marx argues that the proletarians in capitalism share a common class position by the very fact that they are all people excluded from control of the means of production. In Marx's terms, the proletariat forms in this sense a "class in itself" (Marx, 1847:211). The awareness of this common objective position, coupled with a belief in the possibility of change and a concerted desire to seek change, will, despite the repressive power of the state's coercive forces, convert this class in itself to a "class for itself"—a revolutionary force that will fundamentally alter capitalist society (Marx, 1847:211).

Marx, however, is not confident in the proletariat's ability to accomplish revolutionary action without the added assistance, organization, and leadership of others (cf. Avineri, 1968:63). He mentions in particular "a small section of the ruling class," presumably revolutionary intellectuals and enlightened members of the bourgeoisie, who recognize the destiny of the proletariat and go over to its side (Marx and Engels, 1848: 74-75).

Socialism and Dictatorship of the Proletariat

The specific details of how this revolutionary act will come about are never offered by Marx, for, as has been frequently pointed out, Marx is not concerned with providing a blueprint for the revolution or for the structure of the society that will supersede capitalism (e.g., Selsam et al., 1970:20; Singer, 1980:59). Nevertheless, some idea of what Marx envisions for the future can be gleaned from bits and pieces of his writings.

It appears that Marx expects at least two stages in the system that will replace capitalism. The first stage, which may be termed *socialism*, is a temporary one that does not represent the best or highest form of society but is necessary in the transition from capitalism. During this transition, certain residual features of bourgeois society must be retained for a time, particularly some form of state or political apparatus. The state is needed to implement key changes that will eventually make its own existence unnecessary. Political power and decision-making will be centralized in this body; however, unlike the state in capitalism, the socialist state will truly represent the interests of all people and not the special interests of any single group.

This "dictatorship of the proletariat," as Marx sometimes refers to it (Marx, 1875:16), will ensure that important initial policies are instituted: abolition of landed property holdings and inheritance rights, centralization of banking in a government bank, institution of a graduated income tax, partial extension of the state ownership of factories and production, abolition of some forms of child labor, and free education for children (Marx and Engels, 1848:94). Many of these ideas seem rather moderate by contemporary standards and in fact have been put into practice by most capitalist democratic governments. The suggestion of only a partial movement of the state to take over production in this first stage seems especially restrained (cf. Avineri, 1968:206).

However, it is clear to Marx that ultimately the entire productive process must be taken out of the hands of private interests. Marx sees the state-directed socialist system as an initial stage that is required while transitional wrinkles are ironed out. During this period, the truly social or communal nature of humanity and the system of material production will gradually become clear to all. The extraction of surplus by a dominant group for its own purposes will no longer occur. Instead, wealth generated in production will be distributed to all workers, after a common fund has first been set aside to provide education, health facilities, social services, and the like. The distribution of wealth during this first stage of socialism will be done on the basis that each worker "receives back from society— after the deductions have been made—exactly what he gives to it" (Marx, 1875:8; cf. Giddens, 1971:61). This policy suggests that all people will be rewarded fairly but not necessarily equally, since individuals will clearly vary in terms of the ability and effort they put into their work. This system, in Marx's words, "tacitly recognizes unequal individual endowment and thus productive capacity as natural privileges" (Marx, 1875:9).

This does not sound like a classless society, at least in the sense that all people are treated exactly the same. Again, however, Marx sees this as a transitional phase in the move toward the final system. In this first stage, people have yet to overcome all the divisive tendencies instilled in them by the ills of capitalist ideology, all the defects of a changing system that "has just emerged after prolonged birth pangs from capitalist society" (Marx, 1875:10). Marx believed that "it was in general incorrect to make a fuss about so-called '*distribution*' of goods" (Marx, 1875:10). The most important issue for Marx is *relations* between groups, not the *distribution* of wealth to individuals. Marx sees the concern with distribution as a problem stemming from the old bourgeois consciousness and emphasis on individualism. Once the truly social basis of production is recognized, once it is clear that work must be a cooperative enterprise involving every worker and in the interest of every worker, then concerns with the distribution of wealth will dissipate. Differences in ability, effort, responsibility, and so on may continue but will be greatly reduced. People will lose their view of one another as competitors and instead find satisfaction in their differences and in the different roles they play in the collective process of production (Marx, 1847:190; cf. Avineri, 1968:232).

This seems to allow for the continued existence of a division of labor into specific tasks for each worker, despite the fact that elsewhere Marx frequently points to the evils wrought in capitalism by the division of labor (e.g., Marx, 1847:182). It would appear that what will happen as society progresses through the first stage of socialism is a gradual revision and transformation of the division of labor itself. Two key changes in particular may be noted. First, there will be much greater diversity in the jobs that each worker is able to do. Work may be subdivided into specialized segments, but the same worker will not always perform the same segment. Each worker will be able to "hunt in the morning, fish in the afternoon, rear cattle in the evening, criticise after dinner" (Marx and Engels, 1846:47). This seems to be Marx's quaint way of saying that in the future work will be more varied and workers more versatile. Second, it appears that Marx sees the expansion of mechanized and automated production methods as a means to eliminate the routine drudgery imposed by the division of labor under capitalism. The "progress of technology" and "the application of science to production" under socialism will mean that the worker will be a "regulator" of the production process, "mastering it" rather than being enslaved by it (Marx, 1858:705; also Marx, 1847:190; cf. McLellan, 1971:216; Giddens, 1971:63).

Communism

When these changes in the consciousness of people and in the structure of society are engendered and allowed to flourish, the first stage of socialism will have begun to fade, bringing on the highest societal form, true *communism*. The state's role as central decision-maker will have been played out, and the state "will have died away" (Marx, 1875:16). It will be replaced by a decentralized, nonauthoritarian system of administration of the society by all the people. It is not clear what the logistics of this administration are—once again there is no detailed plan—but the new human consciousness, which sees people in their true character, will ensure that the society will function, unencumbered by the distorting effects of bourgeois self-interest, greed, and the pursuit of power. Then it will be possible to implement Marx's dictum of equality and selflessness: "From each according to his ability, to each according to his needs" (Marx, 1875:10).

It is essentially Marx's faith in the potential of humans to act as social beings in a universal society that is the basis for his expectations and visions of the future of society. The views of human nature and the perfectibility of people that Marx learned early in life and retained throughout his intellectual development are reflected here and seem strangely paradoxical, given his own apparent aloofness toward humanity in general and his reluctance to involve himself personally in the revolution (Avineri, 1968:251-252; Berlin, 1963:1-3).

We will see in the subsequent chapters of this book the tremendous influence that Marx's ideas have had on the study of social inequality and class structure in modern societies. We will also see the skepticism that Marx has provoked in some of those who were to write after him. Both adherents and critics, however, readily acknowledge the deep intellectual debt owed to Marx. His analysis of class structure in capitalist society provides a touchstone against which to compare and assess all subsequent views of social inequality in advanced society. In the next chapter, we will consider the second great classical theorist of social inequality, Max Weber. As we shall see, Weber provides a prime example of how both the positive influences of Marx's theory and numerous critical reactions to specific aspects of it can be bound up in the same writer's work.

Summary

In this chapter we have reviewed the key elements in Marx's theory of class and his analysis of capitalism. We began with an outline of some of the significant experiences in his own life that helped shape his thought. We then considered his contention that class struggle has been the consistent basis for social change and inequality throughout history. The remainder of the chapter dealt with the key issues Marx raised concerning the capitalist form of society. We discussed the distorted nature of work under capitalism; the seven processes inherent in capitalism that promote its transformation from within; the various obstacles in the way of capitalism's revolutionary overthrow; and the ultimate end of capitalism, with a brief sketch of the socialist and communist societal forms that Marx anticipated.

CHAPTER THREE

Max Weber and the Multiple Bases for Inequality

"In the last analysis, the processes of economic development are struggles for power." Max Weber, Inaugural Lecture at Freiburg University, 1894

Introduction

Max Weber is the second major classical theorist we shall consider. Weber's analysis is frequently viewed as a distinct alternative to and departure from Marx's theory of class. Indeed, there are significant differences between the ideas of Marx and Weber that cannot be overlooked. At the same time, however, we shall find notable similarities in the interests and conclusions of these two writers. A thorough appreciation of both the similarities and the differences in their work is essential to our understanding of social inequality and of the current state of theory in this field.

Perhaps the most obvious similarity between Marx and Weber is their common concern with examining the origins and development of modern capitalist society using an historical method. In this regard, of course, Marx and Weber share with most nineteenth-century social analysts an interest in how societies have changed or evolved from traditional to modern forms. The two writers are not in total accord about the nature and extent of social inequality, the forces that govern social change, or the likelihood of inequality in future societies. Nevertheless, there can be no doubt that Weber's general conceptions of capitalism, social class, and numerous related ideas are greatly influenced by Marx's writings, virtually all of which preceded his own work. Weber himself identifies Marx as one of the two major intellectual influences (along with Nietzsche) of Weber's time (e.g., Gerth and Mills, 1967:61-62; Giddens, 1972:58; Coser, 1977:249-250).

Sometimes Weber's differences with Marx do not involve substantive issues in sociology so much as they bear on the differing political positions of the two men and their distinct opinions on the likelihood and desirability of socialist revolution. Moreover, often Weber's alleged differences with Marx are really disagreements with certain Marxists of Weber's day, disciples of Marx who interpreted his theories and applied them for their own purposes. Even in these cases it is fair to say that a good deal of Weber's work is a "positive critique" of Marx and Marxism, a "fruitful battle with historical materialism" (Gerth and Mills, 1967:63).

One of the unfortunate parallels between the two writers is that neither one provides a systematic and detailed analysis of social inequality in modern societies. This omission is partly because neither man lived long enough to complete this task and partly because neither thinker is concerned with the issue of social inequality as his principal focus. Indeed, it is somewhat ironic that theoretical developments in the study of social inequality owe so much to two writers for whom the topic was not their primary interest. For Weber as for Marx, then, we must rely on rather short discussions, scattered through his writings, as the means for deciphering his general view of social inequality.

In our analysis of Weber's thought we will take the position that his major contribution to the theory of social inequality lies in his attempt to offer a positive or constructive critique of Marx's ideas, especially as these ideas were interpreted by Marxists of Weber's time. Weber's position entails a number of modifications of the Marxist view. If there is a common theme in his criticisms, it is that the accurate description and explanation of inequality and other social phenomena involve much greater complexity and variability than some Marxists seem to suggest. This is not to imply that Marxism in its many forms is crude and simplistic, though this charge can be made against specific versions of social theory, Marxist or otherwise. Rather, it is to say that Marxist theory proceeds from the conviction that there is a single, ultimate basis upon which social life is built: the economic, material realm of human activity. Other social phenomena—the political or religious, for example—may be worthy of study, but, in the last analysis, these too are explicable in terms of economic forces. To Marxists, then, the study of these aspects of society should not be allowed to cloud our understanding that the real basis of social structure and inequality is economic.

For Weber, however, the range of noneconomic social forces cannot be dismissed as merely secondary to, or determined by, the economic. On the contrary, noneconomic considerations, especially the ideas and interests that emerge from politics, religion, and other institutional structures, have a certain autonomy from the economic in many instances. Moreover, these forces sometimes influence economic structures and behavior as much as they are influenced by them. To many Marxists, such an emphasis on multiple structures only distorts our understanding, because it lays down a smokescreen that masks the underlying material basis for social life. In the Weberian view, these details do not distort our picture of reality. On the contrary, distortion stems from failing to recognize these diverse explanations and multiple causes for social inequality.

A detailed treatment of this general difference between Weber and Marxism, as well as an assessment of the common elements that the works of Marx and Weber share, is the central concern of this chapter. We begin with a brief examination of the life experiences and intellectual influences that affected Weber's thought.

Biographical and Intellectual Sketch

Early Life

Max Weber was born April 21, 1864, at Erfurt, in the German province of Thuringia. By this time, Karl Marx was a forty-six-year-old émigré living in England; hence, the two men never met. There are some broad similarities between the backgrounds of Marx and Weber. Like Marx, Weber grew up in a relatively privileged, middle-class, German household. Weber's father, like Marx's, was trained in law, though he eventually pursued a career in politics and government at the municipal and later the national level. Like Marx, Weber initially followed his father's wishes and enrolled in law school. This was at the University of Heidelberg in 1882, one year before Marx's death. In the same way that Marx spent his early university days carousing and having a good time, so too did Weber enjoy his initial student life for a time. He joined his father's old fraternity and took a regular part in fencing and drinking bouts. Thus, Weber, who had been a sickly, frail, and bookish child, developed into a hearty, somewhat barrel-shaped young man, complete with dueling scars (Coser, 1977:236; Gerth and Mills, 1967:8). At the same time, Weber managed to be an excellent, conscientious student who was popular with his fellows, partly because of his willingness to help them at examination time.

In contrast to Marx, Weber chose to stick with his legal studies, though, like Marx, he became widely read in other areas, including economics, philosophy, history, and theology. His first year in Heidelberg was followed by a year of compulsory military service at Strasbourg, after which he resumed his legal studies, this time at Marx's old school, the University of Berlin. The move to Berlin was prompted mainly by the wishes of Weber's parents, who had settled there some years before. They were concerned about his boisterous behavior at Heidelberg and sought to instill more discipline into his life by having him live at home.

Family Influences

The family emphasis on discipline was particularly evident in Weber's father, a strict, authoritarian, and brutish man who frequently mistreated his wife. One possible effect on Weber of this family atmosphere was a rejection of arbitrary power and a distrust of authority without accountability. The divergence between Weber and his father is evident in his dislike for his father's political beliefs, which favored the conservative, reactionary policies of the German kaiser and chancellor Otto von Bismarck. Like Marx, Weber was a supporter of democracy and human freedom. This is important to recognize because, as Giddens notes, some writers have mistaken Weber's patriotism for Germany and his belief in strong leadership as evidence of right-wing or fascist tendencies (Giddens, 1972:7-8). However, in contrast to Marx, Weber was far less optimistic about the prospects that democracy would survive in future societies. Moreover, as we shall see, Weber suspected that socialism would be an even greater threat to democracy and freedom than would capitalism. Humanity's best hope, according to Weber, lay in a liberal political system, guided by strong but enlightened leaders and operating within an essentially capitalist economic framework. Weber's political views were influenced in this direction by his uncle, Herman Baumgarten, whom he visited frequently during and after his military service at Strasbourg and who retained a strong belief in the liberal democratic principles Weber's father had foresaken.

Weber's visits with his uncle and other relatives in Strasbourg led to other events that significantly influenced his thought. Although Weber's mother was a devout Calvinist, her religious beliefs had not made a notable impression on Weber in his early years. However, in Strasbourg, Weber was in contact with several family members, including his mother's sisters, many of whom were prone to frequent religious and mystical experiences (Gerth and Mills, 1967:9). Thus, Weber witnessed at first hand the power that religious ideas and beliefs can have over people. Though Weber never became a religious man himself, these events helped stimulate his eventual interest in the study of religion and the influence that religious beliefs and other ideas could have in shaping society. Weber's position on this point may be contrasted with that of certain Marxists of his day, who argued that ideas and beliefs are wholly products of social interaction and organization, especially within the sphere of economic production. Weber disagreed with those who adopted this materialist view in the extreme, thereby denying the possibility that ideas could themselves influence and even generate economic structures and behavior, rather than being mere consequences of these material forces.

Success and Crisis

Weber lived at his parents' Berlin home for almost eight years, beginning in 1884. During this period he revealed both tremendous scholarly ability and a voracious appetite for work. He completed law school, worked as a junior barrister, and at the same time followed a rigorous course of study leading to a Ph.D. in law in 1889. Unlike Marx, who was denied an academic career because of his political beliefs, Weber enjoyed a meteoric rise in the university community. He began as a lecturer in law at Berlin in 1891. This position was soon followed by a senior professorship in economics at Freiburg in 1894. In 1896, at age thirty-two, Weber became chairman of economics at Heidelberg.

These successes, however, came at the price of a heavy work load that taxed him mentally and physically. Then, in 1897, a crisis triggered some major changes in Weber's life. During a visit by his parents to his home in Heidelberg, Weber argued bitterly with his father over the continued mistreatment of his mother and drove his father from the house. Not long after, Weber's father died. The guilt Weber felt over these events, coupled with the strain of overwork, led to his psychological collapse. Weber's mental condition was never completely diagnosed and recurred intermittently for the rest of his life. Until just before his death, Weber did not hold another full-time teaching position. Nevertheless, Weber managed a partial recovery and, with regular pauses for travel and recuperation, was able to continue his research. In fact, his most famous and important works really began to take shape only after this initial breakdown.

America and Capitalism

An important surge in Weber's work occurred soon after he traveled to the United States in late 1904. His observation of American capitalist society in action made a lasting impression on his thought in a variety of ways. While his reactions were not entirely positive, on the whole Weber admired the United States. He saw in its mass political parties, voluntary citizens' organizations, and other institutions the possibility that freedom and democracy might be sustained in future societies. Weber was a nationalist concerned with the development of his own country, and some have implied that he perceived in the United States the model for a new German society (Gerth and Mills, 1967:17). However, it appears that Weber saw too many contrasts between America and Germany for any direct imitation to be practicable. Moreover, certain aspects of the American system underscored for Weber the paradoxical and even contradictory nature of mass democracy. In particular, Weber noted that bureaucracy—in the form of political-party machines managed by professional politicians and organizers—was at the same time both essential to democratic action in large-scale complex societies and a threat to democratic principles of equality and participation for all.

Weber was also impressed by the large business corporations in the United States. These enterprises were then coming to the forefront as the dominant forces in the world economy. The movement toward bureaucracy was apparent in the corporations as well, contributing to Weber's ultimate conclusion that bureaucratization is a key process in the general trend of modern societies toward *rationalization*. Weber perceived in all spheres of the social structure—politics, economics, religion, education, and so on—this tendency to develop permanent, organized systems for processing problems and people in regular, routine ways. Weber saw bureaucracy as the only organizational form capable of keeping modern, complex societies operating and thus as both inevitable and inescapable. Yet, at the same time, he regretted its destructive impact on the quality of human interaction and on human freedom (e.g., Bendix, 1962:7, 458-459).

After his American travels, in the period up to World War I, Weber made a notable intellectual recovery. His writing began anew, and in 1905 he published perhaps his most famous work, *The Protestant Ethic and the Spirit of Capitalism*. We have already discussed the Calvinist background of Weber's mother, the religious experiences of his mother's family, and the subsequent impact of religion on Weber's thought. This impact is most evident in *The Protestant Ethic*. In this analysis, Weber argues that the historical development of modern capitalism was significantly shaped by the ideas and beliefs of certain ascetic Protestant sects, particularly Calvinism. This thesis is consistent with his general critique of materialism, for he seeks to demonstrate how ideas, especially religious beliefs, can and do influence economic and social structures like capitalism, rather than simply reflecting such structures. His views on this point were also affected by his visit to America, where he observed the tendency for those of ascetic Protestant backgrounds to be overrepresented among the most successful capitalists (cf. Coser, 1977:239).

Academic and Political Prominence

Weber's academic reputation now began to grow anew. His home in Heidelberg became a regular meeting place for prominent German intellectuals. He was soon writing numerous works on a variety of topics, including several essays on method in the social sciences. His key work for the study of social inequality, *Economy and Society*, was begun around this time (1909) and continued intermittently but unfortunately was never finished (Aron, 1970:305).

One crucial reason for the interruption of Weber's research was the outbreak of World War I. A patriotic German, Weber initially supported the war effort, enlisted as a reserve officer, and served as director of military hospitals around Heidelberg. However, he soon became disillusioned with the war, characteristically, because he questioned the motives and competence of the political regime of the German monarch, Kaiser Wilhelm II (cf. Giddens, 1972:21-22).

Weber had always been interested in his country's political fortunes and gradually became directly involved in them. He unofficially sought to convince the German leadership to stop the fighting, without success, and later acted as an advisor to the German delegation to the Versailles peace conference, which ended the war. His political activities also included participation in the drafting of a new German constitution and an increasingly large role in political campaigns. Some even viewed Weber as a potential candidate for the German presidency (Coser, 1977:241). However, his earlier criticisms of the monarchy and of the kaiser's conservative government made support from this quarter unlikely. His dislike of the opposition socialist factions—some of whom he suggested should be in either "the madhouse" or "the zoological gardens" —was also well-known (Giddens, 1972:25, 17). Thus, Weber's political prospects eventually dissipated.

Instead of a political career, Weber remained with his academic pursuits and was finally able to resume full-time teaching once again, this time at the University of Munich. His scholarly eminence and intellectual vigor reestablished, Weber seemed on the verge of even greater things when in June 1920 he was stricken with pneumonia and suddenly died, at the age of 56. As with Marx, then, death cut short Weber's career before he was able to complete a thorough and systematic analysis of social inequality. As with Marx again, though, it is possible to piece together the major strands of Weber's work on this topic and identify a more or less coherent basis for his emerging theory. A presentation of these main features of the Weberian perspective and how it compares to that of Marx is our next consideration.

The Weberian Perspective: Complexity and Pluralism in Inequality

In the preceding chapter we noted that the central point in Marx's theory of social structure is his conviction that, in the last analysis, societies take shape and change through one key process: the struggle between groups for control of the economy, the system of material production. To recognize Marx's singular emphasis on economics is to deny neither his theoretical sophistication nor his obvious awareness of the complex nature of modern societies. Nevertheless, a tendency does exist to view Marx's position as an oversimplified one. In part, this may reflect a failure by certain critics to acknowledge the polemical, and hence purposely exaggerated, nature of some of Marx's statements. In other instances, the responsibility for oversimplifying the original Marxian formulation must fall on the shoulders of certain Marxist disciples, including some who have attempted to put socialist principles into practice in real societies (cf. Avineri, 1968:252).

In either case, it is clear that Weber's alternative view of social structure stems in part from his reaction to an oversimplified or vulgarized Marxism. Thus, a consistent feature of Weber's sociology is his conviction that social processes and forces are always complex and rarely explicable in simple terms. Weber's emphasis on complexity is evident in a variety of ways that, taken together, form the major substance of our discussion in this chapter. There are six areas in particular that we shall examine because of their relevance to the understanding of Weber's general thought and his perspective on social inequality.

First, there is Weber's overall approach to research and sociological method, with its stress on *causal pluralism* and the *probabilistic* nature of social explanation. Second, there is Weber's sense of the often intricate interplay between ideas and material reality, or between the subjective and objective aspects of social life. The third point concerns Weber's multiple conception of the class structure in capitalist society. Fourth is Weber's pluralist view of the bases for hierarchy and group formation in social structures: class, status, and party. The fifth way in which Weber adds complexity to the analysis of inequality is in his outline of the several types of *power* or *domination* in social life. Finally, we shall assess Weber's contention that the control of economic production is just one means by which some people are able to dominate others. Thus, to understand social inequality, we must recognize the several *means of administration*, especially in the form of rationalized bureaucracies, that wield power in modern societies. This last point leads into the concluding discussion, in which we consider Weber's assessment of the prospects for democracy and the socialist alternative in future societies.

Weber on Method: Probability and Causal Pluralism

Max Weber wrote extensively on the topic of research methods in the social sciences. (See especially the collection of essays in Shils and Finch, 1949.) While it is beyond the purposes of this discussion to consider Weber's methodological orientation in detail, there are certain aspects of his position that are relevant to our analysis. To begin with, we can briefly characterize Weber's approach as a compromise between two opposing schools of thought: those who reject any possibility of applying the techniques of natural science to predict or explain social behavior and those so-called *positivists* who, on the contrary, contend that the methods and assumptions of sociological research should be essentially identical with those of, say, physics or chemistry (cf. Runciman, 1978:65). Weber locates sociology somewhere between the natural sciences and a discipline like history, in terms of both the generality of explanation and the precision of research techniques. Whereas history concerns itself with the understanding of "important individual events", sociology deals with the observation and explanation of "generalized uniformities" in recurring empirical processes (Weber, 1922:29, 19). Unlike history, sociology can offer theories to account for these empirical regularities. However, social explanations typically will not hold without qualification, for all times, all cases, or all conditions. This feature makes sociological explanations distinct from those in natural science to the degree that the latter will hold invariably, assuming appropriate controls for extraneous circumstances.

There are many possible reasons for this essential difference between natural science and social science, including the lesser precision of social concepts and the fact that explanations in social science are subject to constant revision over time, as conditions change (Runciman, 1978:65). Thus, while chemical elements will interact today in the same way as they did centuries ago, individuals or groups, in different historical and social contexts may not, and the social scientist must take this possibility into account. For these and other reasons, Weber raises certain restrictions concerning the application of the scientific method in social research. Two of these restrictions or complications are the probabilistic nature of social inquiry and the inherent pluralism in social causation.

Probability
Weber frequently refers to probability when discussing social phenomena (e.g., Weber in Parsons, 1947:99-100, 118-119, 126, 146). In effect, Weber argues that X *may* lead to Y in some, or even most, instances but rarely without exception. This means that we can assess, and sometimes calculate, the probability that X is a cause of Y, but we cannot establish that

X will *always* lead to Y, since this is not in the nature of social processes (cf. Weber, 1922:11-12; cf. Giddens, 1971:149, 153). If we take, for example, Marx's contention that the dominant ideas in a society are the ideas of the ruling class, this may be true for some or most of the ideas that predominate in a society but probably not for every dominant idea we could examine. The exceptions do not mean, however, that Marx's claim about the origin of ideas is incorrect. Rather, they indicate that the claim is applicable part of the time and that, within a certain probability, we can predict correctly what ideas predominate in society by examining those generated by the ruling class.

Causal Pluralism

And what of those exceptional cases that do not fit our prediction or explanation? These must be examined to determine, where possible, the reasons for their deviation from our expectations. According to Weber there are numerous other factors that inevitably are not taken into account when one poses a simple explanation for something. It is conceivable that these additional factors are responsible for deviant cases; hence, it is essential to search for multiple causes for social phenomena, following a strategy of "causal pluralism" (Gerth and Mills, 1967:34, 54, 61). This method seeks social explanation by means of "a pluralistic analysis of factors, which may be isolated and gauged in terms of their respective causal weights" (Gerth and Mills, 1967:65).

If, for example, we wished to understand why some people are rich and others are poor, we might try to explain these differences in wealth in terms of the family class background of the people involved. Perhaps all rich people were born into wealthy families and all poor people were born into poor families, with no other factors playing a part in economic success or failure. In that case, we would be able to explain economic inequality perfectly on the basis of one factor: inheritance of wealth. However, in a complex society, it is probable that other factors also influence one's economic position, not just inheritance. Perhaps an individual's gender or race has an effect on economic well-being, independent of inherited wealth. Even physical beauty or athletic prowess might be related to economic position. Of course, not all of these possible influences would have the same degree of impact. Presumably, for example, inheritance or race would have a greater effect than beauty in most cases. But, whatever the result of the inquiry, it is imperative that the social scientist look for the several potential causes for social phenomena and assess their relative effects, large or small, by means of empirical observation.

Subjective Factors and the Idealism-Materialism Debate

Subjective Meanings and Explanation

Another one of the complexities that marks social life, and which to Weber must be considered in any social theory, is the subjective nature of human interaction. This point is related to our previous discussion of Weber's method, since these subjective considerations signify another important distinction between natural and social science. One of the advantages of natural science, and another reason for its greater precision, is that it need deal only with objectively observable and interpretable information. Physics and chemistry, for example, analyze the behavior of inanimate objects or forces that, under controlled conditions, can be seen to behave in perfectly predictable ways. In social science, however, the units of observation are individual human beings, whose actions are determined not only by objective conditions but also by subjective forces that lie outside the realm of natural science. Thus, social explanations must take into account these additional subjective aspects of social life: the meanings people attach to their actions, the ideas that govern their behavior, and their consciousness and perceptions of the world around them.

Certain kinds of human behavior can be readily understood by analyzing subjective phenomena. What Weber calls *rational action*, the calculated pursuit of individual interests, is predictable with a high level of certainty because one can successfully assume what subjective motives are at work in most cases. This kind of behavior is epitomized in the actions of capitalists in the marketplace, where subjective interests are geared almost completely to the profit motive or the maximization of wealth (cf. Weber, 1922:30).

However, not all human behavior follows the *ideal type* of rational action. (*Ideal type* refers to a *pure* form here, not necessarily a desirable one.) Some actions are governed by *nonrational* or even irrational considerations—traditional beliefs, love, envy, vengeance, and so on—usually in combination with rational concerns. Now, the more that human actions depart from the purely rational type, the more difficult it becomes to discern, in the external acts of people, the subjective intent of their behavior (Weber, 1922:6). This both adds to the complexity and decreases the precision of social research and social explanation. At the same time, however, it opens up for the sociologist a whole area of inquiry that is closed to the natural scientist and so, in this sense, is an advantage of sociology over natural science. In fact, to Weber it is this special focus of sociology on subjective meaning and explanation that distinguishes it from other kinds of knowledge (Weber, 1922:15).

Ideas and Material Life

Weber's stress on subjective factors as an integral part of social explanation is consistent once again with his rejection of vulgar Marxist theory. In this case, the point at issue primarily concerns the debate over the relationship between ideas and material reality. As noted in Chapter 2, one of Marx's early tasks was to demonstrate the fallacy in Hegel's idealist philosophy, in which ideas are analyzed without regard for the social conditions in which they emerge and operate. Weber and Marx appear in fact to hold very similar positions on this point (Giddens, 1971:209-210). The problem for Weber, however, is that many of Marx's disciples, including Engels, once again have replaced Marx's original formulation with an oversimplified and extreme materialist view, which treats ideas and other subjective phenomena as mere by-products of concrete social conditions, totally irrelevant to the explanation of human action.

Thus, Weber takes pains throughout his work to demonstrate that social life is not understood so simply. In his view, those who employ only material, economic factors to explain social action are doomed to failure, because the subjective meanings and ideas people live by frequently produce effects different from those that a simple materialist theory would predict. One of Weber's early works points out, for example, that peasants in nineteenth-century Germany chose the freedom (but economic hardship) of wage labor over the relative economic well-being (but servitude) of bonded serfdom (cf. Giddens, 1971:122-123). To Weber, this is but one instance of the tendency for people to put a subjective meaning, the idea of freedom in this case, ahead of material conditions when choosing a course of action.

Undoubtedly, the best-known work by Weber which treats this issue is *The Protestant Ethic and the Spirit of Capitalism*. One of the objectives of this study is to show how "ideas become effective forces in history" (Weber, 1905:90). Thus, Weber examines the relationship between the religious ideas and beliefs of ascetic Protestant sects, like Calvinism, and the rise of modern capitalism. Weber observed the Calvinist belief that all people are predestined by God either to salvation or to Hell. He believed that this makes it important to each Calvinist to be successful in this world in whatever *calling* he or she chooses. The action of the Calvinist cannot of course determine whether one is saved or damned, since everyone is predestined. However, the psychological need to *appear* to be one of the chosen, to "shew oneself approved unto God" by being a success in this life, is sufficient motivation. This concerted drive for success, when combined with the belief in asceticism, the rejection of worldly pleasures, means that Calvinists tend to accumulate wealth that cannot be spent on frivolities and so is invested in ever-expanding capitalist enterprises. Thus, *part* of the reason why certain Protestant sects are overrepresented among the capitalist class, and *part* of the reason why capitalism took the specific direction of development that it did, can be traced to certain dominant ideas in these religions.

It is important to note that Weber never contends that Calvinist religious ideas are the *only* reasons for capitalism's emergence or that capitalism would not have occurred without them. He explicitly rejects such a simplistic explanation as "foolish and doctrinaire" (Weber, 1905:91). It contributes little to our understanding if we "substitute for a one-sided materialism an equally one-sided spiritualistic causal interpretation" (Weber, 1905:183). One-sided explanations are obviously inconsistent with his sense of the complexity of social processes and his deep-seated belief in causal pluralism. Instead, there is an intricate interplay between objective social conditions and the subjective meanings of individual persons' actions. This combination is responsible for the direction of social action and the shape of social structure.

Multiple Classes in Capitalism

To this point we have attempted to demonstrate the pluralist nature of Weber's assumptions about sociological theory and method. The same characteristics are evident in his views on the specific area of social inquiry of concern to us—social inequality. We can detect these characteristics first of all in Weber's conception of class, the central idea in Marx's analysis of social inequality.

In Chapter 2 we noted that Marx defines class by distinguishing between two key groupings—the owners of the means of economic production, or bourgeoisie, and those non-owners who must work as wage laborers, the proletariat. Weber's formulation has broad similarities to Marx's definition, for both writers treat classes in the most basic sense as economic entities. One difference, however, is that Marx is concerned primarily with the social *relations* between his two classes in the productive sphere, especially the relations of domination and exploitation of the workers by the owners and the inherent conflict these generate between classes. As we have seen, the simple *distribution* of wealth was a secondary consideration for Marx. Weber's emphasis is somewhat the reverse, at least with respect to the concept of economic class. He also speaks of class struggle and relations of class domination, but his main emphasis in defining classes seems to be on the distribution of valued objects and the bases on which some people get more than others.

To understand Weber's view, we must begin by noting that he sees classes as economic categories, developing out of human interaction in a *market*. A market here is basically a system of competitive exchange whereby individuals buy and sell things of value in the pursuit of profit (Weber, 1922:82). These things of value are in effect equivalent to what Weber calls "utilities", which include both material "goods", especially property and possessions, and human "services", namely personal skills and labor power (Weber, 1922:63, 68-69). Now, a class is simply an aggregate of people sharing common "situations" in this market, and therefore having similar "economic interests" and "life chances" (Weber, 1922:927-928).

We can see Weber's initial discussion is similar to Marx's because his definition leads to a simple distinction between those who have property and those who have only services to exchange in the marketplace: " 'Property' and 'lack of property' are, therefore, the basic categories of all class situations" (Weber, 1922:927). At this point, however, Weber follows his characteristic course, and reasserts his disagreement with contemporary Marxism, by pointing out what he believes are other important complexities that the two-class model hides: "Class situations are further differentiated . . . according to the kind of property . . . and the kind of services that can be offered in the market" (Weber, 1922:928). Thus, the existence of different kinds of property makes for additional classes within the broad propertied group, and different types of services and job skills distinguish segments of the working class from one another. Taken to its logical extreme, this definition leads to difficulties because it implies that each of the various kinds of property people own, and each of the numerous job categories that can be identified in the marketplace, may signify a separate class (Weber, 1922:928). Thus, almost every individual in a complex economic system like modern capitalism could in a sense represent a distinct class; hence, the concept of class would be meaningless (cf. Giddens, 1973:78-79).

In actual practice, fortunately, Weber does not apply his formulation in this extreme manner. In the end, his version of the class structure lies between the simple dichotomy of the cruder versions of Marxism and the uncompromising pluralism that his own definition implies. Nevertheless, to present the Weberian view of the structure of social classes in capitalism is still difficult because of a disjuncture between two of the sections on class in his unfinished work *Economy and Society* (Weber, 1922:302-307, 926-940). These sections were written at different times and seem inconsistent in places, suggesting that Weber may have revised his initial view after some reconsideration (Giddens, 1973:79).

The solution to these difficulties in the last analysis comes down to drawing a distinction between the idea of class and the related but separate concept of *social class*. As we have already discussed, a class is simply a category, a set of individuals in similar economic circumstances and with similar economic interests. Thus, "a class does not in itself constitute a group [or community]" (Weber, 1922:930); individuals in a simple economic class lack the sense of common position and consciousness of common interests that a true group or community possesses. It is when these subjective qualities are added to the aggregate in question and a process of real group formation emerges that Weber's idea of social class becomes operative. In effect, then, social classes are best understood as economic classes that have acquired in varying degrees some subjective sense of "unity" and "class-conscious organization" (Weber, 1922:302, 305). Here again, the importance Weber attaches to subjective processes is evident.

At the risk of some oversimplification, it is worth pointing out that Weber's distinction between class and social class corresponds broadly to Marx's distinction between a class in itself and a class for itself. That is, just as Marx's class in itself signifies a collectivity that is identifiable on purely economic grounds, without reference to group awareness, so too is Weber's concept of class. And, just as Marx's class for itself possesses a consciousness of common position and interests, so too does Weber's social class. The major difference to be noted here is that Marx used his formulation primarily with reference to the proletariat, in order to indicate the two stages through which the working class must move if it is to become a revolutionary political force for transforming capitalist society. However, Weber's discussion is intended to delineate a whole range of social classes, each of which may differ in the degree of group awareness. Moreover, Weber, as we shall see, believed the highest degree of group consciousness and the most potential for political action and control lay not with the working class but with those at the top of the social structure.

With this additional element of subjective awareness included, Weber's potentially countless economic class categories in capitalism tend to coalesce into a limited set of four social classes. In effect, Weber's (and Marx's) distinction between the propertied and the propertyless is supplemented by the addition of two other classes (Weber, 1922:305). What this addition amounts to, first, is separating the bourgeoisie into those who control large amounts of property, the big capitalists, and those who have relatively small amounts of productive property, the petty bourgeoisie. Similarly, the propertyless category is subdivided by Weber, this time according to the level of skill and training required of those who sell their services in the marketplace. The key distinction here is between the "working class", who tend to have labor power alone at their disposal, and those who have more marketable skills as "specialists", "technicians", "white-collar employees", or "civil servants" (Weber, 1922:305). Thus, interposed between the large-scale bourgeoisie and the mass of proletarians we have two middle classes: owners of small, independent shops, businesses, and farms; and a salaried nonmanual class with special education or skills in such areas as law, medicine, and the sciences.

The discussion of middle classes is of extreme importance for our understanding of Marx and Weber and, as we shall see, stands as perhaps the key issue in present debates over the nature of classes in modern societies. If there is one fundamental difference between Marx and Weber on the subject of class structure, it is their discussion of the middle class— more specifically, the salaried nonmanual segment. We should note, to begin with, that the two writers largely agree on the disposition of the petty-bourgeoisie portion of the middle classes. Both writers note the existence of this class in early capitalism but foresee its gradual reduction as capitalism develops. The reader will recall that Marx saw the petty bourgeoisie as a group that would gradually be swallowed up in the growing concentration of productive property in the hands of large-scale capitalists. Weber points out as well how the chance for individuals to become "self-employed small businessmen" has become "less and less feasible" (Weber, 1922:305).

On the question of the salaried nonmanual class, however, Marx and Weber take quite distinct positions. Despite Marx's emphasis on a two-class model of the capitalist class structure, he is aware of this salaried nonmanual group, of "the constantly growing number of the middle classes, those who stand between the workman on the one hand and the capitalist and landlord on the other" (Marx, 1862:573). Because of his emphasis, however, Marx does not deal with them extensively, perhaps because he does not believe they will be a force of consequence in the ultimate shift from capitalism to socialism. To Marx, the salaried middle class is mainly an auxiliary to the bourgeoisie, a set of nonproduction employees who, because of the great surplus wealth generated at this stage of capitalism, can be hired to perform clerical, technical, and minor administrative services for the bourgeoisie (Marx, 1862:571). Their labor may indeed get them more of the distributed rewards than the industrial proletariat. This unjust advantage over regular production workers also makes them a "burden weighing heavily on the working base," while their collaboration with the bourgeoisie increases "the social security and power of the upper ten thousand" (Marx, 1862:573). Nevertheless, they are in key respects akin to the working class, being in a relationship of exploitation by the bourgeoisie and dependent on the capitalist for wages.

The Weberian conception differs in that it stresses the distributive inequalities that Marx downplays. Members of the salaried middle class have better economic life chances and different economic interests that are in themselves sufficient to identify them as a class distinct from the workers, unlikely to take part in fomenting socialist revolution. The salaried middle class, in Weber's view, will continue to expand in numbers and importance as the children of workers *and* of the petty bourgeoisie move into the market for white-collar posts in the growing bureaucratic organizations of modern society (Weber, 1922:305). Besides, some of the nonmanual middle class, in addition to their distributive advantage over the ordinary workers, occupy jobs in middle management, which place them in relations of domination over other workers. This placement of

salaried workers contributes, in Weber's conception, to a clear split between the middle and working classes and sharply reduces the chances
that salaried employees will support or identify with the working class
in revolutionary action.

Multiple Power Bases: Class, Status, and Party

It is clear from our previous review of Weber's conceptions of class and
social class that he departs from Marx primarily in his delineation of
several, not just two, important class segments. This view of the class
structure is but one element in Weber's more general treatment of social
inequality as a pluralist phenomenon. Hence, the analysis of class inequality, in Weber's mind, must be interwoven with, and compounded by,
the examination of two additional ideas that are conceptually different
from class but that can cut across class distinctions in real societies. The
two concepts are *status* and *party*.

As a starting point, we should note that Weber's famous treatment of
class, status, and party is only part of his larger essay on "political communities" (Weber, 1922: Chapter 9). Thus, underlying the important differences between these three concepts, which we will discuss in the next
two subsections, is their common root in Weber's political analysis. A
key concern in all of Weber's work is with the "politics" of social life,
which broadly speaking is essentially a "struggle" or "conflict" between
individuals or groups with opposing interests and different power resources (Weber, 1922:1398, 1414). *Power* here is the chance (or probability)
one has to do as one wills, even against the resistance of others (Weber,
1922:53, 926). More will be said on the subjects of power and politics in
subsequent sections of this chapter. For now, it is important to be aware
of the pivotal roles these two ideas play in Weber's sociology and to
recognize that class, status, and party are all aspects of "the distribution
of power within the political community" (Weber, 1922:926). Each one
represents a potential basis for coalition or organization, in the pursuit
of personal interests.

Classes versus Status Groups

We have already seen that Weber's classes are categories of individuals
differing in economic clout, in "the power . . . to dispose of goods or skills
. . . in a given economic order" (Weber in Gerth and Mills, 1967:181).
Status, however, is something that normally inheres in real *groups*, not
simple categories of individuals (Weber, 1922:932). In fact, Weber speaks
only of *status groups*, not status categories, which reveals how important
the subjective sense of common membership and group awareness is to
his definition of this concept. In addition, status groups tend to have a

distinctive "style of life," or mode of conduct, that separates them from the rest of the population (Weber, 1922:305, 932). Whereas class membership denotes the extent of one's power in the economic order, status groups are delineated by the power that derives from the "social honour, or prestige" distributed within the "status order" (Weber, 1922:926-927). Thus, the economic-class order and the status order are two distinct hierarchies for representing the relative powers of individuals and groups.

Having drawn this distinction, Weber proceeds to complicate his analysis by indicating conceptual overlaps between class and status. The crucial overlap to clarify is the connection between Weber's idea of status group and his concept of social class. It will be recalled that Weber characterizes social classes as economic classes whose members, to varying degrees, have acquired some sense of group consciousness and a subjective awareness of their common class position. But, as we have noted, subjective awareness is also a basic element in what Weber calls a status group. The key difference here is that status groups are distinguishable from one another not on economic grounds but in terms of social honor. However, whenever economic power is also a basis for both social honor and subjective group awareness, then a social class is also a status group. Thus, Weber asserts that "the status group comes closest to the social class" (Weber, 1922:305). Stripped of its subtler details, what this amounts to is a simple equation: when an economic class, a simple category of people with similar economic power, also takes on the subjective awareness and cohesion of a status group, the result is a *social* class.

It is clear from this interrelation between social class and status group that Weber does not seek to portray the economic and status orders as unrelated in actual societies. In reality, the same people can be, and frequently are, ranked similarly in both orders. Thus, for example, those of the highest economic class also tend to possess high levels of status honor. Property ownership in particular is linked to status honor "with extraordinary regularity" (Weber, 1922:932). The subjective awareness basic to status-group membership typically leads to efforts at closure, or the exclusion of outsiders from interaction with members. This interaction can include everything from social activities and gatherings to marriages within the status circle. Here, too, Weber draws some of his examples of status groups from the economic order. Thus, he suggests, at least partly seriously, that because of group closure "it may be that only the families coming under approximately the same tax class will dance with one another" (Weber, 1922:932).

The purpose, then, of drawing a distinction between classes and status groups is not to assert their total disjuncture but to indicate that they are not necessarily related in a perfect, one-to-one correspondence. The power they bestow comes from different sources, and the extent of their correlation is a matter of empirical investigation in real societies. The point is that, as long as it is possible for individuals to derive social honor from noneconomic considerations, then the existence of status groups will "hinder the strict carrying through of the sheer market principle" (Weber, 1922:930). Thus, the leaders of the Roman Catholic Church—the Pope and the College of Cardinals—form a status group to the extent that their power, or ability to influence the actions of others, does not stem primarily from their market position or economic class, which would be below that of the wealthiest capitalists, for example. Instead, the power of church leaders to exercise their will over others is accorded them largely because many people believe them to be worthy of obedience, as God's representatives on earth. This is just one illustration of how considerations of status can cut across and complicate considerations of class. Such an illustration does not deny the great power of those who control the economy, nor does it disprove the possible empirical connections between those people who dominate each hierarchy. But, for Weber, such examples do reveal that the correlation between the economic order and the status order is not perfect and that, as a consequence, the complexity of social inequality must be acknowledged.

Party

The third concept in Weber's three-pronged treatment of the distribution of power in society is his idea of *party*. Typically this concept receives far less attention than either class or status. This is probably because Weber offers only a brief discussion of party himself. Some confusion over the significance of party in Weber's scheme has been engendered by the incomplete nature of his discussion. A related difficulty is that Weber identifies power as the specific concern of parties, leading some writers to conclude, erroneously, that *only* parties are concerned with power and that classes and status groups deal with quite different matters. In fact, as has already been noted, all three concepts pertain to the distribution of power. Each of the three concepts represents a different base through which power inheres in some groups or individuals more than others.

Parties, in Weber's terminology, are voluntary "associations," systematically organized for the collective "pursuit of interests" (Weber, 1922:284-285). The best-known examples are formal political parties, such as the New Democratic Party in Canada or the Republican Party in the United States. But any organization fitting Weber's definition is a party: pressure groups like the Consumers' Association of Canada, unions such as the United Auto Workers, and professional groups like the American Medical Association.

Like the members of status groups and social classes, members of parties possess some sense of group consciousness and solidarity. In fact, status groups or social classes can also be parties in certain circumstances, provided they develop a rational structure, formal organization, and administrative staff. These organizational qualities are what really separates party from the other two concepts (Weber, 1922:285, 938). Thus, not all classes or status groups will be parties, and not all parties will be social classes or status groups, but they *can* and *will* overlap in some cases. The message Weber again conveys here is the pluralist nature of both inequality and the structure of power. Parties, like classes and status groups, are distinct features in the intricate mix of social forces that operate in and shape social structures. In contrast to those Marxists who stress economic power as the single force of consequence in the study of inequality, Weber perceives three major bases for power, according to which different constellations of interests emerge and determine the nature and extent of inequality.

Power, Domination, and Legitimate Domination (Authority)

The complexity of Weber's image becomes more elaborate still when we delve into his analysis of power in social life. Power is probably the most difficult idea to work with and comprehend in Weber's writings. This difficulty is both unfortunate and somewhat ironic, because power is also the central concept in much of his work, particularly that which deals with social inequality. His general view is that inequalities between social actors are traceable primarily to their differential success in the continuing social struggle, the contest between competing or conflicting interests. This struggle is also the essence of what Weber means by politics, in the broadest sense of the term. Essentially, power is the factor that determines the outcome of the social struggle and, hence, the nature and extent of inequality. Power (*Macht*, in German), it will be recalled, is defined as "the probability that one actor within a social relationship will be in a position to carry out his own will despite resistance" (Weber, 1922:53).

The problem with Weber's definition of power is that it is too broad to be very useful. Weber himself concedes that his definition is "amorphous", that "all conceivable qualities of a person" could put that person in a position of power over others (Weber, 1922:53). There also seems to be an allowance here that power relations can be impermanent and sporadic, shifting dramatically on rather short notice.

A key way in which Weber specifies his discussion is to suggest another idea, *domination*, as a "special case of power" (Weber, 1922:941, 53). Domination (*Herrschaft*, in German) refers to those power relations in which *regular patterns* of inequality are established, whereby the subordinate group (or individual) *accepts* that position in a sustained arrangement, obeying the commands of the dominant group (or individual). In fact, one could claim that it is just such continuing power arrangements that are most relevant to our analysis of social inequality as a *structured* phenomenon. What the distinction between power and domination allows us to do, then, is to set aside those power relations that are only transient, temporary, or incidental. These situations after all tell us little about the more general, established, and patterned systems of domination that provide most of the framework for inequality at the societal level.

Remember, though, that not all social analysts adopt Weber's distinction between power and domination, either in their scholarly writings or in everyday conversation. Consequently, the term *power* is frequently employed when discussing situations that to Weber are more precisely considered examples of domination. For practical purposes in our analysis, the two terms may be seen as more or less equivalent, since domination, as defined by Weber, is in large measure the key brand of power that students of structured social inequality consider, especially at the macro level.

We have now outlined Weber's distinction between power in general and the more specific variety of power that we are concerned with, domination. In an earlier section of this chapter we discussed Weber's contention that classes, status groups, and parties are the principal bases for exercising power (or domination) in society. In other words, those who are members of dominant classes, status groups, and party associations are able on the whole to exact compliance to their wills, on a regular basis, from the remaining population. To say this, however, is not to provide the reasons why subordinate factions in these spheres accept or endure their subordination.

There are many possible reasons for compliance to domination. In Weber's terms, some of these are based on *legitimacy*, while others are not (Weber, 1922:904). There are essentially three pure types of legitimate domination, or authority (*legitime Herrschaft*), that are of note. Subordinates may give compliance because they perceive special charismatic qualities of leadership in those who rule them (*charismatic authority*), because they genuinely believe both in the legality of their subordinate position and in the legal right of those in power to be there (*legal authority*), or because they accept the traditional right of certain groups to lead them (*traditional authority*) (Weber, 1922:215).

In addition, however, there are numerous other reasons for obedience which are not legitimate in this sense. In these cases, domination occurs: because, out of custom, habit, or convention, subjects have always been subordinate and entertain no possibility of change; because of opportunities for personal advantage or self-interest; because of fear of the use of physical force or other reprisals; and so on (cf. Weber, 1922:33-36, 753-758, 946-953).

The question of whether one of these types of domination, legitimate or otherwise, is more prevalent than the others is, as usual for Weber, a matter of empirical investigation. His view is that the predominant type of domination will differ over time and from society to society. But the single underlying reason for compliance in virtually all situations, the ultimate sanction that can never be discarded, is the possible application of physical force by the dominant group. The threat of physical force is more prevalent and more blatant, of course, in early, primitive societies, where "violent social action" is "absolutely primordial" (Weber, 1922:904). As societies have evolved, the actual use of force has tended to decrease. This reduction in violence is partly because ruling groups are reluctant to resort constantly to violent means, since these generate resentment and potential rebellion among subordinates. In addition, the actual application of force is unnecessary, with periodic exceptions, because the other reasons for compliance gradually come into play.

It is usually a combination of some or all of the reasons listed earlier that promotes acceptance (Weber, 1922:263). In most cases, the rational calculation of self-interest is quite important, especially in the pursuit of economic rewards and social honor (cf. Giddens, 1971:156). As well, the fact that a "legal order" comes into existence is a significant aspect of domination in modern times. It entrenches in law the rights of certain groups relative to others and so can be used by the ruling group both to justify compliance among the willing and to enforce compliance among the unwilling (Weber, 1922:312, 903-904). But the impact of habit and custom, the "unreflective habituation to a regularity of life," is a particularly important, and frequently overlooked, reason for acceptance of domination among the mass of the population (Weber, 1922:312). We shall deal with these ideas again in subsequent chapters.

Weber's outline of the several reasons that may motivate social actors to accept domination is clearly consistent with his stress on the importance of the subjective meanings that people attach to their behavior. By elaborating the various types of domination, legitimate and otherwise, that can operate in society, Weber is also providing still more evidence of the complex nature of social processes and the need to take this complexity into account in social explanations. His formulations of power and domination make it clear, as well, that the inequalities between individuals or groups arising out of the economic sphere, or the class structure, are but one means by which power is exercised and one means by which some people are able to dominate others.

Rationalization, Bureaucracy, and the Means of Administration

In our analysis of Marx, we noted that his view of social inequality identified the dominant people of society as those who control the means of material production. To Marx, the explanation for how systems of inequality arise and change is ultimately rooted in how classes emerge out of the organization of economic activity. It is more difficult to identify in Weber's work the same sense of a single, overriding force shaping social inequality. In fact, the central theme of our discussion of Weber has been to point out his complex view of social inequality and his skepticism about the existence of ultimate social causes.

Nevertheless, there is some basis for the claim that Weber does stress a recurring, if not a singular, process at work in the generation of social inequality. This claim relates to our earlier observation that Weber sees social action generally as a *contested* activity, a struggle between individuals or groups pursuing their own interests. Factions differ in their power to achieve their interests, and social inequality, in all its guises, is one major result of this imbalance. The contest or struggle for power, which is the crux of what Weber means by politics, is inherent in social action. Thus, if there is a predominant tendency in Weber's approach, it is to explain social action in terms of politics, defined in this broad sense (cf. Giddens, 1972:34; 1973:46-47). Such a perspective differs from Marx's, since Weber views the struggle between economic classes as just one element, albeit a crucial one, in the more universal contest of interests within social structures.

A full appreciation of Weber's power and politics orientation to social inequality requires that we consider three closely connected concepts in his work. These are rationalization, bureaucracy, and the means of administration.

Rationalization
Weber perceives in the historical development of societies a tendency for social action to become increasingly rationalized—that is, to be guided by the reasoned, calculated, or rational pursuit of particular interests. Of course, nonrational actions—those prompted by traditional beliefs or by emotion, for example—do continue to occur in modern societies (Weber, 1922:26). Nevertheless, there is in Weber's view a steady trend toward a predominance of both rationally motivated action and, consequently, rationally organized social structures. This is most obvious in the economic sphere under capitalism, where the calculated pursuit of self-interest reaches an advanced stage (Weber, 1922:71). Economic enterprise becomes geared above all to productive efficiency and its enhancement through the systematic organization of business (Weber, 1905:76). The calculation of profits becomes much more precise with the advent of a money-based economy, accounting procedures, bookkeeping, and the retention of records and files (Weber, 1922:107-108). The growth in the specialization of occupations in the work place and the planned division of labor in large-

scale factories and other enterprises are also key features in this economic rationalization (Weber, 1922:436, 1155-1156).

As we have seen, Marx is well aware of these processes in capitalist development. However, he believes that such changes as the growing division of labor will provide the ultimate impetus toward class polarization and eventual revolution, whereas Weber sees economic rationalization as but one part of a universal trend toward the systematic organization and administration of social action. Weber notes that a similar process of rationalization has occurred in virtually all the major spheres of social action. In religion, for example, he sees a trend toward *secularization*, whereby religious practice becomes structured, routinized, and administered much like the activities of other organizations, with a formal church hierarchy, standardized ritual, and so forth. This process is accompanied by a decline in the significance of the magical and the mystical aspects of spiritual life. The change in religion is perhaps the best illustration of Weber's idea that there is a progressive "disenchantment of the world" (Weber, 1922:538; cf. Gerth and Mills, 1967:51).

In the same way, Weber points out the development of a rationalized legal order and political system. In early societies, a legal system emerges as a basis for legitimizing the monopoly of physical force by those who control a territory. As this set of laws becomes increasingly elaborate and complex, it eventually comprises rules and regulations for a wide range of social action. Thus, the original ruling group gradually takes on a variety of administrative roles, leading to the establishment of the modern *state*. The functions of the state are numerous: the enactment of new laws; the protection of "public order"; the protection of "vested rights" such as property ownership; the administration of health, education, and social welfare; and the defense of the territory against outside attack (Weber, 1922:655, 905, 908-909). Each of these activities in any large-scale society requires a permanent, organized system of problem solving, decision making, and policy implementation. In this manner, the trend to rationalization culminates in the system of formal organizations known as bureaucracies.

Bureaucracy

To Weber, it is the rationalized bureaucracies that have become the key players in the power struggle. Bureaucracies of various types have existed from early times. However, the modern bureaucracy is distinguishable from all previous forms by a particular set of traits. We need not examine these characteristics in detail, but they include the existence of specialized occupations, or offices, with designated duties to perform, arranged in a hierarchy of authority or decision-making power. Management of the organization is based on written documents, or files, and the operation is conducted according to an explicit set of rules or administrative regulations (Weber, 1922:956-958).

In Weber's view, such an organization acts almost like a "machine," providing the most rational and efficient means yet devised for administering social activity (Weber, 1922:973). This claim of rational efficiency may seem strange to those who have been caught up in bureaucratic red tape and who thus equate the term bureaucracy with *ir*rationality and *in*efficiency. Certainly Weber himself speaks of the "impediments" that the bureaucratic apparatus can create in individual cases (Weber, 1922:975). Nevertheless, he firmly contends that the administration of modern societies would be much worse, in fact impossible, without the bureaucratic form, given "the increasing complexity of civilization" (Weber, 1922:972). To Weber, this is not a question of preference or a value judgment but a statement of fact. The modern system of rationalized bureaucracies is for Weber a necessary evil: necessary because it is the only practical means for organizing human conduct in the present day, yet evil because it is an "iron cage" that restricts individualism and threatens democracy (cf. Weber, 1905:181-183). We shall return to this point in the concluding section of this chapter.

The Means of Administration

The significance of rationalized bureaucracies for the analysis of social inequality is that they become the key players in the general power struggle. Bureaucracies are the best examples of what Weber means by enduring structures of domination. They provide the means by which social action is governed on a regular basis and through which a system of inequality is established and sustained.

Once again the contrast with the Marxist conception is noteworthy. Whereas Marxism sees control of the means of economic production as the foundation for class structure and inequality in capitalism, Weber contends that differential access to the means of production is just one of the various ways in which power differences and inequality arise. Each of the major institutional structures of capitalist society has its own sphere of influence and its own bureaucratic system of operation. It is the control of all these various *means of administration* that determines social inequality, not just control in the economic sphere. Hence, in addition to the power deriving from control of the economy by bureaucratically organized corporate enterprises, power inheres in those groups that administer the religious system, the communications media, and so forth (Weber, 1922:223-224).

Perhaps the most crucial structures for Weber are the interrelated set of "public organizations" that make up the modern state: the legal structure, the judicial and executive branches of government, the civil-service bureaucracies, the police, and the military (cf. Weber, 1922:980-989). All of these administrative systems hold power in their own right, so that the Marxist emphasis on the economic structure to the exclusion of others is a distortion. Here Weber clearly rejects the notion that the organizations existing outside the economic sphere are merely superstructural props for a ruling class of capitalists. While acknowledging the great power wielded by the bourgeoisie, Weber appears more worried by the threat posed by bureaucratic officials, especially those found in the state, where the means of administration seem to be increasingly concentrated. As we shall discuss later, the power of the state has become a much more prominent concern, even for Marxist scholars, since Weber's time.

The Future: Democracy, Bureaucracy, and Socialism

Our outline of Weber's work has revealed a complex, multifaceted conception of social structure and the dynamics of social inequality. Modern society is shaped by an ongoing contest or struggle between self-interested social actors. Through control of economic resources, status honor, and the influence deriving from party associations, power is exercised over others. The power struggle gradually is consolidated into a contest involving formal structures of regular, patterned domination. Increasingly, in modern times, these structures take the form of rational bureaucracies, each headed by its own select group of high administrative officials. Social inequality in this context is firmly established, and power is concentrated in the hands of bureaucratic officials in all spheres of influence, not just the economic. A marked concentration of control over the administration of society falls to the various branches of the state, in particular.

It should be apparent from this description of Weber's position that he does not share Marx's optimism about the transformation of capitalism into a new society of universal human freedom and equality. As has been noted, Weber himself is sympathetic to the cause of political democracy. However, because of the structures of domination that have evolved under capitalism, Weber remains pessimistic about the prospects for democratic action and for any reduction of inequality in future societies. Moreover, for a number of reasons he is convinced that socialism cannot alter, and may even intensify, the structure of domination.

Democracy versus Bureaucracy

Democracy, in Weber's definition, is a system of government whose guiding principle is "the 'equal rights' of the governed," a system in which the power of "officialdom" is minimized and the influence of "public opinion" is maximized (Weber, 1922:985). Such a system is most closely approximated in "direct" or "immediate" democracies—those in which persons in authority are obligated to conform to the will of their constituents (Weber, 1922:289). The problem with this brand of democracy is that it cannot function in large-scale systems like a modern society, because of the sheer size and complexity of such structures (Weber, 1922:291). The only alternative is to employ what Weber calls "representative democracy", in which constituents elect individuals who are empowered to act in accordance with the general interest. This "representative body" of elected officials in turn typically appoints or elects a subset of their number as a "cabinet," which itself may be overseen by a premier official for purposes of centralized coordination of action. Such a system of "parliamentary cabinet government" is the most familiar form of modern democracy at the mass level (cf. Weber, 1922:289-297).

But what, after all, is this system of government? It is clearly another instance of bureaucracy, with the same inherent structure of domination that such a designation implies. The dilemma of democracy in the present and future is that "bureaucracy inevitably accompanies modern mass democracy" (Weber, 1922:983). A bureaucratic form of organization is the only means by which democratic action is feasible in complex societies. It is the one structure that assures regular, predictable administration while at the same time providing procedures for the protection of constituents against possible abuses of democratic principles by those who govern. That is, governmental powers may themselves be constrained by a democratic system of laws and regulations that includes appeal procedures, explicitly limited terms of office, multiple parties, provision for elections, and so forth.

Unfortunately, government bureaucracy is also a hierarchy of authority, influence, experience, and expertise. Thus, government leaders are a select group with "special expert qualifications" and have access to more information and resources than any other group, even in a democracy (Weber, 1922:985). This means that the very bureaucratic system that is necessary for democracy in modern society creates conditions that could mean undemocratic action by those who rule. Of course, this is not to say that such abuses of democracy *must* occur. On this point, Weber disagrees with his contemporary Robert Michels, who asserts that an "iron law of oligarchy" operates in organizations, ensuring that they always abandon democratic process in the end (Michels, 1915). Weber's position is more conditional: "democracy inevitably comes into conflict with the bureaucratic tendencies" of modern society (Weber, 1922:985); however, this only means that democracy *may* lose out, not that it always will, with certainty.

This idea comes up again in Weber's observation that political action is always determined by the "principle of small numbers," which gives superior "maneuverability" to "small leading groups" (Weber, 1922:1414). He even says in the same passage that "this is the way it should be," but only as long as leaders are both successful and faithful to essential democratic principles (cf. Weber in Gerth and Mills, 1967:42). For Weber, the key concern in democratic politics is effective leadership (Giddens, 1972:54). His personal preference is for a responsive political democracy, headed by someone possessing special qualities of democratic enlightenment and personal charisma. His fear, however, is that politics in the future will take the form of a "leaderless" democracy, with the mass of the population controlled by a "clique" of bureaucratic officials, a "certified caste of mandarins" (Weber in Gerth and Mills, 1967:113, 71).

The Socialist Alternative

Given all of the previous discussion, Weber's view of the prospects for democracy is, on balance, more pessimistic than optimistic. Even his own preferred version of political democracy contains within it the potential loss of individual autonomy and freedom, because bureaucracy is an "escape-proof" feature of every type of modern society (Weber, 1922:1401). However, any Marxist claim that socialism is both the solution to this dilemma and the means to realize true democracy is, in Weber's view, completely mistaken. The imperative need for systematic organization of social action is universal: "It makes no difference whether the economic system is organized on a capitalistic or socialistic basis" (Weber, 1922:223). If anything, because socialist systems tend to intensify the centralization of decision making in the state and intrude pervasively into all spheres of human activity, "socialism would, in fact, require a still higher degree of formal bureaucratization than capitalism" (Weber, 1922:225). In this way, socialism would further reduce, not increase, human freedom. In other words, any hope for a dictatorship of the proletariat is a delusion. Instead, socialism would be an extreme case of "dictatorship of the official" (Weber in Gerth and Mills, 1967:50).

It appears, therefore, that Weber does not share with Marx the expectation of an eventual end to social conflict and to structured inequality. To Weber, the need for bureaucracy and the factionalism of human interaction make both inequality and competitive struggle inherent features of all societies, socialist or capitalist. The crucial difference between these two great thinkers seems to center on this point. Both give the idea of struggle a key role in their conception of inequality. But for Marx, on the one hand, struggle is not essential to social life. It is part of society only as long as class systems exist and act to pervert the essentially social and cooperative nature of human interaction. For Weber, on the other hand, struggle is basic to social life and operates generally, not just in the sphere of class relations. In his view, inequality emerges from the continuing contest of power, in which individuals and groups pursue, not the general interest, but their own special interests. One can seek to place checks and balances against the usurpation of power by bureaucratic officials, but such efforts may not be successful and, in any case, will eliminate neither inequality nor the self-interest inherent in human nature.

Which of these images of our present and future is the more accurate one, of course, remains a topic of debate to this day. Ultimately, it is a question with no simple answer. In assessing the future of inequality, some deride Marx for the shortcomings of optimism: his failure to discern all the obstacles to revolution; his omission of a clear guide for his disciples to the universal society; and his perhaps excessive faith in humanity. Still, Weber's hard-nosed pessimism is for some more flawed (cf. Marcuse, 1971). Perhaps in predicting for us a future of bureaucratic cages and embattled democracy, Weber has inadvertently helped contribute, in a self-fulfilling way, to the realization of his own worst fears.

Summary

Our concern in this chapter has been to outline and assess Max Weber's conception of social inequality. Weber's work may be characterized generally as a positive critique of Marx and Marxism. A central theme in Weber's writings is his emphasis on the complex, pluralist nature of inequality. This theme was illustrated by reference to a number of Weber's formulations—especially his conceptions of class, power, and domination. We noted Weber's view of society as an arena for numerous contests among social actors attempting to obtain and exert power, and we examined the important role played by bureaucratic structures in these struggles. Finally, the chapter concluded with Weber's assessment of the chances for democracy in future societies, both socialist and capitalist.

CHAPTER FOUR

Durkheim Structural Functionalism and Inequality

"Liberty . . . is itself the product of regulation. . . . Only rules can prevent abuses of power." Emile *Durkheim,* The Division of Labour, *Preface to the second edition, 1902*

Introduction

In this chapter, our task is to assess the third major conception of inequality that has emerged from sociological theory. This conception involves the general orientation known as *structural functionalism*. In contrast to Marxian and Weberian theory, structural functionalism is not clearly identified with any single thinker; hence, its origins are not easily traced to one source. Nevertheless, it is apparent that structural functionalism grew primarily out of a general trend toward functionalist analysis in the nineteenth century—a trend that found disciples in such diverse fields as biology, art, law, and architecture (Kallen, 1931:523-525). Among the social sciences, structural functionalism first achieved prominence in anthropology, especially in the work of Radcliffe-Brown (1922; 1935; 1948; 1952) and Malinowski (1926; 1929). However, its beginnings in sociology can be found prior to these writers, particularly in Durkheim's work at the turn of the century (e.g., Durkheim, 1893; 1895).

Because structural functionalism is a school of thought rather than a single theory, it is difficult both to define it precisely and to review its principles in a manner that everyone will accept. There are many differences in conceptual definitions and theoretical emphases within the rather broad range of writers who make up this school. As a preliminary statement, however, we can say that structural functionalism is characterized by a particular strategy of inquiry. This strategy entails the investigation of society as if it were a system of parts, which are interconnected to form various *structures*, each of which fulfills some *function* for the system.

We will examine the meaning of these two terms in more detail later, but for now we can note that the concept of structure used by structural functionalists is quite similar to that implicit in the formulations of Marx and Weber: an organized pattern of relationships among individuals or social positions (e.g., Parsons, 1951:21; Johnson, 1960:48; Williams, 1960:20; Levy, 1968:22). In fact, this definition of structure is at least generally akin to that used by most sociologists today (but see Lévi-Strauss, 1968; Giddens, 1979). It is the idea of function that really distinguishes structural functionalism from the rest of sociology. Unfortunately, there are certain disagreements over the precise meaning of function. In Durkheim's early view, a function is the "need" that a structure fulfills for society (Durkheim, 1893:49). Some more recent writers define function as a simple "consequence" or "result" of a particular structure's operating in a system (Parsons, 1951:21; Levy, 1968). This definition leaves unsaid whether or not the function is planned or intentional. Perhaps a more forthright approach is to treat a function as the anticipated or expected "contribution" that a structure makes to society or one of its subsystems (Fallding, 1968:77-78).

The diverse and sometimes vague meanings attached to the idea of function are a primary source of confusion and dispute between structural functionalists and their critics. In fact, this allegation of vagueness and imprecision has been applied to the whole structural-functionalist perspective. Like other grand theorists, it is argued, structural functionalists attempt to fit all social phenomena into one scheme, thereby making their analysis too abstract to be meaningful. Important details and features of society are inevitably excluded or deemphasized, especially those things that are not easily explained by the perspective. Thus, in the case of structural functionalism, critics claim that very little is said about such issues as the roles of class and power in social life, the positive part that conflict can play in human interaction, and the beneficial aspects of social change (cf. Mills, 1959:35-42; Lockwood, 1956; Dahrendorf, 1958; Wrong, 1961). Certain structural functionalists have responded to some of these criticisms, in an effort to show that their framework is capable of including such concerns and of seeing beyond vaguely defined functions or general system needs (e.g., Parsons, 1966; Fallding, 1968). Nevertheless, the conviction remains among detractors that structural functionalism ignores essential features of society or pays only lip service to them. (For debate, see Demerath and Peterson, 1967.)

It is not our purpose in this chapter either to examine this debate in its entirety or to attempt a resolution of it. Yet the great influence that structural functionalism has had on recent social thought makes it essential that we consider the main elements of this perspective and the key criticisms they have raised. Our special concern, of course, is with what structural functionalism has to say about inequality. If the critics are correct, the exclusion of such issues as class, power, conflict, and change would make the structural-functionalist view of social inequality and its causes quite different from the theories of Marx and Weber we have already reviewed. At the same time, however, wherever such criticisms are misrepresentations of the structural-functionalist approach, it may be possible to identify similar, or at least compatible, elements in these three perspectives.

Our exposition of the structural-functionalist perspective will proceed in the following manner. First, it is necessary to devote some time to an analysis of Durkheim's work, which, as noted earlier, is typically viewed as a cornerstone of structural functionalism. It will be argued that Durkheim's ideas do provide the beginnings of structural-functionalist sociology in certain general respects but that Durkheim's conceptions of specific issues are often significantly different from the conceptions espoused by current brands of structural functionalism. It will also be revealed that Durkheim says a good deal more about social inequality than is normally acknowledged and that his discussion has some interesting affinities with the writings of both Marx and Weber.

In the remainder of the chapter, the focus will shift to modern structural functionalism, especially the predominant version developed by Parsons (1937; 1951). This discussion will begin with a review of the basic conceptual scheme of structural functionalism. We will then assess the key criticisms of this approach, especially those concerning the concept of function. This discussion of the general orientation will set the stage for our central task: an examination of the famous structural-functional analysis of social inequality, especially as developed by Davis and Moore (1945) and by Parsons (1940; 1953). The important points of similarity and difference between modern structural functionalism and each of Marx, Weber, and Durkheim will be of special concern throughout this section of the chapter.

Durkheim and Social Solidarity

Emile Durkheim was a French sociologist who lived from 1858 to 1917. It is interesting that, despite being almost exact contemporaries, Durkheim and Weber seem not to have been influenced by, or even aware of, each other's work. Durkheim did know of Marx. His thought even reveals some broad similarities with that of Marx, partly because of the influence of Saint-Simon on both writers. However, the affinities between Marx and Durkheim are rarely direct or explicit ones, as evidenced by the infrequent and incidental references to Marx in Durkheim's writings (e.g., Durkheim, 1893:393; 1896:12, 14, 59, 221; cf. Giddens, 1971:97).

This shortage of direct links between Durkheim and either Marx or Weber is to some extent the result of Durkheim's sociological interests— interests that are largely distinct from those of the other two writers. It is true that the three men share a concern with analyzing and comprehending certain aspects of the origin and development of nineteenth-century capitalism. However, each writer concentrates on a particular feature of this societal form. Marx focuses on class struggle—the opposition between owners and non-owners in the productive sphere—and its role in the emergence, maturation, and anticipated demise of capitalism. In contrast, Weber stresses the more general power struggle, especially with regard to the growth of rationalized bureaucracies, which become the principal structures of domination in modern capitalism but which are allegedly inescapable in socialism as well.

To Durkheim, also, problems of class struggle and power inequities in capitalism are important, but he analyzes them primarily with reference to what for him is the prior and more crucial question: how are the social structures, within which power and class struggle operate, even possible in the first place? By what means does a scattered collection of people coalesce to form the ongoing, enduring entity we call society, when so many conflicting and divisive forces are capable of tearing it asunder? Durkheim's focus, then, is on the cohesiveness, or *solidarity*, of social arrangements.

Durkheim's idea of solidarity suggests an image of society as a set of interconnected groups and individuals, interacting with one another in regular, patterned, and more or less predictable ways. Essential to this interaction is *morality*, or moral regulation, by which Durkheim means the set of rules or norms that guide and govern human conduct. The existence of these guidelines means that individuals interact in accordance with their obligations to others and to society as a whole. In doing so, each person also receives some recognition of his or her own rights and contributions within the collectivity. Morality in this sense is "strictly necessary" for solidarity between people to occur; without morality "societies cannot exist" (Durkheim, 1893:51). One of Durkheim's prime concerns is to determine how the forces providing morality, and hence solidarity, have changed as society has moved from primitive forms to modern capitalism (cf. Giddens, 1971:106).

Primitive Societies and Mechanical Solidarity

In *The Division of Labor in Society*, Durkheim presents his central thesis that social solidarity stems historically from two sources, one of which prevails in primitive societies and the second of which predominates in the modern era.

Primitive societies are held together by a "mechanical" or automatic solidarity, a union based on the "likeness" or similarity of people (Durkheim, 1893:70). Such early societies are really aggregations of families or other subunits having certain characteristics in common. These subunits have a structural resemblance to one another, being for the most part economically self-sufficient and capable of providing for their own production and consumption needs. This similarity by itself is not enough to maintain solidarity, since subunits can survive in isolation from one another. In addition, however, primitive peoples also share a "collective conscience" (in French, *conscience collective*), a "totality of beliefs and sentiments common to average citizens" (Durkheim, 1893:79). The moral rules necessary for social solidarity in primitive times are represented in this body of beliefs and sentiments. They provide the social glue that binds together what otherwise would be independent, self-sustaining subgroups. The set of common values is generated within the collectivity and evolves with it over a considerable time, during which adherents presumably come to agree on its central precepts, while dissidents either convert or are excluded.

The collective conscience, which touches all spheres of primitive life, finds its principal repository in religion. Early religion embodies not just purely religious beliefs but also a "confused mass" of ideas regarding "law", the "principles of political organization", even "science" (Durkheim, 1893:135). The connection between religion and law is particularly significant for Durkheim. In fact, he believes law is "essentially religious in its origin," representing customs and beliefs similar to those in the collective conscience, but in a more organized and precise fashion (Durkheim, 1893:92; 65, 110). This link between law and religion is illustrated in the ancient practice of having priests serve as judges and in the medieval concept of the divine right of kings, which granted political and legal powers to monarchs as God's servants on earth.

In Durkheim's view, then, legal, or *juridical*, rules gradually develop out of the collective conscience, especially through the influence of religious beliefs. If there is a close correspondence between these legal rules and the collective conscience, we then have a moral society, one in which individuals acknowledge one another and interact smoothly. However, Durkheim clearly realizes that the formal legal system is not always moral or just. In the course of social change, laws may not change accordingly, making them inappropriate, unjust, and contrary to genuinely moral regulation. Such laws may be maintained only through habit, artificial manipulation, or force (Durkheim, 1893:65, 107-108). Thus, Durkheim recognizes that societies must and will change and that a healthy, or *normal*, society is one in which the regulations that provide the basis for solidarity are suited to the historical period in question.

Modern Societies and Organic Solidarity

The transition of social life from primitive times to the era of modern capitalism entails fundamental modifications in structural arrangements and, hence, in the form of social solidarity. The old mechanical solidarity, based on likeness and a common set of beliefs and sentiments, is assailed on all sides, most importantly by the expanding division of labor. Here Durkheim reveals that, like Marx and Weber, he perceives the division of labor as a crucial force in the historical evolution of social structures. In contrast to primitive societies, where subunits resemble one another both in their economic self-sufficiency and in their common belief system, modern societies comprise individuals who tend to be quite dissimilar, engaged in specialized tasks and activities in their daily lives, and guided by distinct norms and values in their personal conduct.

In such a situation it is difficult to maintain solidarity through the collective conscience, because a "personal conscience", with an emphasis on individual distinctiveness, increasingly comes to the forefront in people's minds (Durkheim, 1893:167). This is not to say that the collective conscience disappears altogether; however, the common beliefs it entails gradually become "very general and indeterminate," acting more as maxims or credos than as detailed guides for conduct (Durkheim, 1893:172). Hence, the collective conscience provides some integrative force in modern society, but of a vague and general sort. Now "each individual is more and more acquiring his own way of thinking and acting, and submits less completely to the common corporate opinion" (Durkheim, 1893:137, 152, 172).

The weakening of the collective conscience is paralleled in the declining influence of religious beliefs. Whereas religion "pervades everything" in primitive society, in the modern era it "tends to embrace a smaller and smaller portion of social life" (Durkheim, 1893:169). Now societies are far more specialized, no longer composed of self-sufficient subgroups but rather of subunits that perform specific "functions" which, taken together, contribute to society's existence (Durkheim, 1893:49). This development of special structures fulfilling particular functions is also evident in the decreasing role of religion: "Little by little, political, economic, and scientific functions free themselves from the religious function, constitute themselves apart, and take on a more and more acknowledged temporal character" (Durkheim, 1893:169). In addition, of course, tasks within each of these special structures or spheres of activity are themselves divided and specialized, producing the complex network of individual positions and roles that is modern society (cf. Durkheim, 1893:40).

It is worth noting here that Durkheim does not mourn the passing of early societies or the decline of the collective conscience. On the contrary, he views the growing division of labor and specialization of functions as normal aspects of modern life. The new emphasis on individualism and personal distinctiveness in modern societies is also a normal development, something which is wholly compatible with, even necessary to, the expanding division of labor. Durkheim believes that this "cult" of the individual personality is here to stay and is a positive development, as long as individual goals and interests do not override collective interests or endanger social solidarity (Durkheim, 1893:172, 400). What is needed is some new integrative force to replace the declining collective conscience—a force that can "come in to take the place of that which has gone" (Durkheim, 1893:173). Otherwise, the individualism of modern life will degenerate into blatant self-interest, or *egoism*—a phenomenon that is destructive of both morality and social solidarity.

Durkheim's principal contention in *The Division of Labor in Society*, and one of the most clever twists in his analysis, is that the division of labor is both the main cause for the weakening of the old mechanical solidarity and the key means by which the new form of solidarity emerges. In Durkheim's terms, the function of the division of labor is to provide solidarity on the basis of *dis*similarity, on the fact that highly specialized individuals and subgroups, are no longer self-sufficient, but must cooperate and depend on one another for survival (Durkheim, 1893:228). Durkheim calls this form of solidarity "organic" because it portrays modern society as similar in key ways to an advanced biological organism, "a system of different organs, each of which has a special role, and which are themselves formed of differentiated parts" (Durkheim, 1893:181; 190-193).

In addition to providing cohesion through this exchange of interdependent services and functions, "the division of labor produces solidarity . . . because it creates among men an entire system of rights and duties which link them together in a durable way" (Durkheim, 1893:406). Increasingly over time, these rights and duties become established in formal laws, because their number and complexity necessitate systematic codification. As noted earlier, Durkheim believes formal law originates with religious beliefs and gradually takes over the task of moral regulation from religion as society evolves. This takeover, however, is never complete. Moral rules, in "a multitude of cases" continue to be based on uncodified and non-legal precepts, on "usage", "custom", or "unwritten rules" which complement and fill in the gaps left by legal rules (Durkheim, 1893:147, 215).

The nature of these moral and juridical guides for conduct and interaction also changes gradually as society develops. In the past their prime purpose was to defend and reaffirm the collective conscience, the common set of beliefs in traditional society. Now, however, they become a complex system of mutual obligations, rights, and duties, which, in ideal circumstances, provide for smooth interaction between individuals, the "pacific and regular concourse of divided functions" (Durkheim, 1893:406).

Durkheim on Social Inequality

At this point, the reader may have the impression that Durkheim's portrayal of modern society is an unrealistically positive one. If social structures are tending toward a new organic solidarity, in which people cooperate and depend on one another in a network of rights and obligations, how is it that other analysts perceive so many social problems? What of Marx's concern with class conflict and worker oppression, or Weber's fear of injustice and servitude through bureaucratic domination?

Some critics might suspect Durkheim of ignoring these problems or of considering them unimportant. However, a closer reading of Durkheim reveals his awareness of and interest in such issues. It is true that Durkheim discusses these problems primarily with reference to their effects on social solidarity, which is always his main concern. Nevertheless, his observations provide evidence that he had a clear conception of the nature and consequences of social inequality, one that shows some surprising parallels with the conceptions of both Marx and Weber. We cannot consider Durkheim's views in all their detail, but several key elements should be briefly examined. These include his distinction between the normal division of labor and its *anomic* and *forced* variants, the role of the state as the moral guardian of modern society, the special problem of the economy and the emergence of *occupational groups*, and the prospects for social solidarity and social inequality in future societies.

The Division of Labor

The Normal Form

When Durkheim stresses the positive functions of the division of labor for modern society, he is speaking of a division of labor that approximates the ideal or normal case. The division of labor is normal if there is genuine moral regulation guiding the interaction between people and if there is justice in the attainment of positions within it. The division of labor is moral if individuals interrelate with restraint, recognizing one another's obligations and contributions, both to other individuals and to the collectivity as a whole. The division of labor is just if each person has an equal opportunity to take on that position that is most appropriate to his or her capacities and interests. Violation of either of these principles produces an abnormal form of the division of labor, a structure that cannot fulfill the functions Durkheim ascribes to the normal form. Though the distinctions are sometimes blurred, insufficient morality produces an anomic division of labor, whereas insufficient justice leads to a forced division of labor (cf. Durkheim, 1893:Book 3). Let us examine each of these separately.

The Anomic Form

Whenever the division of labor fails to underline and reinforce the ties that bind us, moral deregulation, normlessness, or *anomie* can occur. Rather than producing solidarity, the anomic division of labor can promote "contrary results", a situation in which mutual contributions and obligations are denied or overlooked and a lawless, unconstrained struggle ensues (Durkheim, 1893:353). A prime example is in the economic sphere, whenever capitalists and workers become set against each other, with neither side exercising moderation or compromise. The typical consequences are "industrial and commercial crises", marked by "conflict between labor and capital" such that "a sharp line is drawn between masters and workers" (Durkheim, 1893:354-355).

Here Durkheim's discussion sounds very much like Marx's analysis of class polarization in capitalism. Like Marx, Durkheim observes the increasing concentration of capitalist ownership in a few hands, with the result that "enterprises have become a great deal more concentrated than numerous" (Durkheim, 1893:354). This concentration only accentuates the division between owners and workers and makes it even more difficult to build a system based on mutual respect, trust, and moral regulation between classes. The difference between Marx and Durkheim here is that Marx believes such problems are basic to any capitalist division of labor and any class structure. Durkheim, however, believes that class polarization of this sort occurs because the division of labor in this case is anomic—an abnormal form that requires adjustment.

Before proceeding, we should note another interesting parallel between Marxian theory and Durkheim's anomic division of labor. This parallel concerns the working conditions faced by the proletariat in capitalism. We have seen that Marx perceived the capitalist division of labor as a prime cause of alienation in the working class. In a similar way, using similar imagery, Durkheim describes how the anomic division of labor degrades the individual worker, "making him a machine," "an inert piece of machinery" that performs "routine" tasks "with monotonous regularity," "without being interested in them and without understanding them" (Durkheim, 1893:371).

The key difference here between Marx and Durkheim is, again, that Marx apparently believes any division of labor has such consequences, whereas Durkheim identifies this "debasement of human nature" only with the abnormal, anomic division of labor, a system that is itself debased and divested of its moral character. The solution is not the elimination of the division of labor, which Durkheim believes is indispensable to the operation of modern society. Instead, it is essential that each of us perform our roles in the division of labor as best we can, keeping in mind our obligations to our fellows and to society. Not all of us will have equally important parts to play, but such equality is not necessary as long as each person has a sense of obligation and of contribution, a sense that one's labor tends "towards an end that he conceives," and a feeling that one "is serving something" (Durkheim, 1893:372). Moreover, it is not essential that each of us have a similarly broad perspective of how things work. A person "need not embrace vast portions of the social horizon; it is sufficient that he perceive enough of it to understand that his actions have an aim beyond themselves" (Durkheim, 1893:373). These additional elements will alleviate the anomic aspects of the division of labor that have plagued modern capitalism, particularly within the working class.

The Forced Form

The eradication of anomie through moral regulation is for Durkheim basic to any good society. However, regulation alone will not eliminate all the abnormalities that threaten social solidarity. As Durkheim notes, "it is not sufficient that there be rules," for "sometimes the rules themselves are the cause of evil" (Durkheim, 1893:374). This point relates to Durkheim's earlier discussion of the possible lack of correspondence between formal laws or rules and true morality. Rules may exist that are no longer appropriate to the time, but are retained because they serve the special interests of those in a position to keep them in operation through force, manipulation, or an appeal to tradition (Durkheim, 1893:65, 107-108).

It is the application of such inappropriate and unjust rules that characterizes the second abnormal division of labor, which Durkheim calls the *forced* form. In modern society, a key basis for morality and social solidarity is the flourishing of individualism, "the free unfolding of the social force that each carries in himself" (Durkheim, 1893:377). A normal division of labor is one in which one's real self, including one's special "aptitudes" and "natural talents" are allowed to develop (Durkheim, 1893:375). Under such a system people will find their appropriate places in society, thereby satisfying their own desire while at the same time maximizing their ability to perform society's needs. However, under the forced division of labor, people in positions of power act out of self-interest, or egoism, implementing rules that protect their favored positions and that constrain others in roles that are unsuitable and unfair, given their abilities and interests. This forced situation still provides a degree of solidarity, but "only an imperfect and troubled solidarity," threatened by strain and eventual collapse (Durkheim, 1893:376). In such a system, the good of society and of most individual citizens is subordinated to the selfish ends of a few.

Here again we can discern significant parallels between Durkheim and Marx. It will be recalled that Marx viewed the division of labor between owners and workers as the basis for an inherent struggle in capitalism, one that occasionally erupts into open conflict but that usually lies below the surface of everyday life. Similarly, Durkheim sees the forced division of labor as conducive to a sustained struggle between classes. It is most obvious in "class-wars," wherein the "lower classes" seek to change the role imposed upon them "from custom or by law," to "dispossess" the ruling class, and to redress "the manner in which labour is distributed" (Durkheim, 1893:374). Typically, however, the struggle is less open, for "the working classes are not really satisfied with the conditions under which they live, but very often accept them only as constrained or forced, since they have not the means to change them" (Durkheim, 1893:356).

It is apparent from these statements that Durkheim's version of functionalism is neither an apology for nor a defense of the existing economic and political arrangements in capitalist society. As long as the division of labor contains these forced elements, through which the powerful employ "express violence" or indirect "shackle," we have an externally imposed structure in which neither the individual nor society is properly served (Durkheim, 1893:377, 380). Such "external inequality" must be eliminated at all costs, because it "compromises organic solidarity" and therefore threatens the very existence of contemporary society (Durkheim, 1893:379). If this elimination means open conflict in some cases, then so be it. The worst injustice in that event would be "the making of conflict itself impossible and refusing to admit the right of combat" (Durkheim, 1893:378).

The Role of the State

Having just noted Durkheim's acceptance of conflict as one means to produce progressive change, we should also acknowledge that his decided preference is for more peaceful solutions. In Durkheim's view, the most serious problems of anomie and forced inequality can be eliminated, or at least reduced, without such radical actions as full-scale revolution or the utter destruction of capitalism (cf. Durkheim, 1896:204). On this point, then, Durkheim and Marx tend to differ.

But what are Durkheim's suggestions for dealing with these abnormal features of modern society? Both anomie and forced inequality are problems over rules, the former a result of insufficient regulation and the latter a consequence of unfair regulation. Hence, Durkheim seeks an initial answer by considering the structure in which most rules and laws are generated and administered: the political system, or state. We discussed earlier the tremendous growth in the number and complexity of rules that accompany the expanding division of labor, and how these rules are increasingly codified as formal laws. The state is in effect the structural embodiment of this modern, sophisticated system of "administrative law" (Durkheim, 1893:219). Durkheim's discussion here has a strong resemblance to Weber's. Like Weber, Durkheim identifies the state as the "central organ" of modern society, expanding, differentiating, taking on a wide range of duties and a "multitude of functions:" administering "justice," "educating the young," and managing such diverse services as "public health," "public aid," "transport and communication," and "the military" (Durkheim, 1893:221-222; 1896:43; cf. Weber, 1922:655, 905, 908-909).

It is logical that this state apparatus, which creates and implements the rules of conduct in all of these spheres, should also be the key structure for ensuring that these rules are moral and just. The appropriate values of individualism, responsibility, fair play, and mutual obligation can be affirmed through the policies instituted by the state in all these fields. Thus, for example, citizens may be socialized by the education system, the communications media, and so on to embrace moral precepts and to regulate their behavior toward others accordingly. Under normal conditions, state leaders will serve as moral examples for the population, underscoring "the spirit of the whole and the sentiment of common solidarity" in their own conduct (Durkheim, 1893:361-362; 227).

Inevitably, of course, not every individual will adopt the moral code. In those presumably rare instances in which criminal or other elements act against the collective interest, the state has the final recourse of physical coercion, through the police or military, with which to exact compliance (cf. Durkheim, 1893:222-223).

The State, the Economy, and the Occupational Groups

Interestingly, there is one essential function in society that Durkheim believes cannot be infringed on by the state, and that is the economy. The economy is an exception because it has become so sophisticated and complex under the advanced division of labor that only economic specialists can operate it, people who can deal with the "practical problems" that "arise from a multitude of detail"—problems that "only those very close to the problems know about" (Durkheim, 1893:360). State leaders can remind economic leaders of their moral obligations to society and can moderate excesses or correct abuses in some cases. However, for the most part, the impact of state leaders on economic life is "vague" and "intermittent" (Durkheim, 1893:216, 222, 360-361). The specific every-day operation of the economy "escapes their competence and their action" (Durkheim, 1902:5). Elsewhere Durkheim implies that this situation could change in the future. The growth of economic centralization and big industry, a recent development in Durkheim's time, could provide con-ditions necessary for state intervention in the economy, if the state ap-paratus were itself sufficiently developed and sophisticated to take on the task (Durkheim, 1896:42-43). However, barring this uncertain develop-ment, the state cannot intercede in industrial or commercial activities in a detailed way "without paralyzing them" and impeding their "vital" function (Durkheim, 1893:239).

This exclusion of the state's moral safeguards from the economic sphere poses serious problems for Durkheim and threatens the prospects for a normal division of labor. For how can we alleviate social injustice and social strife when the economic structure is exempt from moral constraint? How is it possible to eliminate forced inequality and class conflict when the main arena in which such struggles are fought cannot be regulated?

Durkheim's proposed solution to this dilemma is a system of "profes-sional groupings", or "occupational groups" (Durkheim, 1896:203; 1902:28-29). The exact nature of these organizations is not certain, but they are clearly not unions or occupational associations in the usual sense. That is, their role is not to promote the special interests of particular trades or professions; rather, they are to foster the general interest of society at a level that most citizens can understand and accept (Durkheim, 1902:10). The modern state has become "too remote" in many cases, "too external and intermittent to penetrate deeply into individual consciences" (Durk-heim, 1902:28). However, the occupational groups are situated between the state and the individual, making them capable of affirming in a more immediate fashion those moral principles that the state can foster in only a general and abstract way.

Their special position means that the occupational groups are also particularly suited to dealing with the problem of moral regulation in the economic sphere. Unlike the state agencies, the occupational groups are able to understand the workings of the economy, because they are a part of it. Thus, they can appreciate the problems of business leaders and individual workers alike. They can therefore play a pivotal intermediate role, impressing on both owners and workers the need to act with mod-eration and mutual respect in their dealings with each other. The overall effect should be a morally regulated economy, a normal division of labor, and a reduction of class conflict (cf. Durkheim, 1902:10, 14, 31).

Future Society

It is apparent from the preceding discussion that Durkheim is generally optimistic about the society of the future. His goal of social solidarity based on morality and justice can be accomplished, he believes, provided the capitalist division of labor is adapted to rid itself of anomie, class conflict, and forced inequality.

In part, Durkheim expects that these abnormalities will be alleviated by the natural evolution of the division of labor. The division of labor, in his view, is already responsible for easing similar problems in traditional feudal and caste societies. Those "prejudices" that once gave favored rank to people merely because of aristocratic lineage or ascribed religious superiority have gradually been "obliterated" by the division of labor and its need for special, individual talents (Durkheim, 1893:379).

In much the same way, the "special faculties" required for filling important positions in modern capitalism make it increasingly difficult to obtain these positions solely through inherited class privilege (Durkheim, 1893:312). To be sure, some inheritance does still occur and unfairly restricts those who are deserving but are born "bereft of fortune" (Durkheim, 1893:378). Nevertheless, the growing popular sentiment is for the end of such external inequality. People have come to believe that inequality should not arise from any outside force but instead should reflect differences in individual "merits"—the talents and efforts each person contributes in the service of society (Durkheim, 1893:379; 407-408).

The belief in external equality, in what might be called equal opportunity, is so widespread that it "cannot be a pure illusion but must express, in confused fashion, some aspect of reality" (Durkheim, 1893:379). Of course, the agencies of society should not remain passive while this trend emerges but should actively encourage it. The state, in particular, should institute policies that promote external equality. One key means for doing so is to abolish the inheritance of wealth and property. Economic justice, based on "just contract" between free individuals and a "just distribution of social goods," cannot occur "as long as there are rich and poor at birth" (Durkheim, 1902:29; 1893:388). In addition, Durkheim suggests that various kinds of social welfare may be provided to "lighten the burden of the workers," to "narrow the distance separating the two classes," and to "decrease the inequality" (Durkheim, 1896:57).

Such measures, in Durkheim's view, are important if we are to achieve a normal division of labor, one that is free of forced, external inequalities and capable of promoting the solidarity he so fervently seeks. Nevertheless, economic justice alone is not enough. In fact, we may even endanger social solidarity if we become too preoccupied with such issues. That is, even if our future society is one in which "men enter into life in a state of perfect economic equality," we have other, more crucial concerns that cannot be ignored. These are more pervasive "problems of the environment"—not just our rights within the economic sphere but also our important "duties toward each other, toward the community, etc." (Durkheim, 1902:30).

To harbor an excessive concern with the distribution of economic rewards is to mistake "the secondary for the essential" (Durkheim, 1896:57). Such a concern puts priority on individual interests rather than on the collective good and one's obligations to society as a whole. Here again we see the prime significance that Durkheim attaches to moral regulation of all citizens, by all citizens, and for all citizens. If true morality is heeded, the issue of economic justice will tend to be resolved along with society's other problems. If, however, the concern over economic matters takes precedence, individualism will deteriorate into egoism and self-interest, human desires for gain or power will override moral power, and the "law of the strongest" will be the only law (Durkheim, 1902:3; 1896:57, 199-200). Durkheim's perspective on freedom is particularly significant in this regard. Freedom is *not* the absence of constraint, of moral and legal rules in the economic and other realms: "Quite on the contrary, liberty . . . is itself the product of regulation. I can be free only to the extent that others are forbidden to profit from their physical, economic, or other superiority to the detriment of my liberty. But only rules can prevent [such] abuses of power" (Durkheim, 1902:3).

Durkheim's projections and proposals concerning the nature of future society reveal some important similarities to, and equally important differences from, the projections of both Marx and Weber. In the concluding sections on Durkheim, we will consider some of these major points and their significance for the analysis of social inequality.

Durkheim and Marx

There are several aspects of Durkheim's discussion that, on the surface at least, sound intriguingly Marxian. In particular, a comparison of his normal division of labor with Marx's transitional stage of socialism reveals some noteworthy parallels: the elimination of property inheritance, though not of all property ownership; the removal of unequal opportunity, from the division of labor; though not necessarily of unequal rewards and positions; and the expansion of the state's role as administrator of social services and guardian of the collective good (cf. Marx and Engels, 1848:94; Marx, 1875:8-9).

Of course, these broad similarities cannot mask certain differences between the two men's views. Marx's future society, even the temporary socialist phase, takes us much further from contemporary capitalism than does Durkheim's normal division of labor. Despite the existence in Marx's socialism of a state administration, unequal rewards, and some private property, the impact of such structures and processes is supposed to be curtailed to a much greater extent than in Durkheim's projected society. Moreover, even these vestiges of capitalist society and the bourgeois consciousness will disappear, for Marx, when we move beyond transitional socialism into true communism. In contrast, Durkheim clearly is less concerned that capitalism be radically restructured. The current system may take on quasisocialist elements, but primarily through gradual modification and adjustment: "It is not a matter of putting a completely new society in the place of the existing one, but of adapting the latter to the new social conditions" (Durkheim, 1896:204). Besides, in the last analysis, it is not the precise nature of the economic system, but rather the problem of social solidarity, that is Durkheim's primary concern.

It is interesting that, even on this last point, Marx and Durkheim are again somewhat similar. Both writers desire a society of united individuals, where people interact in a spirit of mutual responsibility, contributing in their own way to the collective interest. Both also believe that problems such as the *distribution* of rewards and resources to individuals can be solved if the social *relations* between people are first geared toward the general well-being of society and all its members. Thus, both theorists really embrace the same primary goal of social solidarity and remain hopeful that it will be achieved. Their disagreement concerns mainly the means or preconditions for its achievement. Whereas Durkheim expects that the collective good can be achieved within capitalism, Marx believes it can never be attained without capitalism's prior demise. Hence, as one analyst has observed, Marxism "finds Durkheimian theory much to its taste *after* the revolution" (Parkin, 1979:180).

But an even more basic disagreement arises from their assumptions about human nature. Durkheim's hopes for the good society are always tempered by his conviction that humanity, though not inherently evil, does require the prior constraint of moral regulation to keep egoistic desires in check: "Human passions stop only before a moral power they respect" (Durkheim, 1902:3, 15). For Marx, however, the problem is almost the reverse; that is, structural constraints, at least within capitalist society, are the greatest threats to the general well-being of people. Left to develop freely, human nature is essentially good, social, and oriented to the collectivity. It is the removal of unjust constraint through the overthrow of capitalism that will permit this natural condition of humanity eventually to emerge.

Durkheim, Weber, and the Problem of Power

Any attempt to compare Durkheim and Weber on the subject of social inequality eventually leads to the problem of power. One basic similarity between the two writers is that Durkheim, like Weber, perceives modern society primarily as a pluralist power system, one in which there are several distinct substructures possessing distinct powers and jurisdictions. While this pluralism is not often explicit in Durkheim's work, it may be inferred from at least two points discussed earlier.

First, there is Durkheim's delineation of the several interdependent functions in the modern division of labor. The economic, political, religious, and other functions correspond to the various substructures that compose society, each with its own sphere of influence and duties to discharge.

The second indication of pluralism in Durkheim's analysis is his expectation that certain occupational groups will emerge in future society. These groups will have their own special roles, mediating between the state and individual citizens and arbitrating economic problems, all in the general interest. Moreover, as separate public organizations, they will have powers that are independent both of private economic interests and of state control (Durkheim, 1896:203-204; 1902:7-8). Hence, they would add to the diversity of power bases in modern times, providing some protection against abuses of power, especially by those controlling the state and the economy.

If there is one important difference between Durkheim and Weber on the question of power, it concerns the disposition of the state, or political structure. Like Weber, Durkheim recognizes the increased role of the state in modern life, because of the expansion over time of legal rules and the attendant growth of a state apparatus to create and administer these regulations in a wide range of activities. Nevertheless, a crucial divergence between the two writers is Durkheim's apparent unconcern with what is Weber's greatest fear: domination and oppression by the state bureaucracy. Here Durkheim resembles Marx somewhat, for both assume that state leaders, under the proper conditions, will be administrators pure and simple, acting out of the same selfless regard for the collectivity as other citizens and posing no threat to democracy or freedom.

For Weber, however, the good will of state bureaucrats cannot be assumed. Those in a legal position to protect the general interest can, instead, use their position to the detriment of the general interest. Like Weber, Durkheim no doubt hoped that the pluralist nature of modern society would provide a set of countervailing forces to control such power abuses. Perhaps the occupational groups, for example, could serve as monitors against improper actions by the state and other structures. In a manner similar to that alleged for the free press or for public-interest pressure groups, they could observe wrongdoings, alert the citizenry against them, and mobilize public support to correct them.

In the end, however, Durkheim's discussion of the entire question of state power is incomplete. This is perhaps understandable, given his basic assumption that the struggle for power is not the principal process shaping social life. Such problems as class conflict and the abuse of power clearly exist, but they are really symptoms of more basic ailments caused by insufficient morality and solidarity. Durkheim maintains his conviction that the members of society are united by more than the struggle between interest groups. Interaction based purely on shared interest is inherently unstable: "Today it unites me to you; tomorrow it will make me your enemy" (Durkheim, 1893:203). Society involves more than a contested activity, with shifting alliances competing for power and rewards. If it is not more than this, society will disintegrate, for then "the state of war is continuous" (Durkheim, 1902:6).

Durkheim and Modern Structural Functionalism

The preceding analysis of Durkheim provides a backdrop for our discussion of contemporary structural functionalism. Structural functionalists claim several theorists among their ancestry, including Weber and occasionally even Marx; however, there is little doubt that Durkheim has had a more significant formative influence on modern structural functionalism than either of these two writers (cf. Parsons, 1937; Fallding, 1968:54; 1972:94). In particular, the tone and emphasis in current structural-functionalist analyses suggest an image of society that generally resembles Durkheim's. Thus, for example, structural functionalists share Durkheim's conception of society as a systematic aggregation of inter-related parts, all fulfilling important tasks for the common good. Structural functionalists likewise retain Durkheim's special interest in organizing and coordinating these tasks in order to maximize social integration and the chances for societal survival.

In addition, structural functionalists point to some of the same forces that Durkheim stresses when discussing the integration of modern society. First, integration is aided by the functional interdependence of individual social actors engaged in their own specialized tasks. This phenomenon is similar to Durkheim's idea of solidarity through the division of labor. Second, functionalists see integration stemming from the collective acceptance by individuals of a system of specific norms or rules that guide social relationships and regulate interactions. These norms correspond to the complex set of moral and juridical rules that Durkheim believes will promote the smooth, cohesive operation of modern societies. Finally, structural functionalists argue that integration is enhanced by popular adherence to a body of common values and beliefs. Like Durkheim's collective conscience, these values are said to pervade social life, providing at least general principles of human conduct and another means for binding society together.

Broad parallels of this sort make it apparent that the similarities between Durkheim's original work and modern structural-functional analysis are both noteworthy and genuine. At the same time, however, several important differences are also evident and must be kept in mind. While there is no single factor or person responsible for these differences, the principal cause is probably to be found in the work of Talcott Parsons.

Parsons was an American sociologist who played a pivotal role in bringing the writings of Durkheim to the attention of English-speaking, especially North American, sociologists. In his early work, *The Structure of Social Action*, Parsons attempts a reinterpretation of Durkheim, which, in combination with his views of Weber and others, he uses as a basis for his own theoretical perspective (Parsons, 1937). Much of what is now the core of structural-functionalist sociology is really Parsons' attempt to filter Durkheim, and to some extent Weber, through his own conceptual framework.

In order to grasp the essentials of contemporary structural functionalism, and in order to discern its major departures from Durkheim and its other progenitors, it is important that we briefly consider the basic conceptual scheme employed by Parsons and most subsequent structural functionalists. We will then assess how this scheme gives rise to the structural-functional analysis of social inequality. In the process we will discuss the key ways in which the structural-functionalist perspective diverges from the outlooks of Durkheim, Weber, and Marx.

Structural Functionalism: The Basic Concepts

Structure

As the name suggests, structural functionalists view society as a system of social *structures*. Structures in this sense are really patterns of relationship or interaction between the various components of society—patterns that are relatively enduring because interactions occur in a regular and more or less organized way.

The structural components of society exist at several levels of generality. At the most general level is society as a whole, which may be viewed as a single, overarching structure. The second level down is a series of more specialized structures that interconnect to form society, rather like the pillars of a building or, following Durkheim, like the organs of a living organism.

Each of these second-level structures is itself characterized by further task specialization. Thus, for example, we can think of the economy as one of these second-level structures. It performs a particular task that is itself a combination of interrelated, even more specialized, tasks: extracting raw materials, such as wood or iron ore; processing these materials into goods, such as lumber or steel; using these goods to manufacture finished products, such as furniture or cars; distributing, selling, and servicing these finished products; and so on. Special economic tasks thus give rise to their own special substructures, and these, taken together, compose the overall economic structure (cf. Parsons, 1953:400).

Status and Role

Ultimately, the decomposition of structures in this way leads to the most basic level of analysis: the individual social actor. In the structural-functionalist perspective, each individual occupies a *status* within the various structures of society. Status here does not refer to the prestige of the individual's position, but simply to the position itself. The individual occupying a status is also afforded certain rights and duties, which are the individual's *role* in that status (Williams, 1960:35-36). Thus, status and role tend to go together in what Parsons calls the "status-role bundle" (Parsons, 1951:25; 1953:393-394).

Social structure, then, *is* the interconnection of statuses that results when actors perform their assigned roles in interaction with one another. Thus, when those who fill the various worker, owner, manager, and related statuses of society perform their roles, we have an economic or occupational structure. When those who are voters, legislators, government officials, and so on fulfill their roles, we have a political structure. The same perspective can be employed to characterize the educational, religious, and other social structures that compose society. One of the unifying aspects of this image of society is that each individual may have a status and a role in all of these structures at the same time. In effect, the individual actor is plugged into numerous structures, rather like a multiple electrical outlet. A related image is to see the individual as segmented into several roles, almost like the slices of an orange (cf. Williams, 1960:517).

Norms, Values, and Institutions

Under the label *social structure* some structural functionalists include not only the status-role interactions but also the specific rules and general beliefs, the *norms* and *values*, that regulate these interactions (e.g., Johnson, 1960:51). A more prevalent view among structural functionalists, however, is that norms and values are not structural but *cultural*, existing in a different conceptual space that overlays social structures. In other words, norms and values are really ideas or symbols that individuals keep in mind as codes and sanctions for their interactions (cf. Parsons, 1951:327; Williams, 1960:20-30).

This disagreement over whether norms and values are structural or cultural parallels the confusion over the meaning of *superstructure* in Marxian theory, an issue discussed in Chapter 2. Just as superstructure can refer both to sets of ideas and to the structures that embody them, so too are norms and values sometimes equated with the structures that represent them. This equation occurs especially when structural functionalists speak of *institutions*, which are the most permanent, pervasive, and obligatory systems of norms and values in society (Williams, 1960:30-31; cf. Parsons, 1937:407; 1951:39; Levy, 1968:27). There is, for example, a common tendency to equate religious institutions, the system of religious rules and beliefs, with the religious structure, the administrative apparatus that has evolved for the nominal purpose of implementing these religious beliefs. The same may be said concerning economic institutions and the economic structure, education and the educational system, or political institutions and the structure of the state (cf. Williams, 1960:517).

This rather loose equation of ideas and realities, of institutions and social structures, is sometimes a useful device, for it aids in organizing one's thinking about social arrangements. However, one must be careful to look for cases where stated values or norms and *actual* structural relations do not correspond. An example would be when a dominant value, such as equal economic opportunity in capitalism, is not served by, or is even impeded by, existing social structures.

Function

This brings us to the last key concept in structural-functionalist analysis: the idea of *function* itself. We have noted that there is a correspondence between social structures and the institutions that guide their activity. In a similar way, there is a rough correspondence between these two conceptions and the various functions of society. Thus, for example, a structural functionalist would characterize the economy in capitalism as a structure, or system of structures, operating according to a set of corresponding economic institutions, such as private-property ownership, in the performance of its main function—the provision of the material means of existence for society's members.

But what, precisely, is meant here by the term function? Is this the economy's intended purpose in society, as planned by some agent or leader, or is it simply an unintended consequence of economic activity? Is the provision of the means of existence the actual contribution the economy makes to society, or is it merely the stated goal attributed to it by some people and not others? Such questions inevitably arise when the term function is used in sociology. Moreover, as noted at the start of this chapter, structural functionalists and their critics alike cannot agree on how to answer them, because of the confusion and disagreement over the definition of function. Problems are further compounded by the use of several ideas that are related to function but somehow distinct from it, including "functional requisite", "functional prerequisite", "functional imperative", and "functional problem" (cf. Aberle et al., 1950; Parsons, 1951; 1953; Johnson, 1960).

Even if it were possible, it is well beyond our purposes here to sort out the conceptual wrangles involved in the idea of function. And, in any case, most of these disagreements do not undermine at least a basic consistency in the use, if not the definition, of the term. For most structural functionalists, a function is really a *social task*, an activity that must be performed with some degree of adequacy if social groupings are to exist and to sustain their members. Among these tasks are a range of operations: socialization and education of the young, administration of economic and political affairs, regulation of criminal behavior; and so on.

Presumably, most sociologists would agree that such activities are indeed essential to any society (cf. Giddens, 1979:113-114). Hence, if a straightforward definition along these lines were to be employed consistently, there might be fewer problems with the meaning of the term function. Instead, however, the ambiguity surrounding this central concept in the structural-functionalist scheme has provoked serious suspicions regarding the intentions of structural-functionalist analysis. Among the numerous allegations that have been made, two in particular will be noted here.

First of all, some observers believe that, when structural functionalists describe the tasks of society as functions, they are really promoting the view that the existing structures and institutions of society are good or ideal, functioning properly in fulfilling society's needs. The implication is that any alteration in the established arrangements must, in their terms, be *dysfunctional*—that is, disruptive of the stable operation of society. Thus, detractors believe that structural functionalists implicitly adopt an uncritical acceptance of the current social structure, sometimes combined with an outright distrust of social change.

A second key problem involving the idea of function concerns how we decide if something is functional or not. Critics argue that structural functionalists judge structures or institutions solely on the basis of whether they meet the needs of society *as a whole*. To critics, judgment on this basis alone implies that a structure or system of rules will be deemed functional as long as it fulfills some important societal task, regardless of its consequences for particular groups or individuals *within* society.

Thus, for example, an important task for society is to control crime, violence, and other forms of antisocial behavior. Structures such as the police and the military may be in place to perform this task. However, if these structures employ policies, official or otherwise, that control crime and violence by means of strict curfews, imprisonment without trial or evidence, and so on, the social-control function may be achieved, but at tremendous cost to other segments of society. These organizations and rules could become tools not only to regulate crime but also to eliminate peaceful dissent—to oppress political dissidents, racial minorities, or other legitimate factions who may not hold favor with the society's leadership. Thus, if we were to judge the functionality of a structure *only* in terms of the vague abstraction called society, these dysfunctional aspects of that structure might be ignored, unintentionally or otherwise. Moreover, it would be possible in such a circumstance to hide what are really the *special* goals and interests of certain groups, particularly those in control of the economy or the state, by representing them as society's goals or the general interest.

One important feature of these criticisms is that they result more from what structural functionalists fail to say than from what they actually say, from what they imply more than from what they explicitly advocate. This is not to argue, of course, that all the disagreements between structural functionalism and its critics are simply misunderstandings. As we shall see, there are several fundamental differences, especially in the analysis of social inequality, that seem irreconcilable. However, it *is* contended here that the concept of function in sociology has become a loaded term, detested by some and embraced by others, primarily because of the implied meanings attached to it over the years. There is nothing inherent in the concept that should provoke such feeling, especially if the term is used mainly as a synonym for social task, as discussed earlier.

It is interesting to note in this regard that some Marxist scholars have been among the strongest opponents of the concept of function as employed by the structural-functionalist school; yet there seems to be nothing intrinsic in the term that explains this opposition. In fact, both classical and contemporary Marxists have been known to use the concept of function (or *Funktion*) themselves (e.g., Marx, 1894:379; Engels, 1890a:490; Habermas, 1975; Poulantzas, 1975; Weiss, 1976; Carchedi, 1977; Wright, 1978).

We should also note that at least some structural functionalists have attempted to allay the problems raised by their critics. That is, although structural functionalists admittedly place greater stress on the importance

of stability in society, some do try to incorporate a discussion of progressive social change into their scheme. In addition, some structural
functionalists do not always judge the functionality of social phenomena
in terms of the vaguely defined needs of society as a whole. These writers
recognize that one must be explicit about who is being served or not
served by particular structures and institutions in a social system (e.g.,
Johnson, 1960:70; Levy, 1968:25; Fallding, 1968:77-78).

Only One Sociology?

As the preceding discussion reveals, the structural-functionalist conceptual scheme portrays society as a complex system of social structures,
which operate under the guidance of institutionalized norms and values
in the performance of special, vital functions for society and its members.
Although the terminologies sometimes differ, it should be apparent from
the earlier analyses that Marx, Weber, and Durkheim share an interest
in these same concerns: how social structures are arranged, how they are
regulated or governed, and what they do for (or to) the people who live
within them. In fact, it could be argued that virtually all sociologists,
past and present, are involved primarily in examining these phenomena.

This very general resemblance between structural-functionalist concerns and those of other sociologists seems to be responsible for a bold
claim on the part of some structural-functionalist writers: that there is
only one sociology and that it is functionalist. In other words, structural
functionalism is not a special version of sociology at all but rather an
equivalent term for sociology itself (Davis, 1959; cf. Fallding, 1968:54-
55; 1972:93; Levy, 1968:22).

Some aspects of this assertion, on the surface, may seem plausible.
To begin with, it is true that the basic sociological approach until recent
years has been broadly similar to the structural-functionalist strategy.
Sociologists do tend to look at society as if it were a system of interconnected parts, of individuals and groups organized in more or less regular
interrelationships. Secondly, this apparent affinity is compounded by the
fact that even structural functionalism's critics tend to voice their opposition to it using a functionalist vocabulary (cf. Giddens, 1979:60). A
third point that seems to favor the structural-functionalist claim is that
a generally similar strategy is used outside the social sciences (cf. Levy,
1968:22). When other scientists wish to understand how something works,
they typically perceive the phenomenon in question as if it were a system
of interrelated segments. The component pieces can then be separated,
analyzed, and mentally reconstructed in an effort to comprehend both
the parts and their interconnections. Medical science, for instance, studies
the human body as a complex of cells, organs, and subsystems operating
in concert to create and sustain life. Biological science examines plants

and animals using similar assumptions. The sciences of physics and chemistry likewise proceed from images of chemical and physical matter as composites of elements and particles organized into a systematic whole.

However, a closer look reveals some basic flaws in the argument that structural functionalism is the universal approach in sociology or in science generally. This assertion seems, in particular, to mistake the lesser for the greater. That is, the vaguely similar strategy used by structural functionalists and other sociologists is taken to mean that all sociologists are structural functionalists, whereas it really demonstrates the simple fact that all structural functionalists are sociologists. This reversal introduces some unfortunate misrepresentations. Among structural functionalists, it can produce an unfounded self-assurance, a strong conviction that their particular view is the only one to take. As an aside, we might note that a similar conviction, that their own perspective is the only correct one, sometimes occurs in other theoretical camps as well.

An equally serious misrepresentation in this regard is one which occurs among certain critics of structural functionalism. Some critics automatically assume that any perspective that represents society as a structured system, even in very general terms, is merely another brand of structural functionalism and therefore to be completely dismissed. The point to stress here is that this assumption is just as mistaken as the structural-functionalist assumption that it is the universal approach in sociology. Both views fail to recognize that using a similar strategy of inquiry—one that amounts to sociology itself—does not amount to having the same theory of society. Using this very broad sociological strategy, it is possible to develop numerous theories for how social structures are generated, sustained, and transformed, each of which has a distinct emphasis and draws distinct conclusions. Our task is to determine which of these sociological theories is most useful, or seems most accurate, for explaining the phenomenon under investigation. There are few topics in sociology in which these distinctions between theories are more apparent or more crucial than in the analysis of social inequality. In the remainder of this chapter, we will examine the structural-functional approach to social inequality and assess the key ways in which this unique view can be compared with and contrasted to the theories of Marx, Weber, and Durkheim.

Structural Functionalism and Social Inequality

Because there are several variants of the general structural-functionalist perspective in sociology, it is not surprising that there are also several different ways in which structural functionalists have approached the subject of social inequality. Among these formulations, the principal versions are Parsons' early "analytical approach," which he later revised, and the better known though less comprehensive treatment by Davis and Moore (cf. Parsons, 1940; 1953; Davis and Moore, 1945).

There is no doubt that these analyses diverge on certain points (cf. Münch, 1982:815-816). Nevertheless, the essentials of the various structural-functionalist approaches to the topic of inequality are generally similar. Thus, we will not attempt a detailed review of what, for our purposes, are minor distinctions between these formulations. Instead, we will proceed with an outline of the major themes held in common by the several structural-functionalist discussions of social inequality. In addition to noting these central themes, our second task will be to assess the key areas of similarity and dissimilarity between the modern structural-functionalist perspective on inequality and that posed by each of the three early writers we have considered—Marx, Weber, and Durkheim. Obviously, the number of possible comparisons is very large; therefore, in the interests of clarity and simplicity, only the crucial points of convergence and divergence will be highlighted. The discussion throughout is organized around three principal issues: the differing conceptions of inequality as class structure or as individual *stratification* ranking, the relative importance of consensus and conflict in generating and sustaining social inequality, and the parts played by power and authority in social hierarchies.

Social Inequality: Class Structure or Stratification?

The predominant strategy for studying social inequality over the years has been to focus attention on issues of class. However, as an alternative to the class perspective, researchers will sometimes use a different view, one in which society is perceived as a hierarchy composed of layers, or *strata*. In this stratification perspective, individuals are ranked along a continuum or ladder and divided into discrete categories, which are, in effect, the strata for that particular analysis.

The stratification criterion varies depending on the researcher, but in most cases it is some objective indicator of economic rank, such as income, education, or occupational level. Often researchers will attempt to combine these separate rankings into some overall hierarchy. Perhaps the most common procedure is to calculate a single score for every occupational title, based on the average income and education of those engaged in each occupation. Thus, the occupational structure is transformed into a scale of overall "socioeconomic" rank (e.g., Blishen, 1967; Blau and Duncan, 1967; Blishen and McRoberts, 1976; Pineo et al., 1977).

Another approach is to rely on the *subjective* assessments, by representative samples of the population, of the general *social standing*, or *prestige*, of occupations. These occupational-prestige scores have also been used as indicators of the individual's overall stratification position (e.g., North and Hatt, 1947; Inkeles and Rossi, 1956; Hodge et al., 1964; Hodge et al., 1966; Goldthorpe and Hope, 1974; Treiman, 1977).

These various forms of the stratification perspective can be quite useful for students of social inequality. To take a simple illustration, imagine that we wished to determine the degree of income inequality in society. We could proceed by ranking people according to their annual incomes, dividing them into deciles (ten strata of equal size), and then comparing the total amounts of income earned within each stratum. If we determined for example, that the top tenth of the population receives fifty percent or more of the total and the bottom tenth earns only one or two percent, this would suggest an extremely unequal society, in terms of the distribution of income.

Stratification research along these lines has been done extensively in sociology. In fact, some researchers use this approach almost exclusively; however, it is also common for the same researcher to employ a class view at certain times and a stratification view at other times, depending on the researcher's purposes or interests. Thus, for example, some Marxist scholars, despite being concerned primarily with class issues, will occasionally take a stratification perspective in their empirical investigations (e.g., Kolko, 1962; Johnson, 1979).

The structural-functionalist approach to social inequality is really a special version of this stratification perspective. Structural functionalists also conceive of inequality as a general, continuous hierarchy along which individuals can be ranked (Barber, 1957:77). In their conception, people are stratified on the basis of the various status-roles they perform in society. People tend to fulfill numerous status-roles in life, so that one's ranking is "the general resultant of many particular bases of evaluation" (Parsons, 1951:132). In most cases, however, structural functionalists focus on the status-role the individual adopts in the occupational sphere. Occupation is seen as the best single indicator of general stratification rank, partly because it correlates with many other bases of ranking, such as income and education, but mainly because it is, for most people, the "functionally significant social role" one plays in society (cf. Barber, 1957:171; 184-185).

What this approach means is that, for structural functionalists, the stratification system is really a consequence of collective *judgments*, by which society (presumably, people in general) *evaluates* the worthiness of a person with regard to his or her importance or contribution to the collectivity (cf. Parsons, 1940:76-77; 1953:386-387). This approach corresponds loosely with the occupational-prestige variant of the stratification perspective noted earlier, for both views stratify society in terms of a *subjective* evaluation by others of one's prime social role or status. Of course, all prestige researchers are by no means structural functionalists; nevertheless, this idea of prestige ranking does appear to be the crucial element in structural-functionalist conceptions of stratification (e.g., Davis and Moore, 1945:242; Parsons, 1951:132; Barber, 1957:73; Johnson, 1960:469-470; Williams, 1960:97).

That structural functionalists perceive inequality in terms of one's value to society is, of course, consistent with their general viewpoint, especially their overriding concern with collective sentiments and societal needs. This concern is not in itself particularly objectionable. However, as we shall discuss later in this chapter, one may wonder whether it is possible to achieve collective agreement on which occupations are more important or worthy than others. Furthermore, if collective agreement is not possible, who makes these crucial ranking decisions?

One of the most serious weaknesses in the structural-functionalist conception of inequality as prestige stratification is that it becomes interwoven and confused with questions of class. These prestige strata— ranked categories of people with similar occupational prestige—come to be equated with the class structure. Class is then defined as "a more or less endogamous stratum consisting of families of about equal prestige" (Johnson, 1960:469; cf. Barber, 1957:73; Parsons, 1951:172). The prestige—and, hence, the "class status"—of all family members is judged by the occupation of the household head, who is usually the "husband-father" (Parsons, 1953:426-427).

Conceptual problems arise when the stratification and class perspectives are confused in this way, when strata are erroneously equated with classes (cf. Stolzman and Gamberg, 1974). While the two perspectives focus on similar topics, especially economic inequality, they differ in certain key respects. For one thing, a stratum, unlike the original idea of class, is not meant to be studied as if it were a real *group*, a set of people interacting with one another or having some sense of common affiliation. Of course, classes are not always real groups either, but there is at least some possibility that classes will form groups in certain circumstances. Thus, for example, a precondition for the overthrow of capitalism in Marxian theory is the development of a revolutionary working class— individuals who, in addition to their common economic position, also have a common consciousness, a sense of group solidarity, and a collective will to mobilize for political and social change. In contrast, when stratification analysts examine socioeconomic ranks, income deciles, or other types of strata, these cannot be, and are not intended to be, real groups. Instead, they are statistical aggregates, categories of individuals lumped together for particular research purposes.

Second, class and stratification analysts tend to emphasize different aspects of the inequality they study. On the one hand, class analysts are interested primarily in the *relational* consequences of inequality—that is, in the domination or exploitation of one class by another and the impact of these relations on social structure or social change. Recall, for example, that Marx viewed the relationship between owners and workers in capitalism as the driving force behind social change, because of the conflict inherent in this relationship between classes. On the other hand, stratification analysts typically focus on *distributive* inequalities, on the differential allocation of income, prestige, and other rewards or advantages to individuals in society (cf. Goldthorpe, 1972; Curtis and Scott, 1979; Hunter, 1981).

We shall have more to say on these issues later. For now, it is important to note only that the class and stratification perspectives differ and that the structural-functionalist approach tends to blur or ignore the difference. The failure to make this distinction is rather curious. The structural-functionalist view departs completely from Marx's classical treatment of class as defined by relationship to the means of production. Moreover, despite claims by structural functionalists of an affinity between their work and the formulations of both Weber and Durkheim, there is really very little common ground in either case. One structural-functionalist analysis explicitly argues that Weber adopts a prestige-stratum definition of class (Barber, 1957:73). However, as should be clear from Chapter 3, for Weber class is primarily an *economic* concept, related to market position and control over goods and services. In Weber's scheme, the concept closest to the structural-functionalist idea of class as prestige stratum is probably the status group. But the prestige strata in the structural-functionalist scheme are not groups, whereas Weber's status groups obviously are. Besides, Weber goes to great lengths to show that status groups and classes are *not* the same in any case, asserting the conceptual independence of economic class and status honor.

We might expect the structural-functionalist affinity with Durkheim to be very close on this issue of class and stratum, given their broad similarities in general approach, and given the conventional assumption that Durkheim's work is a prototype of modern structural functionalism. However, there are significant disparities. Presumably, Durkheim would agree with the structural-functionalist argument that ideally inequality arises through the differential evaluation of what individuals do in and for society. However, this individual stratification has little or no theoretical connection with the idea of class. In fact, in those relatively rare instances where Durkheim speaks of class, his remarks, as we have already seen, are rather close to Marx's and Weber's. His emphasis in discussions of class is, like theirs, on the *economic* differentiation of people, not on their differential prestige or moral worth.

Our intention in this section has been to outline the major differences between the class and stratification perspectives on inequality, especially as these relate to certain conceptual difficulties in the structural-functionalist approach. Structural functionalism's particular view of social inequality seems to comprise selected and modified elements of traditional class-based theories, which have been grafted to the more recent stratification school of social research. This attempted amalgamation has really only confused these two important, but quite separate, formulations. The failure to recognize these distinctions is a serious flaw and underscores our earlier conclusion that structural functionalism, despite its claim to the contrary, is *not* capable of subsuming all of sociology in any satisfactory and complete fashion.

Conflict, Consensus, and Social Inequality

A second important issue to address in any discussion of structural functionalism is the debate over whether society is characterized primarily by underlying conflict and struggle or by general consensus and agreement among its members. More specifically, we need to examine whether it is mainly through conflict or through consensus that individual and group inequalities become established in social structures.

To understand the structural-functionalist position on this issue, and to compare it with the other theories we have examined, a simple strategy is to locate each approach along a continuum, according to the relative importance each attaches to conflict and consensus. On such a scale, Marx probably would fall closest to the conflict end, with Weber nearby. Durkheim would be some distance away from Marx and Weber, but not at the consensus extreme. The modern structural-functionalist school would lie closest to the consensus pole. Let us briefly examine the reasoning behind each of these placements.

Marx, Weber, and Durkheim

Marx's conflict emphasis is most evident in his central premise that unequal relations of power and privilege are the products of a continuous historical struggle for control of the means of production. Although there may be extended periods of time when open social unrest does not occur, this relative stability is not a sign that there is a general consensus on the justice of existing social inequalities. In most cases, this apparent acceptance is a mere illusion and instead reflects a variety of other processes including successful ideological manipulation of the population by the ruling class, lack of awareness in the lower classes of the causes of and remedies for their subordinate position, or simple despair in the lower classes that inequities can ever be alleviated.

Compared to Marx, Weber seems somewhat more likely to conclude that there is *some* general agreement about the justice of social inequality. To a limited extent, at least, people have conceded that bureaucratic hierarchies and other institutionalized inequalities are a fact of modern life. Nevertheless, claims of consensus should not be overstated on these grounds. First of all, to say that one accepts the inevitability of inequality is not to say that one agrees with how particular hierarchies arise. Moreover, the ultimate origins of this acceptance should not be overlooked. For Weber, from the earliest times it is the monopoly of physical force that has generated inequality and the domination of one group by another. This coercive aspect of inequality may become less obvious as societies develop and power is formally institutionalized, but the ability to force compliance from subordinates nevertheless remains the underlying basis of social inequality.

Thus, to Weber, considerable conflict and antagonism often lie at the root of what on the surface are stable social hierarchies. Some citizens will actively embrace these existing social arrangements, but others will abide them for a mixture of quite different motives: habit, custom, fear, or a failure to discern alternatives. Such motives have little to do with a general consensus on the justice of the social order. Moreover, even in those societies where there is evidence of harmony and agreement, social action regularly includes a struggle for advantage among opposing factions and competing interest groups.

Analysts tend to identify Durkheim more with a consensus view of society, and less with a conflict perspective, than either Marx or Weber. This view probably stems from Durkheim's concept of the collective conscience, the commonly held values and beliefs that he perceived as a unifying force among early peoples. While there is little doubt that Durkheim is interested in such consensual aspects of society, we should not overlook the departures from consensus that he also perceives in social structures. First, we shall remember that Durkheim sees the collective conscience as necessarily weaker in modern times. To be sure, shared sentiments, such as a belief in freedom or equal opportunity, may still set a general moral tone for social action. Beyond this, however, consensus is unlikely, because the growing division of labor makes the legal and moral guides for conduct too specialized, elaborate, and complex for everyone to agree on, or even comprehend.

Thus, although Durkheim envisions a just and moral future society, it will not be characterized by some thoroughgoing consensus. What accord there is will stem mainly from *differences* between people in the division of labor, coupled with the recognition by most citizens of the need for mutual cooperation, obligation, and interdependence. We should also note that this differentiated basis for social harmony, the normal division of labor, "is far from being on the verge of realization" (Durkheim, 1893:408). In the interim, forced inequalities and class antagonisms persist beneath the orderly facade of present-day societies, calling into question the view that social hierarchies somehow arise out of a collective consensus among the people.

Structural Functionalism

It is here that structural functionalism enters the discussion. It would be inaccurate to claim that the entire structural-functionalist school ignores the existence of conflict in its portrayal of society (see, for example, Davis, 1949; Fallding, 1968, 1972). Nevertheless, there is little doubt that structural functionalism deals with conflict mainly as a secondary issue and that, more than any other perspective, it sees consensus as the principal foundation of social structures. On this basis, for example, Parsons disagrees with Durkheim's view that moral consensus, as reflected in collectively held beliefs, has waned in modern times. Instead, Durkheim's collective conscience has simply changed character and is now embodied in the "ultimate value system" (Parsons, 1937:400-401). This value system is "inculcated from early childhood" into the individual personality and fundamentally shapes even those specific normative rules, rights, and duties that govern social action (Parsons, 1940:73-74).

Hence, as social structures develop, their inherent properties tend, on the whole, to be consistent with a collectively held value system. According to structural functionalism, one such inherent property of society is the existence of inequality or stratification. Stratification is a universal aspect of social life, something that has occurred in virtually all known societies (e.g., Davis and Moore, 1945:242; Davis, 1949:366; Parsons, 1951:188; Williams, 1960:88). To structural functionalists, this prevalence of inequality is evidence of its inevitability and of its acceptability, at least in principle, to social actors.

Even more important to the consensus argument is the claim that there is a high level of agreement in the population about how specific status-roles or occupations should be ranked. At times, of course, structural functionalists concede that people's judgments will not correspond perfectly (e.g., Parsons, 1953:390). Nevertheless, it is argued, consensus on stratification rankings is quite high, at least in stable, democratic societies (e.g., Parsons, 1940:71; 1953:388; Davis and Moore, 1945:242; Williams, 1960:93).

And what of the criteria for ranking occupations? What are they, and to what extent is there general agreement on them? As discussed in the section on class versus stratification, structural functionalists envision stratification as a subjective scale of prestige, social standing, or moral evaluation. Various other factors can influence this evaluation of occupations or status-roles, including the power, possessions, or family background of incumbents (Parsons, 1940:75-76; 1953:389-390; Davis and Moore, 1945:244-248; Barber, 1957:30-48). For the most part, though, one's worth to society is the key factor, and it is judged by two overriding concerns: the "functional importance" for society of one's occupation and the "differential scarcity" of people with the talent or training needed for its performance (Davis and Moore, 1945:243-244; cf. Davis, 1949:368;

Parsons, 1953:403, 410). In other words, because such jobs as doctor or scientist are allegedly more important and harder to fill, compared to such jobs as dishwasher or waiter, they are more highly ranked in the stratification system. Here, too, people are said to be in considerable agreement in their judgments, even for the numerous and complex set of occupations in the modern division of labor (but see Davis and Moore, 1945:244 fn.).

One might ask at this point whether there is any evidence to support these allegations of consensus in the stratification rankings that people make. The most commonly cited evidence is the strong correlation (frequently above .90) that various researchers have reported between occupational-prestige rankings done by samples of respondents in different countries or at different times in the same country (e.g., Inkeles and Rossi, 1956; Barber, 1957:105-106; Lipset and Bendix, 1963:14; Hodge et al., 1966; Treiman, 1977).

However, we should note that these results have been criticized on methodological and statistical grounds. For one thing, researchers derive prestige scales by combining the disparate ratings of a sample of respondents, thereby averaging out significant disagreements between respondents in their ratings of some occupations (e.g. Guppy, 1981, 1982; Nosanchuk, 1972; Stehr, 1974; Coxon and Jones, 1978; for debate see Balkwell et al., 1982; Hodge et al., 1982). Thus, it appears that the high correlations between such scales really mask considerable dissensus in the popular evaluation of status-roles. Therefore, while it is unlikely that the observed correlations are totally the result of such measurement problems, it is also unlikely that, beyond certain obvious distinctions, there exists a general stratification scale that most people will agree on (cf. Parsons, 1940:86).

Before concluding our discussion of conflict and consensus, we should consider one additional point. Let us imagine, for the sake of argument, that there *is* a consensus on the way occupations rank with respect to prestige, moral evaluation, functional importance, or scarcity. We might still wonder why this scale should also give rise to other inequalities— for example, in access to such material advantages as income, wealth, or property. That is, is it not possible that the rewards of prestige and recognition for service to the collectivity might be sufficient distinction for the deserving, thus eliminating the need for material and other inequalities (cf. Tumin, 1953)? The response to this question varies somewhat, depending on which structural functionalist one consults. On the whole, however, the structural-functionalist view is that material inequalities *will* occur and that, in stable societies at least, these differences *should* correspond generally to the scale of evaluation.

This view stems from a particular conception of human nature and motivation (cf. Wrong, 1959:774; Wesolowski, 1966). The structural-functionalist assumption here is that most social actors are oriented to the good of the collectivity, but also to their own "self-interested elements of motivation" (Parsons, 1940:73; Davis, 1953). Stratification serves the function of satisfying both these needs, one collective and one individual, at the same time. However, this is so only if the material and evaluative hierarchies tend to correspond. According to Davis and Moore (1945:244), unequal material rewards motivate the best-qualified and most talented to take on those positions that are the toughest, most important, and hardest to fill. Any distribution of economic rewards not based on one's contribution and worth to society will only act as a disincentive to an efficient division of labor, especially because it will discourage rare and able people from assuming the sacrifices and responsibilities of high office (cf. Parsons, 1953:404-405). Note again the implicit assumption of consensus here, this time about the perceived justice of unequal rewards for service and the injustice of alternatives. Especially in western societies like the United States or Canada, these inequalities are seen as consistent with popularly held beliefs in such values as efficiency, freedom, achievement, and equal opportunity (e.g., Parsons, 1953:395-396; Williams, 1960:415-470).

In the end, however, structural functionalists believe that people see these material incentives and economic rewards as of secondary priority anyway, at least in comparison with the primary rewards of prestige and recognition from others. Wealth, while important in its own right, really has a *symbolic* meaning, as an index of achievement and high evaluation in society (Parsons, 1940:83; 1953:404-405; Barber, 1957:44). The idea that the distribution of economic advantages is really secondary to recognition for one's contribution to society sounds vaguely like Marx's view that distributive issues will be relatively unimportant in the popular mood that prevails under true communism. Even more, however, this idea resembles Durkheim's image of society under the normal division of labor. In that hypothetical system, there will be an interplay of individual competition for rewards and group cooperation for collective ends. Thus, self-interest exists but is restrained and harnessed for the good of all. Although it involves some exaggeration, one could almost conclude that structural functionalists in North America see Durkheim's future society as an imminent occurrence. The normal division of labor, with equal opportunity and rewards based on merit and contribution, seems to have gone from a nineteenth-century hope to an emerging twentieth-century reality (cf. Parsons, 1953:433-439).

The Conception of Power
in Structural Functionalism

So far, we have found that structural functionalists see social inequality as a stratified hierarchy of individual status-roles, ranked primarily by their value, in most people's minds, to society. Individuals compete for access to the higher of these status-roles because of the greater prestige they carry, and, secondarily, because of the greater material and other rewards they offer. At least in democratic societies, this competition for rank is relatively open, because people have a reasonable opportunity to excel at what they do best. Such an arrangement is functional in that it ultimately serves both the individual's need to achieve and society's need to have vital positions filled by the most competent and qualified persons. In addition, the resulting stratification system also serves an *integrative* function, by mapping out where people fit in society and by providing a systematic pattern of norms for interaction with others (e.g., Parsons, 1940:73).

But what is to ensure that people either accept where they fit in this structure or agree to the normative rules of the game that place them there? In particular, what is to stop certain individuals or groups from wresting away rewards belonging to others, usurping privileges not rightfully theirs, or otherwise forcing their will on the collectivity? This question really comes down to the role of power in social structures. In this final section, we will examine the approach taken by structural functionalists to the concept of power and the implications it has for their views on social inequality.

Power and the Problem of Social Order

Structural functionalists certainly discuss the idea of power, although their treatments tend to be rather brief and incidental to other issues. It is typical of structural functionalists to tie the concept of power directly to the fundamental question noted above: how do we maintain societal stability in the face of internal factions who might disrupt the social structure for their own ends? This so-called *problem of social order* is, in particular, an overriding concern for Parsons, who consistently raises it in his own writings and who attributes a similar preoccupation to Durkheim as well (e.g., Parsons, 1937:89, 307 fn., 314-315, 402-403; 1951:36-37, 118-119; cf. Giddens, 1971:106).

The general conclusion reached by Parsons and other structural functionalists is that, apart from isolated incidents, the use of coercive power cannot be the means by which social order is attained, because force itself can only breed disruption and disorder in the end (e.g., Parsons, 1966:246). Thus, to understand how stable societies exist, we must look for the source of social order elsewhere.

According to structural functionalism, social order arises mainly from legitimate and generally accepted bases of social control (e.g., Parsons, 1953:418). A key process here is socialization, whereby most people learn and adopt a set of prescribed rules and norms that permit orderly, mutually beneficial social interaction. This point, of course, relates to the structural-functionalist emphasis on popular consensus discussed earlier in this chapter. The crucial item to stress here is that these rules and norms are obeyed, in the structural-functionalist view, not out of fear of coercion or punishment by those in power, but primarily because the populace is instilled with the need or obligation to do what is right and to eschew what is not (cf. Parsons, 1940:74). Hence, the use of force in stable societies is rare, because of the pronounced feeling among the people that both their rules and their rulers are essentially legitimate.

Power and Authority

This sense that legitimacy is the ultimate basis of social order is reflected in structural functionalism's conception of power. On the surface, most structural functionalists appear to employ Weber's classical definition of power: the capacity to exercise one's will, even in the face of opposition (e.g., Parsons, 1966:240; Johnson, 1960:62; Davis, 1949:94-95; cf. Weber, 1922:53). Typically, however, structural functionalists then draw a key distinction. *Power* does not in fact refer to all such instances of exercising one's will despite resistance, but only to those instances that are "illegitimate" or "not institutionally sanctioned." The term *authority* is reserved for those situations where power is legitimate, institutionally recognized, or supported by "social consensus" (Parsons, 1940:76; 1953:391-392; 1966:240, 249; Barber, 1957:234; Williams, 1960:96). Thus, for example, the government in a democracy exercises authority when it collects property tax, provided that taxation is legally under its jurisdiction; however, the government is exercising power if it seizes a portion of one's property without recourse to legal statutes or some popular mandate.

This distinction between power and authority may seem reasonable enough. But, unfortunately, the tendency is for structural functionalists to believe that the concepts of power and authority exhaust all the situations in which some people hold sway over others. Thus, except for transitory cases of open, illegitimate coercion (power), most social relations are based on legitimate influence (authority), since subordinates must harbor some degree of acceptance if they regularly obey their superiors. Yet such a broad view of what constitutes authority clearly subsumes a wide range of instances in which people obey others out of habit, custom, self-interest, a lack of real or perceived alternatives, and so on. While these situations do not entail coercive power, neither are they examples of truly legitimate control (cf. Habermas, 1975:96). Structural functionalists thus tend to blur important differences in both the intent and the meaning of the influence operating in these cases. It is notable that this failure to acknowledge fully the wide range of situations in which neither power nor authority operates parallels a similar failure, noted earlier in this chapter, to appreciate completely the wide range of situations that involve neither open conflict nor general consensus.

Authority versus Domination

This tendency to emphasize the existence of authority, rather than other forms of influence, in social hierarchies is sometimes presented by structural functionalists as if it were consistent with Weberian theory. However, it is obvious from our discussion in Chapter 3, that this is not the case. The key difference between the structural-functionalist conception and Weber's analysis is that Weber does make an explicit distinction between authority, or genuinely *legitimate domination*, and other forms of domination based on habit, self-interest, and the like. The failure of structural functionalists and others to discern this crucial difference probably stems from Parsons, whose early translation of Weber's German works incorrectly treats domination (*Herrschaft*) and authority (*legitime Herrschaft*) as equivalent terms (cf. Weber, 1922:62 fn.; 299 fn.; Giddens, 1971:156).

These concerns over translation and terminology may seem like minor quibbles, but in fact they lead to fundamental difficulties in the way structural functionalists conceive of power and domination in social hierarchies. Of course, we should remind ourselves again that we are dealing with a school of thought, and that not all writers in this school are the same. Nonetheless, the impression given by most structural-functionalist analyses is that virtually all enduring structures of domination are basically legitimate. While this is a view that Weber would never espouse, it occurs rather consistently in structural-functionalist discussions. Thus, for example, Davis (1949:95) asserts that "the whole social structure, the whole system of positions, may be viewed as a legitimate power system." The reasoning here is that "the line of power corresponds roughly with the hierarchy of prestige"—that is, with the popularly held ranking of what are the most important positions in society (Davis, 1949:95). In other words, if the populace agrees that the most powerful positions also have the highest evaluations of importance, then the power structure is legitimate by definition.

However, the crucial question that should be raised here is one we have already noted: who decides what positions are most important and prestigious in society? The structural-functionalist assumption, as discussed earlier, is that society, or everybody in general, makes these decisions. If that were true, then the stratification system and its corresponding power structure would indeed have a legitimate and consensual basis in the popular will. But a plausible alternative is that it is largely the *people in power* who decide which positions are most important and thus most deserving of prestige and other rewards. In that event, the close correspondence among one's power, prestige, and privileges would have little to do with legitimacy or consensus but instead would flow mainly from the capacity of people in positions of domination to establish and maintain their own advantages, through force or other means.

This alternative image of power's role in social hierarchies is generally similar to the views of Weber and Marx, which we reviewed in earlier chapters. It is apparent, then, that structural functionalism departs significantly from these classical perspectives. Although some structural functionalists concede that there are coercive and nonlegitimate aspects of power at times, there is little doubt that these factors are seen as of secondary importance for generating inequality. Power, in most cases, is not a *zero-sum* relationship, wherein people struggle for scarce resources and some win only if others lose. Rather, as modern social structures continue to develop and expand their mastery of the environment, there will really be more power for everyone, because of the increased opportunities to exploit and resources to control (see especially Parsons, 1966; also Parsons, 1953:436-437).

The Pluralism of Power

The last element in the structural-functionalist treatment of power that we should briefly discuss is its decidedly pluralist tone. As we have already seen, structural functionalists view modern society as a complex of structures and substructures, each of which performs important tasks for the overall system. This portrayal in itself implies a pluralist power structure, for it suggests numerous centers of jurisdiction, decision making, and control over resources. As well, each of these structures is in some sense another stratification system, with its own distinct distribution of powers and responsibilities to groups or individuals (e.g., Parsons, 1940:86-87; Davis and Moore, 1945:244 fn.). Thus, while we may speak of "the total 'power' system of a society," it is really made up of multiple components, "a plurality of other systems" which, when coordinated, ensure that societal problems are solved and goals achieved (Parsons, 1953:388-389). Moreover, none of these structures by itself is seen as having "monolithic" or "paramount" control. The overall effect is a "separation of powers," so that no one interest group or elite has a "monopoly of influence" (Barber, 1957:241-242; Parsons, 1953:418, 426).

For the individuals and subgroups of society, this pluralism means a great deal of opportunity for mobility into positions of value and authority. If, for example, an individual has little or no power in the political sphere, he or she nonetheless may attain high rank and influence in one or more of the economic, religious, or other substructures. Thus, the overall effect, both on the stratification system and the pattern of power, is considerable "openness," "looseness," and "dispersion" (Parsons, 1940:86-87; 1953:407, 430-432).

This portrayal of the modern power structure as fluid and open is of course entirely consistent with the other central tenets of the structural-functionalist perspective we have outlined in this chapter. Equally clear are its departures from Marx's formulation. For Marx, the apparent dispersal of power in modern societies is largely a superstructural illusion, masking the underlying economic basis for all social domination.

The view of power among structural functionalists may seem vaguely similar to Weber's pluralist analysis. Even here, however, Weber's case for the multiple bases of power in society is different, because he sees the dispersion of power as more limited. Moreover, Weber retains a concern over the very real possibility that the domination of social life may eventually be centralized in a massive, omnipotent state bureaucracy. Structural functionalists do not seem to acknowledge the threat that state centralization poses for pluralism, at least with respect to capitalist liberal democracies such as the United States or Canada. It is only with respect to totalitarian societies such as the Soviet Union or Nazi Germany that this threat is identified (cf. Parsons, 1953:407, 418; Barber, 1957:241-242). It is probably no surprise that structural functionalism has achieved its greatest following and its best-known proponents in western capitalist countries, especially the United States (cf. Wrong, 1959). In these societies, the dominant belief system tends to accept social inequality as legitimate and normal as long as it results from equal opportunity, individual performance, and an absence of coercive power.

Thus, we see once again that the structural-functionalist view of modern democratic societies seems much closer to Durkheim's vision of the future than it does to the predictions implicit in Marx or Weber. But is the moral, just, and normal division of labor an impending reality? The more skeptical among us may wonder just how close any society, including the United States or Canada, has come to achieving such a system. This is a question that we shall raise again.

Summary

In this chapter we have taken an extensive look at the view of social inequality that has developed out of the so-called structural-functionalist school of sociological theory. We began with a review of Durkheim's classical discussion of the division of labor in society. We saw that Durkheim's work is in some ways a prototype of the modern structural-functionalist approach but that in other ways it has a closer affinity to the works of Weber and Marx. As a result, Durkheim represents an important bridge between these two classical writers and the more recent structural-functionalist perspective.

In our discussion of modern structural functionalism we reviewed its major concepts and some of the key criticisms that have been leveled against it. Our central concern, however, was to examine the particular manner in which structural functionalists conceive of inequality, especially as it compares with the conceptions of Marx, Weber, and Durkheim. We found that there are significant discrepancies between the structural-functionalist approach and each of these classical writers on most points. Among the crucial differences are the tendency for structural functionalists: to see inequality mainly as a matter of individual stratification rank rather than class structure; to depart widely from the classical usage of class when they employ this concept; to perceive far more consensus, and far less conflict, in the processes that lead to inequality; to play down the importance of coercive power, compared to legitimate influence, as the basis for inequality; and to see a significantly more open and equitable system of power and opportunity in present day societies than is typical in earlier analyses.

The treatment of structural functionalism here has no doubt seemed much more critical and skeptical in tone than was evident in our assessments of the other writers. This critical stance, however, should be partly tempered by the realization that we have had to examine the sometimes diverse school of thought that constitutes structural functionalism as if it were a single, consistent approach. Because of the need to summarize and distill the ideas of so many writers, some oversimplification has been inevitable. Thus, in some instances, the criticisms apply to certain writers more than to others and should not be seen as a categorical rejection of all the ideas and analysts identified with this school. This caution is important to note because of the tendency among some critics to present a mere caricature of structural functionalism and then to dismiss it entirely. The proposal here is to avoid an outright rejection of structural functionalism, at least until we have been able to examine the key issues again. Our final judgment of the structural-functionalist viewpoint, and of the views put forth by the earlier writers as well, should first take into account the most promising recent attempts to conceptualize the problem of social inequality. A review of these efforts is the task to be addressed in the next chapter.

CHAPTER FIVE

Recent Perspectives on Social Inequality

"Class power is the cornerstone of power." Nicos Poulantzas, State, Power, Socialism, *1978*

"All social interaction involves the use of power." Anthony Giddens, A Contemporary Critique of Historical Materialism, Volume 1, *1981*

Introduction

We have now examined the principal approaches to social inequality that have emerged from classical sociological theory. Clearly, there are many other perspectives we could discuss, including the numerous accounts of more recent times. However, an exhaustive review of these approaches is unnecessary, since the great majority of them tend to be variations on the key ideas and themes we have already outlined from the classical perspectives. Still, some of these other viewpoints, particularly in the current literature, are of special note for their attempts to build upon the classical formulations and reorient them to fit contemporary conditions.

The central goal of this chapter is to assess the most promising or prominent of these newer approaches to social inequality. The writers to receive special attention here include Dahrendorf and Lenski, whose works probably are the best-known departures from structural functionalism to come out of the 1950s and 1960s; Poulantzas and Wright, who are arguably the foremost among a range of neo-Marxist thinkers who have achieved distinction in the 1970s and 1980s; and finally Parkin and Giddens, whose efforts represent the best of what has been loosely termed a neo-Weberian upsurge in the 1970s and 1980s.

Inevitably, the selection of these six writers over others is to some extent not a matter on which complete consensus is possible. This choice omits, for example, Marxists such as Lenin (1917), Mills (1951; 1956), and more recently Habermas (1975) and Offe (1974), as well as certain power theorists such as Lukes (1974; 1978), Blau (1964; 1977), and Wrong (1979). Nevertheless, the view taken here is that the key insights of these writers are largely represented in the works of the six analysts chosen for review. On specific points, of course, reference to such additional theorists will be made when necessary.

Throughout the chapter, the reader should remain alert to the key areas of similarity and dissimilarity, not only among the six selected approaches but also between them and the classical views we have already examined. Obviously, our discussion would be much too involved were we to deal with these comparisons in all their minute aspects. Hence, rather than a comprehensive exposition of all six conceptual schemes, we shall conduct a much more selective investigation, one that critically evaluates each approach but focuses almost exclusively on the four major topics that were outlined in the opening chapter. These four points include each author's stance on the concept of class or class structure; the significance of power for explaining structured inequality in society; the interconnection of the state with the economic and other structures of society in modern times; and the prospects for reducing or ending social inequality in the future, through socialist revolution or other means.

The six recent perspectives to be considered in this chapter, combined with the classical views already discussed, occupy a wide theoretical spectrum that, if analyzed in detail, reveals countless subtle differences in conception and emphasis. Yet, when these perspectives are examined on a more general level of analysis, one can argue that their similarities are at least as striking as their differences. The approach taken here is to adopt a middle ground between these two levels, one in which the essential distinctions among perspectives are acknowledged, but where the presentation is simplified and clarified whenever possible. As a step in this direction, it is instructive to array the various theorists along a general continuum between two poles that, for want of more precise terms, are labeled *left* and *right*. To take the most extreme illustration, those at the left pole see social inequality arising purely out of conflict or struggle between antagonistic groups; trace the root of inequality to the single factor of class location or control of economic power; and stress the major social problems that inequality engenders, problems that can be alleviated only through radical social change. In contrast, those at the right pole see social inequality wholly as the result of consensual interaction between individuals competing with one another according to agreed-upon rules of conduct; believe that inequality flows from an extreme plurality of factors, not one or a few sources; and stress the positive effects of inequality, especially for societal stability and integration.

Although no theorist under scrutiny here precisely fits either of these two extreme images, we can estimate each one's *relative* position on the continuum between the poles, as shown in Figure 5.1. Note that each writer's location on the left-right scale is cross-referenced with the approximate time of his emergence or prominence, especially in North

Figure 5.1

The Chronology of Major Theories of Inequality and Approximate Locations on Loosely Defined Left-Right Continuum

Period of emergence
or prominence:

prior to 1900	Marx, early Marxism			
1900 to 1920		Weber	Durkheim	
			Structural	
1920 to 1950			Functionalism	
1950 to 1960		Dahrendorf		
1960 to 1970		Lenski		
	Poulantzas			
1970 to present	Wright Giddens Parkin			

Left _____ Right

(inequality based on struggle, rooted in class or economic power, must be changed by radical action)

(inequality based on consensus, has extremely pluralist roots, provides stability and other benefits for society)

American sociological circles. This procedure produces an interesting pattern, one that roughly resembles a *U* laid on its side.

We must avoid grand explanations for this pattern, but one way to make some sense of this apparent trend is to consider the manner in which leading intellectuals respond to the climate of the times in different historical periods. We have already discussed how Weber's work in many respects was a critical reaction to Marx, or at least to the manner in which Marx's main premises were represented by the subsequent groundswell of Marxist thinkers in the late nineteenth and early twentieth centuries. Weber's critique, which is paralleled in Durkheim's writings to some extent, was meant to be a positive, or constructive, one. However, it seems to have set in motion a much wider swing away from the left pole than Weber intended. This swing was accelerated significantly by Parsons' peculiar interpretations of Durkheim and Weber, which eliminated from these writers' works most of the affinities with Marx that we have outlined in previous chapters. The culmination of this trend was the emergence of the structural-functionalist school as the dominant force in sociological thought by the 1950s, especially in the United States.

At about this time, as was noted in Chapter 4, certain influential writers came to react against the inaccuracies they perceived in the more extreme versions of structural functionalism. Dahrendorf was one of the leading critics of what was seen as a false, utopian representation of societal harmony, stability, and consensus by the structural-functionalist school (e.g., Dahrendorf, 1958; 1959; 1968; see also Mills, 1959; Wrong, 1961). The work of Dahrendorf and others provided a catalyst that sent the pendulum swinging back again, away from the right end of the continuum and into a broad middle range of rather diverse viewpoints. Lenski is among the most notable here, as someone who himself moved from a functionalist stance to a "synthesizing," partly Weberian position in the 1960s (Lenski, 1966:435).

Although they differ in other respects, writers like Dahrendorf and Lenski share a desire to combine in one perspective key elements from both the left and the right poles, from Marx or Marxism on the one hand and from structural functionalism on the other. There are at least two important developments that have followed in the wake of such efforts. First of all, the changes they have stimulated seem to have come more at the expense of structural functionalism than of Marx. In other words, whereas Marx's ideas have had a continuing influence to the present day, structural functionalism has virtually abandoned the topic of social inequality, at least since the 1960s. This abandonment may be a tacit admission by structural functionalists of fundamental difficulties in their approach to inequality, or it may reflect the simple truth that, after all, the subject is of secondary concern to them and not deserving of sustained attention. Whatever the reason, structural functionalism has been largely supplanted as a serious alternative to Marx in the current literature on social inequality.

The second important consequence of Dahrendorf's and Lenski's work has been a revival of Weberian thought. As we shall see, their focus on power and their plural conception of class and power structures return us to some version of the Weberian perspective. Thus, the pendulum moves back to Weber and the renewal of an old rivalry: the theoretical debate between Weber and Marx. In fact, it has been argued that even now the trend of thought in the study of social inequality oscillates between these two writers, that "the all-pervasive influence of Marx and Weber . . . is, if anything, more pronounced today than at any other stage" (Parkin, 1978:601). Generally speaking, this is the argument that will be put forth in this chapter. The ideas of Marx and Weber, especially as they have been refurbished in current debates involving Poulantzas, Wright, Parkin, and Giddens, provide the most fruitful basis for examining inequality in modern societies.

Depending on the relative emphases of these four writers, it has been typical to classify them as either neo-Marxists or neo-Weberians, with Poulantzas and Wright in the former category and Parkin and Giddens in the latter. Such a classification is not unhelpful, provided it is applied cautiously and at a very general level of discussion. Thus, it is fair to refer to Poulantzas and Wright as neo-Marxists, because they provide us with new or fresh analyses based on Marx's first principles. However, it is also the case that, with each succeeding generation, their title as *new* Marxists inevitably must be relinquished to the next cohort of Marx's followers that comes along. We should also note that these categories exhibit wide internal variations. This is well illustrated by Parkin, who readily accepts the neo-Weberian label but disagrees with several other writers to whom he gives the same title (Parkin, 1979:112; 1972:29-33).

But probably the greatest difficulty with such simple classifications is that they do not deal precisely with those, like Giddens, who prefer to be allied with neither camp (Giddens, 1981a:296-297; 1981b:1). Certainly, although Giddens acknowledges the contributions to his thought from both classical thinkers, some of the subtler elements of his work do not stem from either Marx or Weber. And yet, at a broader level of discussion, there is justification for locating Giddens relatively near the neo-Weberian circle. As we shall see, Giddens, like Weber, is greatly concerned with offering a critical but constructive appraisal of Marx's historical materialism (see especially Giddens, 1981b). Like Weber, Giddens places considerable stress on the complexity of social inequality and the various forms it can take. Finally, like Weber, Giddens uses as his conceptual centerpiece the idea of power and its role in the structures of domination that shape social interaction in modern societies. For these reasons and others, the neo-Weberian label is not without some provisional foundation.

With this preamble, we are now in a position to review each of the six more recent perspectives on social inequality. It is possible to proceed chronologically at the outset, beginning with Dahrendorf and then Lenski. The other four writers, however, are part of an ongoing debate, with the latest round ending in the neo-Weberian camp. Consequently, it is useful to consider the neo-Marxist views of Poulantzas and Wright next, and follow them with Parkin's neo-Weberian critique of their positions. Finally, we shall examine Giddens' formulation, which is the most inclusive of all in many respects.

Ralf Dahrendorf
Class Conflict
in Industrial Society

Dahrendorf's *Class and Class Conflict in Industrial Society* (1959) is the most complete presentation of his position on social inequality, the essentials of which he has more recently reaffirmed (Dahrendorf, 1979). Dahrendorf makes the central claim that neither structural functionalism nor Marxism is adequate by itself as a perspective on society, since the former pays too little attention to the realities of social conflict, while the latter ignores the obvious evidence of consensus and integration in modern social structures (1959:122-124, 158-160). As an alternative, Dahrendorf proposes to "draw from Marx what is still useful" and to incorporate it with certain promising elements of the structural-functionalist viewpoint (1959:118). Hence Dahrendorf contends, following Marx, that conflict is still a basic fact of social life and can have positive consequences for society, as a spur to progressive social change. In this way, Dahrendorf seeks to dissociate himself from those structural functionalists and others who saw an "end of ideology" during the 1950s, who proclaimed a complete end to the conflict of ideas and class interests that preoccupied Marx in the nineteenth century (e.g., Riesman et al., 1953; Bell, 1960; for discussion see Giddens, 1973; Benson, 1978).

Even so, Dahrendorf's affinities with Marx remain minor in the end and distinguish him only partially from the structural functionalists he criticizes. For Dahrendorf ultimately shares with these analysts the same general optimism and faith in existing institutions that arose out of the prosperity and stability of the post-World War II era. In fact, according to Dahrendorf, several important changes and improvements in the capitalism of Marx's age signal the emergence of a new social structure called "industrial" or "postcapitalist" society (1959:40-41). In general, postcapitalism involves a much more complex system of inequality than can be captured by the simple split between capitalists and workers, the "two great and homogeneous hostile camps with which Marx was concerned" (1959:48). It is marked, first, by a diverse class structure and, second, by a very fluid system of power relations. Moreoever, it is a society in which the resolution of class conflict has been "institutionalized"—legitimately incorporated within the state and economic spheres—so that the drastic class strife of Marx's time has been made obsolete. Let us briefly consider each of these points and their relevance to Dahrendorf's views on the future of inequality in postcapitalist society.

Class Structure in Postcapitalism

Dahrendorf rejects Marx's dichotomous, two-class system because it is too simplistic to be applicable in postcapitalist society and because its stress on property ownership as the single distinguishing class characteristic has become outdated. For one thing, the capitalist class has been "decomposed" by the rise of the "joint-stock company," which separates simple ownership from actual control of economic production. Although Marx was certainly aware of this new form of business organization, owned by stockholders and run by managers or corporate executives, Dahrendorf claims that Marx underestimated how much power this arrangement would take from owners and give to executives, who may own no part of the enterprise but still make the crucial business decisions (1959:47).

A second important complication in modern class structures concerns diversification within the working class itself. Like Weber, Dahrendorf criticizes Marx's view that the proletariat will eventually become a homogeneous collection of relatively unskilled machine operators. On the contrary, there are now increasingly elaborate distinctions among workers regarding skill levels, life chances, and prestige, with a need for more, not less, skilled personnel to run and maintain the sophisticated machinery of industry. The result is "a plurality of status and skill groups whose interests often diverge" (1959:51, 277).

The third major factor in this pluralism of classes involves those categories of people who are neither bourgeois nor proletarian precisely but are lumped by various writers under the title "new middle class." To Dahrendorf, some of these people, including salaried white-collar employees, overlap partly with the old working class, while others, including some bureaucrats and the executives noted earlier, may have vague affinities with the old capitalist class. In both cases, however, these intermediate groupings are distinguishable in key respects from capital and labor, confirming once again that "the pleasing simplicity of Marx's view has become a nonsensical construction" (1959:57).

For these reasons and others, Dahrendorf contends that Marx's idea of class can be salvaged only if its entire meaning and definition are altered to reflect the changes in modern social structures. Dahrendorf thus makes an alternative proposal. Because of the separation of ownership and control, the growth of corporate and state bureaucracies, and other manifestations of complex organizational hierarchies, it is apparent that the crux of social inequality is no longer the antagonistic property relations between capital and labor, but the *authority* relations arising within a wide variety of social and organizational settings (1959:136-138). Authority relations are crucial because, while it is possible to imagine an end of inequality in property holdings, or in such advantages as income and prestige, it is impossible to conceive of social organization without inequalities in authority (1959:64, 70-71, 219). Moreover, "authority is the more general social relation," with property "but one of its numerous types" (1959:137).

According to Dahrendorf, then, any useful definition of class in post-capitalist society should include the key idea of authority, and the term class relations should refer not only to the conflict between economic groupings but to *all* situations of struggle between those who have authority and those who do not. Hence, Dahrendorf explicitly defines classes as "social conflict groups," distinguished from one another by their "participation in or exclusion from the exercise of authority" (1959:138, 247). These conflicts are most telling within the major institutions and organizations, especially in the economic or industrial sphere and in the political structure or state. In theory, however, they can occur in any hierarchical authority structure, any "imperatively coordinated association" (1959:138-139).

Dahrendorf's redefinition of class in this manner is intriguing and, on the surface, may appear to have merit. His claims that inequalities in authority are inevitable, and that property relations are but one manifestation of such inequalities, seem difficult to deny. Indeed, most analysts, including Marx and Engels, acknowledge both of these points from time to time (e.g., Marx, 1867:300-331; Engels, 1872, 1890b:463-465).

But does the recognition that authority is an important factor in social relations justify its equation with the concept of class? Surely, the answer to this question must be no. Now, Dahrendorf allows that his proposal for defining all authority relations as class relations is "pragmatic" and "reversible" (1959:201). However, even such a temporary or tentative definition can serve no useful purpose for our cumulative understanding of theory in this area. Dahrendorf's class definition has no consistency or connection with the classical views of Marx and Weber or with established usage. In addition, it has inherent logical problems, for, if every conflict over authority is a class relation, then there are an infinite number of classes, making class virtually meaningless as a concept. As others have pointed out, Dahrendorf's definition also leads to certain ludicrous conclusions, because every confrontation over authority, even between parent and child for example, is by definition a class conflict (cf. Giddens, 1973:73). Such difficulties are somewhat ironic, since Dahrendorf is critical of theorists who confuse the general with the specific; yet, by seeing all authority relations as class relations, instead of viewing class relations as really one crucial type of authority (or power) relation, Dahrendorf commits precisely the same error himself (1959:137).

Dahrendorf on Power and Authority

It should be apparent by now that Dahrendorf's general conceptions of class and inequality are closely tied to his view of authority or power. This emphasis is reminiscent of Weber, with whom Dahrendorf shares certain broad affinities, including his pluralist view of class and power structures; his belief that authority hierarchies are inevitable in all advanced societies, capitalist or otherwise; and his interest in the growing concentration of influence within formal bureaucracies, especially in politics and industry (1959:299).

It is only when we examine Dahrendorf's actual definitions of power and authority that his differences with Weber become apparent. A curious aspect of Dahrendorf's discussion is that he claims to adopt Weber's view of power and authority but, in the end, uses a terminology that is much closer to Parsons and the structural-functionalist school. This inconsistency is most serious in his treatment of Weber's idea of domination (Herrschaft). Like Parsons, Dahrendorf simply treats all situations of domination, of patterned or structured power relationships, as if they were legitimate (1959:166). Thus, he fails to distinguish between authority (truly legitimate power) and those cases where subordinates give regular obedience to superiors, not out of a belief in the justice or legitimacy of the relationship, but for a variety of other reasons. At times, Dahrendorf seems to acknowledge the difference between domination and authority, but on the whole he blurs this distinction and so creates considerable confusion (1959:176; 1979:117).

An additional difficulty with Dahrendorf's approach to power is his contention that all situations of conflict must involve two and only two contending parties (1959:126). This means that all class conflicts, and all authority or power relations, must involve a "dichotomy of positions" between those who possess power and those who are deprived of it (1959:170, 238). Such a view obviously departs from Weber, who saw power as a graded phenomenon, varying in degree within bureaucracies and other hierarchies. More important, this dichotomous view is also at odds with social reality. It is not difficult to think of illustrations that run counter to such a perception. The complex authority network of a modern corporation, comprising owners, top executives, middle managers, and salaried employees, among others, cannot be reduced to a simple set of dichotomous relations. The numerous examples of multiparty political systems, as in Canada or Great Britain, are further evidence against the claim that confrontations over power always involve only two factions. Dahrendorf's insistence on the dichotomous nature of power relations seems especially peculiar in the light of his generally pluralist view of social structures and his passing references to "gradations" of power or authority in society (1959:196).

The Institutionalization of Class Conflict

Unlike some of Marx's more extreme critics, Dahrendorf readily accepts that conflict is inherent to social structures and treats it as a definitive feature of all class and power relations. However, what distinguishes him from Marx, and what explains his location toward the structural-functionalist end of our left-right continuum, is Dahrendorf's special conception of modern class conflict. Today such conflicts are "far removed from the ruthless and absolute class struggle visualized by Marx" (1959:66). Rather than violent class warfare, the contending parties in postcapitalism engage in regulated, or "institutionalized", conflict. In other words, they have "agreed on certain rules of the game and created institutions which [have] provided a framework for the routinization of the process of conflict" (1959:65, 225-227).

This institutionalization of class struggle is most crucial within the economy and the various legal and political organs of the state. In the economic sphere, it is best illustrated by the spread of unionization and collective bargaining, whereby labor and management pursue their conflicting interests and resolve disputes through conciliation, mediation, or arbitration. In the legal-political sphere, institutionalized conflict is apparent in the settlement of grievances through the law courts and the negotiation of legislation and policy decisions through parliamentary debate (1959:66, 228-231). In this form, conflict is an essential force for social change, as Marx believed, but also is an important source of coherence and unity, because of its problem-solving function (1959:206-208).

Thus, even though Dahrendorf speaks of conflict at least as much as Marx does, Dahrendorf's stress on the regulated nature and integrative function of conflict reveals that his affinities with Marx are far more tenuous than his ties to structural functionalism. Dahrendorf's closer ties to structural functionalism are evident in his very definition of conflict, which is so broad that it could include everything from outright war to friendly competition, even sports contests and games (1959:135). Such a diluted view of conflict, combined with Dahrendorf's implication that class and power relations are all somehow rooted in authority structures, leads his portrayal of social inequality in quite a different direction from Marx. Social inequality under postcapitalism *is* a product of the contest for advantage among conflicting interests; however, this contest occurs generally according to institutionalized regulations within both the economy and the state, and under conditions of considerable pluralism and legitimacy. The conflict or struggle that arises is more a means for keeping contemporary industrial society healthy and progressive than a cataclysmic force for the revolutionary overthrow of capitalism (1959:134).

The Future of Inequality

Given Dahrendorf's stress on the constructive and progressive nature of modern social struggle, it is not surprising that he has a generally optimistic view of the future of inequality in postcapitalist society. Not only has class conflict been institutionalized, but equalities of opportunity and condition are themselves becoming part of the established institutions of society. The state has played a key role here through the implementation of public education to increase the mobility chances of the lower strata. Although complete equality of educational opportunity is still to be achieved, sufficient advances have been made that class barriers are gradually weakening and "no social stratum, group, or class can remain completely stable for more than one generation" (1959:59). The state has also acted to narrow the inequalities between top and bottom, by establishing social-welfare programs and tax laws that redistribute wealth from the rich to the poor. Thus, Dahrendorf sees a continued reduction of inequality over time, since "the process of levelling social differences cannot be denied" (1959:63, 274).

Since that optimistic interlude of the 1950s, many analysts have despaired that the promised reduction of inequality will ever come true. Dahrendorf, however, maintains more than two decades later that the drive for equality has continued apace (1979:128). In fact, although Dahrendorf supports this alleged narrowing of the social hierarchy, his fear is that it may be *too* successful. Total equality carries with it considerable dangers, "for a society in which all are equal in all respects is one devoid of realistic hope and thus of incentives for progress" (1979:123).

Ultimately, then, Dahrendorf sides once again with the structural-functionalist view of inequality, seeing it as necessary to motivate individuals to the pursuit of excellence in a free society. In the end, the real fear for the future is that totalitarian, state-socialist forms of society will predominate (1959:318). Such systems impose equality through a gray sameness that stifles progress and freedom. It is Dahrendorf's fervent belief that hope and liberty are indispensable to any just society but that "hope springs from difference rather than sameness, and liberty from inequality rather than equality" (1979:140).

Summary Observations

In this section, we have reviewed and evaluated the major elements in Dahrendorf's discussion of class conflict in industrial society, with special reference to his views on social inequality. It is apparent that there are some basic difficulties in Dahrendorf's conceptions of class, power, and conflict. It is also the case that many of his claims concerning the reduction of inequality in modern times and the separation of ownership from control in advanced capitalism are matters of considerable dispute. Nevertheless, Dahrendorf's analysis is notable as the first prominent attempt to move away from a doctrinaire structural-functionalist perspective by incorporating aspects of Marx and Weber into a new orientation to social inequality. Although the final result takes us only part of the way toward a more balanced perspective, and never relinquishes its basic structural-functionalist leanings, Dahrendorf's formulation is a prime stimulus for several of the approaches that follow.

Gerhard Lenski
Social Inequality as Power and Privilege

The second important perspective on social inequality in the more recent literature is Lenski's analysis of *Power and Privilege* (Lenski, 1966). Rather like Dahrendorf before him, Lenski proceeds on the assumption that a comprehensive approach to social inequality must take into account the entire spectrum of views between "radicals" such as Marx on the one hand and "conservatives" like the structural functionalists on the other. He portrays his own formulation as an initial step toward a "synthesis of the valid insights of both the conservative and radical traditions," a stance that he readily acknowledges brings him very close to Weber (1966:17-18). The final result is a position roughly midway between the poles of our left-right continuum.

Lenski's proposed synthesis is really a selection of certain basic premises from both the left and the right, moderated and amalgamated in a generally pragmatic fashion. His overall conclusion is that some degree of social inequality is inevitable, as conservatives argue, in part because humans differ in their effort, strength, intelligence, and so on and tend to use these favored traits to further their own interests or those of special groups to which they belong. This does not mean that all inequalities result from differences in "natural endowment;" in fact, most do not. Neither does this mean that people are incapable of the altruism and collective orientation that Marx and other radicals have stressed. But partisan interests do normally receive first priority because of natural tendencies in human nature, and a good deal of the apparent co-operation and selflessness that radicals point to occurs more from "enlightened self-interest" or necessity than from a universalistic orientation to the common good (1966:25-32, 441-442).

Where Lenski differs markedly from the conservatives is on their insistence that such selfish tendencies in human nature can somehow produce just and legitimate social hierarchies. Thus, Lenski rejects the structural-functionalist view that most people agree on the value or prestige attached to positions in society and that this common evaluation gives rise to differences in both power and material rewards. On the contrary, Lenski argues the reverse view: that differential access to power is ultimately what determines inequalities in material privilege and that power and privilege together determine most of the prestige attached to various groups or individuals in society (1966:44-46). On this crucial point, then, radicals like Marx seem nearer the truth. They recognize that the outward stability of social structures may say little about the extent to which such structures are endorsed by the populace and may instead mask fundamental antagonisms between dominant and subordinate factions. Of course, some level of genuine legitimacy is likely to be accorded the power structure, especially by citizens of western democratic countries; yet even here legitimacy is often far from complete, and the general acceptance of existing social hierarchies seems to result from at least two additional influences: the potential coercive force of the dominant group; and the "inertia" of custom, habit, or conventional beliefs that holds back the impetus for struggle and change (1966:32-35, 41).

It is clear, then, that Lenski considers differences in power to be the pivotal factor responsible for the structure of inequality in society. Because of this, it is preferable to begin with a review of Lenski's conception of power and then trace its influence on his discussion of class, the role of the state, and, finally, the prospects for social inequality in the future.

Power and the Multidimensional View of Inequality

It is immediately apparent that Lenski adopts a largely Weberian conception of power, though he reveals certain differences with Weber that should also be noted. Like Weber, he begins by defining power as the capacity to carry out one's will despite opposition. Following Weber, he also maintains that coercive force is "the most effective form of power." Of course, any enduring system of domination must minimize violent upheaval, so that force should not be used exclusively or imprudently but should "recede into the background to be used only when other techniques fail." Nevertheless, Lenski echoes Weber's position that force is the "ultimate guarantee" and "the foundation of any system of inequality" (1966:50-51).

Eventually, the factions that control the use of force try to have their power officially entrenched, or formally established, by creating or rewriting laws to protect their general interests. In modern democracies, such laws are not blatantly self-serving in most cases but, on the contrary, are frequently couched in universalistic terms that give them an air of popular legitimacy. Typically, for example, they not only spell out the powers of those who rule, but also specify the formal rights of subordinates. Thus, a small minority may control the political structure, but there are provisions for the mass of the population to voice their wishes or their grievances through regular elections, referenda, or other means. Still, despite this apparent two-way flow of power between the top and the bottom, the relationship is decidedly *asymmetrical*, with power running more strongly and with far greater effect from the dominant to the subordinate faction (1966:52-53, 58).

Lenski's discussion of power leads him finally to Weber's conclusion that power in modern times stems mainly from the ability to establish, and to enforce if necessary, certain special *rights* relative to others. As already noted, these rights are embedded in legal statutes for the most part, although the informal forces of custom, convention, and traditional beliefs or prejudices frequently supplement the official bases for power differences (cf. 1966:32, 89). The most prominent illustration of the legal basis for power is the formal right to private ownership of productive property. In addition, however, there are numerous examples from societies past and present of the legal establishment or denial of power for different races, sexes, religions, and so on. The supplementary influence of nonlegal conventions and prejudices is also apparent when, for example, certain racial minorities or women are excluded from positions within the ruling faction despite the removal of legal barriers.

From the foregoing discussion, it should be apparent that Lenski shares with Weber a generally pluralist view of both power and inequality. Power derives from a combination of control over coercion and access to legally or conventionally sanctioned rights. Consequently, power differences can generate a wide range of social inequalities, depending on the variety of social categories that come to be accorded or refused such rights. Thus, a fundamental feature of Lenski's approach is that inequality is *multidimensional*, involving multiple criteria for ranking groups or individuals in terms of their power and, thus, their material privilege and prestige. The exact criteria for ranking obviously vary by country and historical period but usually include such diverse bases as property ownership, occupation, education, religion, ethnicity, race, gender, and age.

In many respects, Lenski's multidimensional view is both the key contribution and the most significant difficulty in his overall approach to social inequality. Predictably, Lenski sees Weber as the pioneer of this view, although Sorokin also deserves mention (1966:18; cf. Sorokin, 1927, 1947). However, subsequent critics argue that Lenski's multiple dimensions are different from Weber's delineation of class, status, and party in several key ways (e.g., Parkin, 1972; Giddens, 1973; Hunter, 1981). In particular, Weber's scheme is not explicitly intended to represent different ways for *ranking* people in society but rather to suggest the various bases around which interest groups may coalesce in society's continual power struggle (recall Chapter 3). Another way to express this is to note that Lenski is more clearly a *stratification* theorist than is Weber and that, compared to Weber, he is more concerned with *distributive* inequalities in material and other rewards than with the *relations* between groups that underlie this distribution (1966:2-3, 84-86).

Nevertheless, despite Lenski's apparent confusion of these points, the one undeniable similarity between his multiple dimensions and Weber's ideas of class, status, and party is that they are all derivative from the central concept of power. This makes it possible to conceive of both distributive and relational inequalities in terms of one key idea. It also suggests that our understanding of virtually all social hierarchies, whether they refer to class, race, gender, or any other social criterion, can be tied to the analysis of power, of access to enforceable rights. Whether these multiple forms of inequality are labeled *dimensions* or some other term is, in a sense, immaterial. The important and useful aspect of Lenski's approach is precisely his recognition that such multiple forms exist and that, in one way or another, they are manifestations of power. This modified version of Weber's conception takes us significantly closer than earlier analyses to a general strategy for conceiving of social inequality.

Lenski on Class Structure

The one real difficulty with Lenski's multidimensional perspective concerns his conception of class and class structure. At times, his discussion is not unlike Weber's once again, for Lenski visualizes a pluralist class structure, composed of a dominant propertied class, a subordinate working class, and a range of middle classes, as typical of capitalist countries like the United States. If there is a notable difference from Weber at all here, it is Lenski's tendency to be, like Dahrendorf, more convinced of the reduction of class inequality and the dispersion of wealth in modern society (1966:308, 338-382).

Unfortunately, rather than confine his use of the term class to these standard economic concerns and treat class as one of the multiple dimensions of inequality, Lenski introduces considerable confusion by labeling all such dimensions as different types of class systems. In other words, he perceives "property classes", "educational classes", "ethnic classes", "religious classes", and so on as constitutive of the overall class system (1966:74-82). This strategy is oddly similar to Dahrendorf's view of class, since all power structures come to be defined as class structures, leading to a proliferation of different "classes" in society. Use of this terminology confounds class with power and renders the class concept virtually meaningless. The saving factor here is that we can expunge this weakness from Lenski's approach without abandoning its useful elements.

The Role of the State

Given Lenski's focus on law and the formal institution of power, it is not surprising that, like Weber once again, he places considerable stress on the role of the state in modern systems of inequality. It is the state and its agencies that are responsible for creating, administering, and occasionally imposing by force the laws and formal rights that give power to some and not others. Because of this key role, and because of "the tremendous increase in the functions performed by the state," one might expect that the state's leaders would be central players in the overall power structure. In fact, Lenski does concur with Weber that power has been concentrated in the government, especially its growing bureaucracies; moreover, he also seems well aware that a dominant economic elite is typically able to turn the power of the state to its advantage on most key issues (1966:304, 310, 342).

And yet, in the end, Lenski is more optimistic than Weber that the cage of state bureaucratic control can be escaped, at the same time that exploitation by the ruling class is reduced. To Lenski, the complexities of modern society, and the consequent intervention of the state into numerous spheres of life, have led to a greater, not a lesser, dispersion of power. The elaborate machinery of government has itself created diverse centers of jurisdiction and administration. Of course, the economic elite and other dominant factions will continue to gain disproportionate privilege from these agencies and the laws they uphold. But there is a limit beyond which such concentration of privilege cannot proceed without provoking public outcry, and it is the state structure itself that is now the key vehicle in this process. The people can oppose the policies of the ruling faction and resolve their own internal disputes through the state government, since it "has become the object of a never ending struggle between a variety of organized groups which, in their totality, represent the special interests of most of the population"(1966:314-318). Here Lenski seems to share Dahrendorf's confidence that the power struggle can be legitimately institutionalized and acted out, no so much *by* the state as *through* the state, with government a "mere switchboard of authority" (Dahrendorf, 1959:306). We shall encounter this image of the state again in subsequent sections of this chapter.

The Future of Social Inequality

As one might expect, Lenski's projections concerning the future suggest a guarded optimism, the same middle course that characterizes his overall analysis. Lenski devotes much of his discussion to an investigation of the historical trend of inequality. His central conclusion is that social inequality has tended to increase since primitive times but that there is reason to believe the trend is now reversing with the rise of advanced industrial societies. Among the many factors contributing to this alleged reversal are significant improvements in technology, which have made possible a vast increase in surplus wealth, and the spread of democratic ideas, which have captured the imagination of most people. These and other developments make it possible to redistribute both privilege and power to more and more citizens in the modern era (1966:308-317, 428-430).

Such positive expectations sound in some ways like Dahrendorf's favorable predictions for postcapitalist society. However, Lenski's views are tempered by his conservative assumptions about humanity and social organization, which make the complete elimination of inequalities in power and privilege unlikely in *any* society. Lenski retains his conviction that social rankings are to some degree inevitable because of people's "natural tendency to maximize their personal resources" at the expense of others. In addition, hierarchies seem unavoidable given the importance of coordinated decisions in complex social structures and the differences in power or authority that result. Ultimately, then, the reduction of political and economic inequality should continue in the long term, but "will stop substantially short of the egalitarian ideal in which power and privilege are shared equally by all members of society." In Lenski's opinion, radical thinkers who see socialism as the path to complete equality are destined to be disappointed (1966:327, 345).

Summary Observations

Our purpose in this portion of the chapter has been to review Lenski's perspective on social inequality as the relationship between power and privilege. Despite certain difficulties in his conception of class, a weakness he shares with Dahrendorf, Lenski's attempted synthesis of radical and conservative views provides some important insights. In particular, his multidimensional strategy suggests a rudimentary means for thinking about social inequality as a generalized phenomenon, a process that is critical for understanding class relations but that arises and endures in numerous other forms as well. Moreover, in stressing that the differential power to enforce rights is the common thread linking all these manifestations of inequality, Lenski achieves a significant advance over Dahrendorf and his contemporaries. As we move through the remainder of this chapter, the importance of Lenski's contribution should become increasingly evident.

Recent Marxist Views
Nicos Poulantzas

In the century since Marx's death, there have been countless attempts by Marxist scholars to build on the ideas expressed in his extensive, but largely unfinished, writings. In recent years, the most promising of these discussions have primarily been those that connect in some way to Althusser, a Marxist philosopher who has questioned the simplistic readings of Marx by certain early Marxists (cf. Althusser, 1969; 1976; Althusser and Balibar, 1970). Within sociology, Poulantzas and Wright, whose works will be reviewed in the next two sections of this chapter, have been the most successful in applying a broadly similar interpretation (see also Hindess and Hirst, 1975; 1977; Carchedi, 1977). Poulantzas is notable in that, like Althusser, he rejects the dogmatic economic determinism of other Marxists, those who completely reduce social analysis to an investigation of capitalist relations of production. While this issue is crucial, in Poulantzas' view, there are other forces operating within society that must be grasped if the Marxist goal of revolution is to be realized. Moreover, Poulantzas argues, it is clear that "Marxism alone cannot explain everything," that the decisive role it plays in explaining social processes can still be enhanced by other valid insights (1978:23).

With this in mind, Poulantzas seeks to supplement and redirect the traditional Marxist treatment of class, the capitalist state, and several other topics of import for the study of social inequality. Despite certain obscurities and inconsistencies in Poulantzas' formulation, it is instructive to review and evaluate his attempt to accommodate the complications in modern systems of inequality with the essentials of Marx's original analysis. As with the other theorists we have considered, our review will focus on four principal concerns: the concept of class or class structure; the meaning and significance of power in social hierarchies; the role of the state, especially in capitalist society; and the prospects for inequality in the future, with particular reference to the transition to socialism.

Classes in Contemporary Capitalism

Like most recent Marxists, Poulantzas conceives of class primarily as a set of "places" in a structure, although he sometimes uses class to refer to the "men" or "social agents" who fill these places (Poulantzas, 1973b:27; 1975:14, 203). The distinction between classes as people and classes as structured locations is, of course, paralleled in the structural-functionalist insistence that stratification refers mainly to the ranked status-roles individuals occupy rather than to the individuals themselves (Davis and Moore, 1945). While such a distinction is artificial, to Poulantzas and others it is seen as crucial for demonstrating that the *distribution* of people into classes is really a separate problem from the more pressing issue of how the structured *relations* between class locations are generated in the first place. For, even if we could imagine a capitalist society where people have an equal chance to move up or down the class structure, this mobility would do nothing to alter the structure itself or the exploitative relations built into it (1975:33).

In any case, both the class places of capitalism and the people within them are defined principally by their location in the productive, or economic, sphere. In addition, however, Poulantzas maintains along with Althusser that both Marx and his more discerning followers recognize how *political* and *ideological* forces can simultaneously act with the central economic factor in the formation of classes. The simultaneous nature of economic, political, and ideological influences on class structure is important to stress here if one is to avoid fruitless "chicken-and-egg" debates over whether the political and ideological superstructures are "caused" by the economic infrastructure or vice versa (recall Chapters 2 and 3). To Poulantzas, it is important to retain Marx's discovery that economic forces are decisive "in the last analysis" for shaping classes and the other structural relations within capitalism; but such a view is far different from the vulgar Marxist stance that the political and ideological systems operate in perfect coordination with the economic and are automatically and completely determined by it (1975:14, 25; 1978:26).

In delimiting the class structure, then, Poulantzas begins with the standard Marxist claim that there are two basic classes in advanced capitalism, the bourgeoisie and the proletariat, and these are divided primarily by their economic relationship, by the fact that the bourgeoisie exploits the productive labor of the proletariat for profit. But the class structure is also sustained over time by political and ideological processes. Like most Marxists, Poulantzas generally identifies the bourgeoisie's political control with the governing and coercive power of the state and sees its ideological influence operating in the religious, educational, and other structures of society. As well, though, Poulantzas uses these two terms in less conventional ways: bourgeois political control is also embedded in the economic system, in the "politics of the workplace" created by capitalist rights of supervision and discipline over labor; bourgeois ideological control is likewise present on the job, in its monopoly of scientific ideas and technical knowledge, which deprives most workers of the means of "mental" production. Poulantzas perceives in Marx's writings this same wider sense of what political and ideological control mean and how these forms of bourgeois domination conjoin with economic relations to reinforce, perpetuate, or "reproduce" the essential class dichotomy (1975:227-236; cf. Marx, 1867:331, 361).

Having affirmed the Marxist view that the essential split between capitalists and workers is not blurred, but rather highlighted, by political and ideological forces, Poulantzas nevertheless notes that political and ideological factors can act to generate secondary splits *within* the two major classes, in the form of "fractions" or "strata" (1975:23, 198). In the working class, for example, internal fragmentation can arise from skill differences that ultimately cede "political" supervisory power and "ideological" control of special information to a distinct fraction of skilled laborers within the proletariat (1975:15, 245). Even in the bourgeoisie such political and ideological disunities can occur, for despite their common interest in exploiting the working class, large-, medium-, and small-scale capitalists, as well as industrial, commercial, and finance capitalists, often break ranks because of differences in political clout, policy preferences, or their ideological commitments to such beliefs as free enterprise versus monopolistic efficiency. Such divisive tendencies can breed competitive or even antagonistic relations within capital, calling into question "the mythic image of the bourgeoisie as an integrated totality" (1975:139; 1978:143-144). This is not to deny the truth of Marx's two-class system, but to attack any simplistic representations of it.

Still, there is one aspect of Poulantzas' discussion of class fractions that has raised some questions about the dichotomous view of class and caused some controversy with other recent Marxists. Poulantzas identifies various class places near the boundary between bourgeoisie and proletariat that do not fall clearly into either class because they resemble the bourgeoisie on some political, ideological, and economic criteria but resemble the proletariat on others. In the end, he subsumes these intermediate locations under Marx's term, the *petty bourgeoisie*, to signify that they are indeed part of the bourgeoisie but play a petty or marginal role within this class. This designation does not completely solve the problem of classifying these positions, since they are themselves a heterogeneous mix, fragmented by political, ideological, and economic differentiation. Hence, out of this melange Poulantzas identifies two major subcategories: the "old," or "traditional," petty bourgeoisie, a declining category of independent owners and craftspeople that both Marx and Weber refer to; and the "new" petty bourgeoisie, a growing array of technicians, supervisors, salaried "white-collar" employees, and "tertiary" wage earners (1975:193, 208, 285-289).

It is Poulantzas' designation of a new petty bourgeoisie in advanced capitalism that has generated much of the debate over his work, both inside and outside Marxist circles. His new petty bourgeoisie represents a significant departure from other Marxists, most of whom treat such positions as working class because their occupants are both propertyless and dependent on the capitalists for wages (e.g., Mills, 1951; Braverman, 1974). Poulantzas concedes this dependence to some extent and notes that the new petty bourgeoisie, like the proletariat, is exploited by the capitalist class; nevertheless, the supervisors, engineers, and other segments of the new petty bourgeoisie share considerable political and ideological ties with the capitalists because of their control over workers in the productive setting and their grasp of technical knowledge and expertise denied to the proletariat. Their provisional resemblance to the bourgeoisie is further enhanced by their economic function, which produces no surplus value in Poulantzas' view and is paid for out of the surplus generated by the proletariat. In other words, they share with the capitalist class the bourgeois trait of being "unproductive" (1975:210-216, 235-250).

Other Marxists remain unconvinced by Poulantzas' distinction between productive and unproductive activities because so many class locations are mixtures of both, and because it is not clear that technical knowledge and supervision are irrelevant to the creation of surplus. Besides, all such activities are proletarian to the extent that they place their occupants in a situation of exploitation by capitalist employers. The most distressing aspect of Poulantzas' scheme, for Marxist thinkers, is that his new petty bourgeoisie would form the largest single segment of the class structure and leave a comparatively small and insignificant working class to fight for the overthrow of capitalism (e.g., Wright, 1978:46-53). Poulantzas himself sees in this no threat to revolutionary action, since the new petty bourgeoisie is likely to increase its proletarian allegiances and weaken its ties to capital with time (1978:242-244).

Poulantzas' overall portrayal of the capitalist class structure nevertheless raises difficulties for any Marxist sympathetic to his analysis. This is primarily because, in the end, Poulantzas comes surprisingly close to an essentially Weberian viewpoint. Like Weber, he wishes to acknowledge both the essential truth of Marx's two-class model and the intricacies that are overlooked if it is taken too literally. Like Weber, he is also faced with an infinite number of classes if he draws all the political, ideological, and economic distinctions possible within each class. Finally, like Weber, he ultimately settles on four key categories: the bourgeoisie, the proletariat, the traditional petty bourgeoisie of small owners, and the new petty bourgeoisie of salaried white-collar, technical, and supervisory personnel (recall Chapter 3). The principal difference, of course, is that Poulantzas rejects Weber's treatment of these latter two categories as distinct *middle classes* in their own right, for this would contradict the basic Marxist precept that there are only two real classes in advanced capitalism (1975:196-199, 297).

Poulantzas on Power

It has been typical of Marxist discussions to avoid any detailed attempt to conceptualize the notion of power, perhaps because Marx himself devoted little effort to this task. Poulantzas does use the idea of power in his analysis, but in an ambivalent manner. His initial definition treats power solely as the capacity of a *class* "to realize its specific interests in a relation of opposition" to another class (1978:36; 1973a:99; 1975:277). Poulantzas seems to be affirming the conventional Marxist preoccupation with class issues here, since by definition all situations of opposed interests that do not involve class are not worthy of being called power struggles. This usage poses conceptual problems that are almost the reverse of those found earlier in Dahrendorf and Lenski. As we have seen, the latter two writers label all power relations as different types of class relations, thereby making class a meaningless idea. Poulantzas chooses to ignore all power relations that are not class relations and thus makes power the superfluous term.

Yet, on closer inspection, the ambivalence and inconsistency of Poulantzas' view of power is evident, for elsewhere he reveals a wider sense of power that is oddly similar to Weber's conception. First of all, his contention that power is a capacity to realize interests despite opposition is very similar to Weber's, apart from its restriction to class issues (cf. Weber, 1922:53). Moreover, even this restriction appears to disappear at times, since Poulantzas allows that "power relations stretch beyond class relations" to include problems of race, gender, and so on (1978:43-44; 1975:305-306). On these grounds, at least, Poulantzas' neo-Marxist approach to power, like his analysis of class structure, is not incompatible with a limited form of Weberian pluralism. If there is a real quarrel, it is with more extreme pluralists who fail to recognize that economic power is central "in the last instance," that "class power is the cornerstone of power" in the other areas (1973a:113; 1978:44).

The Capitalist State

Poulantzas distinguishes himself from most early Marxists by his attempt to include the state as an important factor in the structure of advanced capitalism. Unfortunately, his discussion is often obscure, primarily because he once again walks a nebulous line between orthodox Marxism and some variant of Weberian pluralism. To begin with, his definition of the state as the "condensation" or "fusion" of class struggle is too cryptic to be very informative. He seems to mean that the state is an organizational *shell* for society, a vast framework of rules and principles that ensure bourgeois domination in all those spheres not immediately part of the economy (1973a:53-55; 1978:26-30). At a concrete level, the state thus comprises a network of organizations or "apparatuses" that are of two related types: the political apparatuses, including the executive, legislative, judicial, civil-service, police, and military arms of government; and a range of ideological apparatuses such as education, the mass media, and so on. This portrayal resembles the conventional views of Weber and even Durkheim, except for Poulantzas' curious inclusion of religion, the family, and other structures within the state's ideological apparatuses (1975:24-25). As others have noted, this means that virtually everything but the material production process is subsumed under the capitalist state according to Poulantzas (Giddens and Held, 1982:193).

Given this image of the state as an all-encompassing framework for bourgeois domination, one might suspect that Poulantzas accepts the crude economic determinism of those Marxists who see the state as an appendage or tool of the capitalist class. However, Poulantzas wishes to dissociate himself from this viewpoint while at the same time avoiding charges of pluralism. His compromise is to argue that the state apparatuses are not totally independent operators in the capitalist power structure but nevertheless are *relatively* autonomous from the bourgeoisie (1973a:256; 1975:158; 1978:13). The heads of the state apparatuses are themselves bourgeois for the most part, while the rest of the state personnel are mainly members of the new petty bourgeoisie, white-collar civil servants with varying political and ideological ties to the capitalist class (1975:187; 1978:154-155).

Such inbred allegiances mean that the state will uphold the general interests of the bourgeoisie. Nevertheless, the state is too large and, like the class structure, too fragmented by special interests to exercise a unified political will on all issues. On the contrary, the complex bureaucratic amalgam of state agencies generates an intricate mix of "diversified micropolicies," many of which are "mutually contradictory" (1978;132-135, 194). The overall result is that certain specific policies of the state may produce "short-term material sacrifices" by the bourgeoisie: being required to pay for the improved health and safety conditions of workers; contributing through taxation to public education, social security, or unemployment benefits; and so on. Still, these actions by the state really benefit the capitalists in the end, by defusing potential revolt, promoting a compliant and dependable work force, and thus securing the "long-term domination" of the bourgeoisie (1978:30-31; 184-185).

Poulantzas' determination to find a middle ground between the state as a tool of capital and the state as an independent force in society ultimately leads to his paradoxical claim that the state, on the one hand, is the very "center" of power in capitalism but, on the other hand, "does not possess any power of its own" (1973a:115; 1975:81; 1978:148). Given his peculiar conception of power as an exclusive aspect of class relations, it does of course follow that the state by definition has no power, since it is not a class (cf. Connell, 1979). And yet Poulantzas must reconcile this with his view that the state is now the prime setting in which power is exercised, because of massive state involvement in social services, public administration, and, increasingly, the operation of the capitalist economy itself (1975:81; 1978:168). His insistence that the state has no power is justified primarily by the fact that the state does not control the means of production, even if it does have an expanded role in taxing and spending the surplus generated. Besides, state incursions into the economy never go beyond certain limits, for fear of eroding the profit motivation of the bourgeoisie on which the state's own funds depend. Often, in fact, state involvement is really a desperate attempt to help the bourgeoisie out of economic crisis or depression. It represents the dilemma state leaders face in trying simultaneously to placate a discontented working class and a capitalist class concerned mainly with its own gains. In short, the state is far from omnipotent under advanced capitalism but instead stands with "its back to the wall and its front poised before a ditch" (1978:191-192, 244).

There is at least one key difficulty with this assessment of state power that should be noted. Poulantzas' own definition of power indicates that it involves the realization of a faction's interests in the face of opposition. But control of material production does not exhaust the means by which interests can be realized or opposition quelled. In particular, one should not overlook the use of coercive force or repression to exact compliance from one's opponents. In fact, Poulantzas follows Weber, Lenski, and others in acknowledging the fundamental role of repression in *all* power relations and notes that power in its most basic form entails physical force, quite literally "the coercion of bodies and the threat of violence or death" (1978:28-29; 1973a:225). But who has the capacity to employ repressive power? Clearly, it is the state that monopolizes this resource, especially through the legalized actions of the police, the military, and the official justice system. In addition, the activities of virtually the entire state bureaucracy enjoy the legal sanction and, if necessary, the coercive aid of these agencies. Poulantzas seems to recognize this point and credits Weber with being the first to establish it (1978:80-81). Yet Poulantzas fails to appreciate fully that this makes state power a distinct force to be reckoned with in society.

Of course, in rejecting Poulantzas' claim that the state has no power, one must not simply take the opposite stance that the state in capitalism has a monopoly of power. Thus Poulantzas is correct to note, along with Lenski and others, that organized state repression is subject to limitations, particularly in nominally democratic societies. The laws that establish state powers in modern times can also restrict them, delimiting the state's jurisdictions and spelling out popular rights. Blatant disregard for these limits to power risks public outrage and possible open rebellion against state control (1978:82-83, 31-33). The crucial point to stress is that the state's powers are indeed constrained but that neither these restrictions, nor its ceding of ultimate economic control to the capitalist class, leaves the state's apparatuses without inherent influence. The major weakness in Poulantzas' entire perspective is that he emphasizes the relative autonomy of the state and yet cannot admit the distinct state power that this implies. In addition, his interest in the abstract framework of state apparatuses leads to an insufficient awareness that they are also concrete organizations, run by real people who have considerable say in the running of society.

The Prospects for Socialism

As a committed Marxist, Poulantzas wishes primarily to understand and promote the transformation of capitalism into socialism. Here Poulantzas addresses a question faced by all modern Marxists: why have so many attempts to create an egalitarian society through socialist revolution led to systems bearing little or no resemblance to Marx's version of communism? Interestingly, Poulantzas believes the problem lies with the state. Such perversions of socialist principles as Stalin's Russia, for example, occurred because of the misguided belief of Lenin and others that an utter smashing of the capitalist state can solve the administrative problems of socialist society. Instead, the administrative void is filled by a "parallel" socialist state, one that does not wither away but too often is more resilient, more bureaucratic, and more repressive than its bourgeois predecessor (1978:252-255).

Poulantzas' alternative strategy is really to work within the existing capitalist state to transform it gradually. Briefly, this entails the spread of trade-union activities, workers' political parties, and other new forms of "direct, rank-and-file democracy" (1978:261). In addition to the working class, a key force for change is the new petty bourgeoisie, especially many middle- and lower-level state employees, whom Poulantzas expects to ally with the proletariat as economic crises occur and their material conditions worsen (1978:242-244). To be sure, the eventual use of force cannot be ruled out as necessary to final success. Moreover, it remains to be seen whether current leaders on the left are yet capable of enlisting and organizing mass action. But, in any event, no truly democratic socialism is possible without this base of "broad popular alliances" to counteract totalitarian tendencies (1978:263).

Even in his prescription for the future, then, Poulantzas shares a certain vague similarity with Weber, for both have a distrust of socialism that is really bureaucratic *statism* in disguise, and both advocate working within existing bourgeois structures to change them. Of course, they are unalterably opposed on both the extent and the vehicle of social change.

Whereas Weber supports rather minor revisions to bourgeois liberal democracy and sees an enlightened political leadership as the key force to curb bureaucratic domination, Poulantzas desires like Marx the fundamental shift from liberal democracy to democratic socialism and considers the mass of the people as the principal factor in this transformation.

Summary Observations

In this section of the chapter, Poulantzas' neo-Marxist perspective has been examined. We have seen that Poulantzas' image of inequality, as reflected in his analyses of class, power, and the capitalist state, falls somewhere between conventional Marxism and a limited form of pluralism broadly suggestive of Weber. Perhaps the key strength of Poulantzas' approach is his attempt to sustain Marx's basic emphasis on control of material production as the source of power and inequality, while also observing the important political and ideological forces that sometimes escape notice. Where there are weaknesses in Poulantzas, they emerge mainly from his lack of conceptual clarity and his ambivalent handling of the problem of state power. We are left with a contradictory impression of a state that pervades more and more of our lives but somehow has no substantive power of its own. The major omission here is the realization that the state personnel are themselves social actors with powers of legal and physical coercion at their disposal.

Recent Marxism
Erik Olin Wright

The second neo-Marxist scholar we have chosen to consider in this chapter is Wright. Like Poulantzas, and Marx himself, Wright's concern is not primarily to devise a theory of social inequality, but to investigate the prospects for socialist revolution, given the inherent characteristics and recent developments in advanced capitalism (Wright, 1978:26). Nevertheless, in approaching this central task, Wright also provides several insights of use for our general understanding of the forms and sources of social inequality.

Wright's general orientation parallels that of Poulantzas in some respects, in part because Wright also reflects Althusser's desire to offer a sophisticated reorientation of early Marxism. Wright devotes his discussion to several of the same issues that are of crucial concern to Poulantzas and that tie closely to the analysis of inequality in advanced societies. For our purposes, the topics of note are the capitalist class structure, especially those anomalous "places" or "locations" that are somehow distinct from the bourgeoisie and proletariat; the origins of power; the role of the capitalist state; and the outlook for a socialist transformation of capitalism in the light of these other considerations.

The Capitalist Class Structure

Like Poulantzas, Wright wishes to retain the standard two-class model of nineteenth-century Marxism, but in an updated form that incorporates important modifications and extensions of recent times (cf. Wright and Perrone, 1977). However, while Poulantzas sees these developments in terms of "fractions" within the two main classes, Wright uses a more systematic strategy that goes back to the classical Marxist criterion of control over economic production.

According to Wright, capitalism in its most "abstract" or "pure" sense does indeed generate only two classes: those in control of economic production, the bourgeoisie and those excluded from control of production, the proletariat. However, in real capitalist societies, complications arise, first, because a third class, the old petty bourgeoisie, continues to exist (albeit in a declining form) and, second, because modern economic control has become more complex than in the earlier stages of capitalism. Wright suggests that control of production is now divisible into three key elements: (1) "real economic ownership," which is most crucial and refers to control over all the economic surplus — the profits, products, and other resources of capitalism; (2) command of the physical apparatus of production, which entails supervisory control over the machines, factories, and so on that are used to make products; and (3) command of labor power, which means supervisory control over workers (1978:73; 1979:24).

Now, in Wright's formulation, the modern bourgeoisie subsumes every class location in which all three types of control are retained, while the contemporary proletariat includes those class positions where all three types of economic control are absent. The third class in capitalism, the petty bourgeoisie, is a carry-over from earlier times and comprises those people engaged in small businesses and others who generate and control their own surplus (control 1) and manage their own enterprise (control 2) but who do *not* employ workers (control 3).

As for the rest of the class structure, it is composed of positions that, strictly speaking, do not form classes at all because they have some elements of economic control but not others. Wright sees these as "contradictory" locations arrayed between the three main class clusters, as in Figure 5.2. Thus, between the bourgeoisie and proletariat are all those positions filled by people who resemble proletarians in that they do not own or control the economic surplus (control 1) but have varying degrees of supervisory command over both the physical plant and the employees of the enterprise (controls 2 and 3). Along this line, top-level managers are closest to the bourgeoisie, since they control the most workers and large segments of the apparatus, while toward the proletarian end of this continuum are minor supervisors and foremen, who oversee only small sectors of production and a few workers.

The other two ranges of contradictory class locations include small-to medium-scale capitalists, positioned outside the bourgeoisie and toward the petty bourgeoisie primarily because they employ relatively few workers; and "semiautonomous" wage earners, a mix of scientists, professors, and other salaried professional or technical personnel who are located between the petty bourgeoisie and the proletariat because, like the latter, they employ no workers, but, like the former, they have some command over the products of their labor and over the physical means used in their creation (controls 1 and 2) (1978:80-81; 1979:46-47).

In this rather innovative manner, Wright poses an alternative strategy for conceiving of places in the class structure that do not fit precisely into the Marxist two-class model. Wright avoids lumping these positions into a single new middle class like Dahrendorf or a single new petty bourgeoisie like Poulantzas. Instead, he locates them systematically along three separate ranges that vary according to both the type and the degree of economic control enjoyed by their incumbents.

Figure 5.2

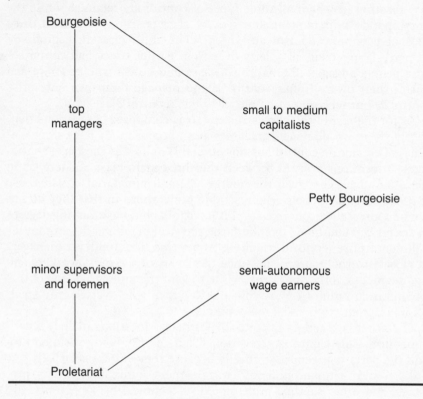

Wright's Model of Capitalist Class Relations
Source: Erik Olin Wright, *Class, Crisis, and the State*
(London: New Left Books, 1978), p. 84. Reprinted by
permission.

But what of people employed in spheres outside the production process, in the political and ideological structures of society? Here Wright also shuns Poulantzas' simple treatment of all such positions as unproductive elements of the bourgeoisie or petty bourgeoisie. In classifying these locations, Wright applies the same rationale used for the sphere of economic production. Thus, within the political and ideological apparatuses of capitalism, class position is also defined by control of production, but here *production* refers to political and ideological creations, especially the policies, laws, ideas, and beliefs generated and communi-

Figure 5.3

The Intersection of Class Relations across
Economic, Political, and Ideological Structures

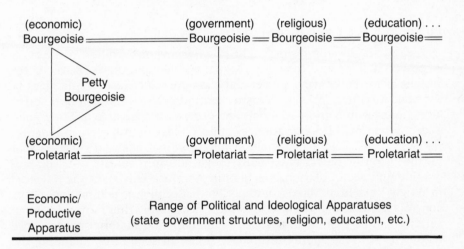

cated by such structures. Hence, most of the political and ideological personnel are proletarians, because they are excluded from control over the creation and implementation of policies and ideas. A few at the top — political leaders, supreme magistrates, the heads of education, religion, and so on — control both creation and implementation and therefore are members of the bourgeoisie. The remainder have some partial control over such matters and so occupy contradictory locations between the bourgeoisie and the proletariat. The one apparent difference between these class alignments and those within the economy itself is the absence of any political or ideological counterparts to the petty bourgeoisie (1978:94-97; 1979:54).

Apart from this discrepancy, however, Wright's scheme allows us to envision an entire array of political and ideological apparatuses, running side by side with the economic structure and representing all the major spheres of capitalist society. The bourgeoisie is really the intersection of positions at the top of all these structures, the proletariat is the intersection along the bottom, and the various contradictory locations lie between these ends (Figure 5.3). It is worth noting that this feature of

Wright's formulation bears some resemblance to conventional sociological portrayals of society as a series of interconnected structures, each engaged in a particular task within the larger system. Wright's view enables us to conceive of class structure as a phenomenon that cuts across every sphere of social organization and that, in a sense, joins them all together (cf. Wright, 1980:190).

Power and the Capitalist State

One element missing from Wright's analysis is any explicit conception of power and its link to social inequality. Perhaps this is because, for Wright as for Poulantzas, power and class are really inseparable ideas in the end. At times, Wright seems to contradict this impression: he criticizes, for example, those Marxists and others who perceive racial, sexual, and other forms of domination as simply class domination in disguise (1979:197, 227-228). Nevertheless, Wright's final position suggests that for him genuine power is virtually indistinct from control over the production and accumulation of economic surplus. This stance is reflected in Wright's essential Marxist assumption that economic domination means control over material resources, without which no other forms of human activity can be sustained. Because of fundamental material needs, those who control the economy ultimately shape all social life, including the political and ideological arrangements of capitalism (1979:15).

It is from this perspective that Wright examines the role of the state in capitalist society. First of all, we should note that Wright diverges from Poulantzas, for he favors a more conventional and less inclusive image of the state as mainly the government-run apparatuses of society: the political structure, its civil-service bureaucracies, and certain ideological arms such as public education and any state-administered mass-media organizations. Like Poulantzas, however, Wright generally sees the state structure as one that is severely constrained in its actions by its economic dependence on the capitalist class. Because it generates no surplus of its own, the state relies primarily on taxation of privately accumulated profits and wages for its funds. This is not to say that the state apparatuses are therefore unswerving servants of their capitalist benefactors. Again, Wright parallels Poulantzas in arguing that sectors of the state can and will act against bourgeois wishes at times, out of a commitment to the general welfare or in order to appease discontent within various interest groups in the public at large. Yet these actions rarely threaten bourgeois dominance in the long term, because most state leaders are themselves bourgeois and because the state as a whole requires a contented capitalist class, possessed of the economic incentive necessary to amass profits, employ workers, and thus ensure the state's vital operating revenues.

Hence, the state leadership and the bourgeoisie have a common interest in maintaining a stable, unimpeded capitalist economy. According to Wright, however, the state in advanced capitalism is increasingly required to intervene in the economic sphere, usually against its will, because of the inherent tendencies toward crisis and depression that regularly disrupt the capitalist economy. Such crises are even more serious in advanced capitalism because, as Marx foresaw, economic control has become concentrated in a relatively few giant corporations. Whereas in the past economic depression led to the failure or absorption of small enterprises, now it is these large-scale businesses that are threatened in economic declines. Thus, when Chrysler or Dome Petroleum faces bankruptcy, major portions of the capitalist class are endangered, as well as the jobs of thousands of workers. As a result, the state is compelled to step in to protect capitalist interests, avert popular unrest, and preserve its own tax base. But the state's actions in these cases usually involve short-term solutions that create new problems. Bailing out weak companies, giving preferential treatment to troubled businesses, and increasing taxes to provide more unemployment benefits simply put more burdens on the system, for they subsidize inefficient, unproductive elements at the expense of the healthy sectors and also drain economic surplus through the creation of costly state bureaucracies to administer the programs. In Wright's view, these added burdens eventually engender new crises and force the state to intercede still further in a continuing cycle of intervention that satisfies neither the bourgeoisie nor the majority of workers (1978:156-163, 174-179).

The Prospects for Socialism

Because of the growing inability of the state or the bourgeoisie to ease economic crises, one might expect an increase in popular discontent and in the chance of socialist revolution in future society. Wright contends that a successful shift to socialism is possible, but unlikely as long as two key problems are unresolved. First, the proletariat must come to realize that it has a fundamental interest in the socialist cause; second, the proletariat must become actively involved in changing capitalism from within its own existing structures, especially the state apparatuses. Let us briefly assess each of these points.

Wright argues that workers in most countries continue to be distracted from their fundamental interest in overturning capitalism because of a preoccupation with immediate interests such as wages and job security. Such distraction is understandable, given workers' material deprivation, but Wright is convinced that the proletariat would surely engage in struggles for socialism if only its members had a complete comprehension of their exploitation by the capitalist class (1978:88-90). There are at least two difficulties with such a claim. To begin with, it really assumes, rather than demonstrates, that workers have a fundamental stake in socialism. While such an assumption could be correct, as it stands here it is simply a Marxist axiom, a statement that must be true by definition. Because of this, it ignores other explanations for working-class inaction, including the possibility that workers themselves are capable of judging the merits of socialism and have found them wanting. It is plausible that many workers, on observing the Soviet Union, Poland, and other instances of socialism in practice, have chosen capitalism as the lesser of two evils, despite its exploitation and injustice. In that event, capitalism would be more suited to both the immediate *and* the fundamental interests of workers, at least in comparison with current brands of socialism.

The other difficulty in Wright's treatment of class interests is that, by his own definition, only a minority of the population appears to be located presently within the working class proper. In the United States, for example, Wright estimates that roughly forty to fifty percent of the class structure is proletarian, using his criteria for classification. Even if all these members of the working class take a strong interest in socialism, a point we have already questioned, a majority or near-majority remain whose class interests partially or completely oppose capitalism's demise. Of these only one or two percent are in the bourgeoisie, while another five percent are in the petty bourgeoisie. Thus, the prospects for socialist revolution seem to hinge on those who occupy the numerous contradictory locations that form close to half of Wright's class structure (1978:84; cf. Wright et al., 1982). If all the people in these positions were to resolve their ambivalent interests in favor of the proletariat, the massive support necessary for revolution could be achieved. Wright does perceive signs of "proletarianization" among some of the technical, white-collar, and other employees in these locations, for some have seen their objective conditions of labor come more and more to resemble those of the working class. However, compared to Poulantzas and others, Wright seems less certain that all such intermediate positions will become proletarian; instead, it is likely that many will remain distinct for the time being, and new locations of this sort will continue to be created as technology advances (1979:28-32; Wright and Singelmann, 1982; see also Gagliani, 1981). The persistence of these contradictory locations, coupled with whatever disaffection exists toward socialism in the proletariat itself, makes it less than probable that a majority desire for the overthrow of capitalism is imminent.

Assuming that the working class is eventually able to overcome these and other impediments to achieving revolutionary consciousness, Wright then raises the second key concern: that workers be allowed a real part in shaping revolutionary change, especially through the political apparatuses of the state. Like Poulantzas, Wright rejects the old view that successful revolution means a sudden and total smashing of the capitalist state, since this typically leads to a totalitarian socialist regime that excludes workers from power and subverts the very principles it is supposed to uphold. Wright offers no detailed alternative strategy, but, like Poulantzas, he holds the basic hope that working-class community councils and similar organizations will arise to establish "direct democracy on the fringes of the state administration" (1978:245). Then, as the state increases its involvement in running the economy and the rest of society, workers will be in a position to apply their developing organizational skills and other "capacities" by participating in state programs directly, ultimately achieving their rightful majority influence through democratic means.

Nevertheless, as Wright himself notes, this smooth and democratic achievement of a society ruled by all workers is likely to encounter considerable opposition, depending on whether the state's repressive branches — the police and military — are used against it and on whether possible economic reprisals by the bourgeoisie — the flight of businesses out of the country, for example — are successful in impeding its course (1978:250-251). Apart from these potential obstacles, however, the final hurdle for the universal society of workers may well be organized socialist political parties themselves. To Wright, these are a necessary focal point for concerted proletarian action, and a successful transformation of the capitalist state from within seems inconceivable without them. Yet they are subject to the same pressures for administrative hierarchy and bureaucratic decision making as any other organization and therefore threaten to undermine the broadly based worker involvement in planning and running society that socialism stands for (1978:247, 252).

On this final point, then, Wright comes down closer to Weber than many other Marxists would like, for he suggests that, even if workers actively seek the socialist transformation, and even if it succeeds, organizational exigencies persist that make a truly democratic socialism difficult (1978:216, 225). Nonetheless, in keeping with Marx, Poulantzas, and Marxist thinkers in general, Wright would rather risk the future on the possibility that workers can overcome these hurdles than on Weber's hope that some enlightened political elite can save capitalism from bureaucratic abuses and its own internal contradictions. Workers must develop and retain the capacity to rule themselves if human societies are to progress, and the chances of this occurring are, in the Marxist view, clearly better under socialism than under any form of capitalism.

Summary Observations

In this section, we have considered Wright's attempt to reorient traditional Marxism to the analysis of modern class structure, the capitalist state, and other topics relevant to the study of social inequality. Overall,

Wright's discussion is more clearly conceived and internally consistent than Poulantzas' neo-Marxist formulation, especially with respect to the problem of class structure. While both Poulantzas and Wright provide noteworthy treatments of the state, a topic ignored by most early Marxists, here too Wright's analysis seems preferable to Poulantzas' rather obscure account. The principal weakness in Wright's viewpoint is his omission of any systematic treatment of the concept of power and his consequent tendency to play down the role of repression and other means for domination apart from economic control. A second problem is his failure even to question the assumption that socialism must always be in the fundamental interest of the working class. His certainty on this point is especially surprising in light of his sensitivity to the bureaucratic and totalitarian threats to democratic action that are internal to socialism itself. Skepticism on this issue in particular provides the backdrop for the next perspective to be considered: Parkin's neo-Weberian critique of Marxism.

Frank Parkin
The Bourgeois Critique of Marxism

Parkin's work is the clearest contemporary attempt by an avowed neo-Weberian to provide a renewed perspective on social inequality. In his analyses, Parkin dissociates himself from certain early Weberians, especially those structural functionalists who have erased from Weber's original analysis his important affinities with Marx (Parkin, 1972:17-18; 1978:602-604; 1979:48). At the same time, however, Parkin is highly critical of most Marxists as well because of their inordinate preoccupation with one aspect of social inequality: capitalist economic production and the division between bourgeoisie and proletariat arising within it. Parkin's prime purpose is to act as a non-Marxist or "bourgeois" sociologist and criticize the flaws in this narrow focus. His own position is that there are other important class cleavages in modern society to consider, as well as numerous other forms of exploitation that are distinct from class and that persist independently of the class structure itself. These other forms of exploitation involve a range of social criteria that vary in importance across different societies but typically include race, ethnicity, gender, and religion, among others (1979:9, 89).

To Parkin, it is instructive that, whenever Marxists such as Poulantzas and Wright try to incorporate such complications into the conventional two-class model of Marxism, they produce perspectives that invariably resemble Weber's in key respects. This prompts Parkin to note that "inside every neo-Marxist there seems to be a Weberian struggling to get out" (1979:25). Consequently, Parkin concludes that all manifestations of structured inequality can and should be examined using a single, essentially Weberian, conceptual framework. This unified scheme treats power relations, not class relations, as the elemental factor generating inequality but elaborates Weber's original notion of power by linking it to his related but less familiar idea of *social closure*. Because of its central role in Parkins's analysis, we begin with an assessment of his discussion of power as social closure. We then consider Parkin's treatment of class, the modern state, and the outlook for inequality in future society.

Power and Social Closure

Parkin concurs with the view put forward in Chapter 3 that, for Weber, the overall structure of inequality in society stems from a general and continuing struggle for power (1972:46; 1979:44). According to Parkin, however, it is unclear in Weber's discussion precisely what the source or location of power is in society, particularly because his definition of the term is never completely satisfactory (1979:46). Parkin's remedy for this problem is to combine the idea of power with social closure, a less prominent concept in Weber that refers to the various processes by which some social groupings restrict others from "access to resources and opportunities." From this viewpoint, power is really a "built-in attribute" of any closure situation, denoting one's degree of access to these resources and opportunities (1979:44-46).

Parkin suggests two basic forms that social closure can assume: *exclusion*, which is the prime means by which dominant factions deny power to subordinates, and *usurpation*, which is the key means by which subordinates seek to wrest at least some power back from those who dominate them. Of the two, exclusion is by far the more effective form in modern societies, for it is largely established in legal rules and regulations that enjoy the official sanction of the state's justice system and, if necessary, its repressive agencies as well. The obvious example of exclusion in capitalism is the legal right to own private property, which excludes workers from power over the production process. As for usurpation, it is a secondary process for the most part, through which those subordinates denied power by formal exclusion attempt to consolidate themselves and mobilize power in an "upward direction." In its most extreme guise, usurpation could mean a complete overthrow of the ruling faction, as in a proletarian revolution to oust the bourgeoisie from power. Typically, however, usurpation involves more moderate and less potent kinds of action, the most common being a collective withdrawal or disruption of services through strikes or demonstrations. In contrast to exclusion, such usurpationary acts are less often given formal recognition or protection by the state. Such tactics are frequently accorded only grudging or partial legitimation and may even be outlawed in some circumstances. Thus, like Lenski before him, Parkin envisions a two-way flow of power in social hierarchies, but one that is asymmetrical in that the exclusionary powers of the dominant faction generally override the usurpationary responses of subordinates (1979:45, 58, 74, 98).

So far, we have used examples of class relationships to illustrate Parkins's two forms of social closure. However, Parkin stresses that closure processes are the common factor behind all structures of inequality, including ethnic, religious, sexual, and other forms of exploitation in addition to class relations. Once again, Parkin is critical of Marxist analysts here, most of whom ignore these other forms or simply give them passing mention as phenomena that obscure from view the "real" struggle between classes. But, to Parkin, the struggles between blacks and whites in South Africa, Catholics and Protestants in Northern Ireland, or women and men in most every nation are all conflicts over closure, over access to resources and opportunities. Moreoever, such antagonisms and the inequalities connected with them occur in both capitalist and socialist societies, regardless of whether class inequality exists or not, so it is incorrect to assume that they are somehow secondary to or derivative from class struggle (1979:113-114). On the contrary, these other bases for inequality are frequently more important than class in explaining social change or collective action in some countries (1978: 621-622). What is required, then, is a recognition of these other clashes between interest groups and an analysis of how they reinforce, negate, or otherwise interact with class closure.

Closure and Class Structure

Having noted the general process of social closure and the various systems of power and inequality it can engender, Parkin gives particular attention to the problem of class structure. Despite his criticisms of Marxist analysis, Parkin clearly holds with Marx, as well as Weber, in emphasizing the pivotal role of property relations in defining classes. In fact, control of productive property continues to be "the most important form of social closure" in society, since it can mean exclusion from access to the material means of survival itself (1979:53). However, following Weber, Parkin notes that the class system is increasingly being shaped by a second key type of exclusion: the use of formal "credentials," especially educational certification, to close off privileged positions from others (1979:54; Weber, 1922:344; see also Collins, 1979). Particularly in such fields as medicine and law, a few incumbents have gained license from the state to special forms of knowledge and practice, resulting in a legal monopoly over professional services. Parkin believes these credentials are so important that those who hold them are the second layer of the dominant class, just below those who have exclusive control of productive property (1979:57-58).

Outside the dominant class, the class structure in Parkin's view seems to form a graded structure of people who have varying degrees of usurpationary influence, occasionally combined with a partial capacity for excluding others. Workers without property or credentials form the subordinate class, although they vary internally according to whether or not they enjoy usurpationary influence because of union affiliation and according to the strength or "disruptive potential" of their union relative to others (1979:80, 93). Between the dominant and subordinate classes, Parkin also notes a range of "intermediate groups" who exercise incomplete forms of both exclusion and usurpation, in what Parkin calls "dual closure". The lower end of this middle range includes skilled tradespeople, workers who are unionized and can also invoke limited exclusionary

closure through apprenticeship systems and other credential mechanisms. Such certificates are less exclusive than those given doctors and
other professions but still provide workers who have these papers some
advantages over workers who do not. The remaining intermediate positions primarily involve white-collar "semiprofessions", a mixture of
teachers, nurses, social workers, and the like, who may shade into the
more established professions at the upper end but normally fall short of
the complete exclusionary closure doctors and lawyers have attained.
Such semiprofessionals are often state employees, without a true monopoly over the knowledge or services they dispense, and thus may resort
to unionization and other usurpationary tactics to defend or improve their
position in the collective struggle of interest groups (1979:56-57, 102-
108).

In total, then, Parkin's portrayal of the class system comprises a dominant class of people with exclusionary rights to property and to special
credentials, a subordinate class of workers with only varying amounts of
usurpationary power, and a middle range or semiprofessions and skilled
workers with different mixes of both types of closure at their disposal.
Despite the emphasis on closure, Parkin observes that this structure is
open or permeable to some extent. The dominant faction in modern liberal
democracies harbors a degree of ideological commitment to individual
opportunity, so that some with talent will be allowed and even encouraged
to move up from humble origins, while others of privileged background
who lack ability must eventually move down. Nevertheless, this sifting
process does not alter the closure principles themselves and falls far short
of negating the advantages of those who inherit property and other rights
of closure. In addition, any commitment to individual opportunity is
belied by the tendency for collective or ascriptive criteria such as race or
gender to become interwoven with considerations of merit and performance. Thus, blacks or women could be denied entry to the dominant class
irrespective of their personal qualifications or abilities and could be rel-
egated to the lowest reaches of the subordinate class by white male workers, who may jealously guard what few prerogatives they have themselves
(1979:63-68, 90-91). These latter possibilities suggest some of the ways
that other bases of social closure can be overlaid with or embedded in
the class structure.

The Role of the State

Parkin considers the upsurge of interest in the state the most novel feature
of recent discussions of social inequality (1978:617). His own emphasis
on exclusionary closure, established and upheld by the legal and repressive
branches of the state, suggests that Parkin also sees the state as crucial

to contemporary systems of inequality. However, Parkin contends that the concept of the state has been misused or misunderstood by many theorists, especially those on the left. There is an apparent inconsistency in those Marxists such as Poulantzas who argue for the state's relative autonomy, as if it were a separate force in society, and yet claim that it has no power of its own (Parkin, 1978:618; cf. Miliband, 1969). Parkin's own view is generally closer to the latter, for he suggests that it is *people* who have power *through* the state, especially those factions who are most able to infiltrate state positions or influence state personnel from the outside. This means that the state itself is mainly "an instrument of social domination" — in fact, an elaborate cluster of such instruments that subsumes the "administrative, judicial, military, and coercive institutions" of society. These structures are subject to separate and even contradictory manipulation by the various antagonists in the struggle for social closure. Using a different metaphor, Parkin also compares the state to a "mirror" that reflects the overall outcome of conflicts involving classes, races, genders, and the other key interest groups in society (1979:138-139; 1978:619).

Nevertheless, despite this image of a complex contest to acquire power through the state, Parkin also contends that a few dominant factions, particularly the dominant economic class, are typically able to gain majority control over the means of social closure (1972:181-182). In addition, despite Parkin's apparent stance that the state is without power of its own, he seems to allow for one crucial exception: where a single political party is able to take complete control of the state, as occurs in state-socialist systems, for example. In these situations, the will of a single political faction becomes "fused" with the entire state apparatus into one totalitarian, omnipotent "party-state." Under socialism, this means the end of bourgeois class domination, but it can also mean the centralization of all power within the party-state (1979:140). The serious problems Parkin perceives in such a system provide the basis for his assessment of the future of inequality and the relative merits of capitalism, socialism, and social democracy.

Capitalism, Socialism, and Social Democracy

Notwithstanding the acknowledged exploitation, injustice, and other flaws in capitalism, Parkin is not surprised that workers in most developed countries appear to find the prospect of socialism even less palatable. Massive disinterest in the socialist cause in many capitalist countries is less attributable to "false consciousness" or "mystification" within the working class than to the regrettable examples of socialism in action provided by the Soviet Union and other contemporary state-socialist nations. First of all, although organized repression is found in all societies to some extent, the fusion of party and state within totalitarian socialist regimes on the left (and, of course, totalitarian fascist regimes on the right) seems far more conducive to the sustained use of violence and terror than is typical of western capitalist societies. It is partly because of this specter of violence on the left, of Stalinist purges and "the possibility that the Red Army might be mobilized for other than purely defensive purposes," that workers in other nations have been suspicious of putting socialist doctrines into practice (1979:201).

A second impediment to popular support for socialism is the evidence that early Marxist revolutionaries, including Stalin, Lenin, Lukacs, and others, placed much greater faith in an elite "vanguard" party than in a general groundswell of workers' involvement in shaping and directing socialist transformation. Certainly, Lenin and others expected this elite dominance to be only temporary, and recent Marxists such as Poulantzas and Wright strongly advocate broad proletarian participation in any future socialist initiatives. Nevertheless, the impression among many workers, that the dictatorship of the proletariat is still a euphemism for totalitarian control by the party-state, is partly responsible for their disavowal of socialist revolution. Even such minimal freedoms under capitalism as the right of political dissent or the choice of more than one political party to vote for imply, by comparison, a much more democratic system (1979:153-155, 178-182).

A final factor acting against socialist success is the perception among many workers that the elimination of private control over production has not eradicated inequalities in power or in the distribution of resources and opportunities. Removal of property rights under socialism has meant that other forms of exclusionary closure have become the salient bases for inequality, especially between the mass of the population and an elite category of intellectuals, scientists, officials, and bureaucrats, who have special educational credentials or strategic positions in the party hierarchy with which to exact privilege. In addition, although the differences between top and bottom are probably smaller under state socialism, workers in capitalist countries still have the perception that there is less wealth to spread around in socialist economies, so that being more equal under socialism may still mean having a more meager material existence than under capitalism (1979:185-187). If this situation prevails or is perceived to prevail, and if workers put greater stress on distributive issues than some Marxists would prefer, it is unlikely that state socialism can serve as a sufficiently attractive replacement for capitalism.

Although Parkin's assessment implies that neither capitalism nor socialism offers a particularly rosy future, there is at least one other possibility to consider, one that Parkin himself appears to support. Increasingly, in his view, the real choice has become one of state socialism on the one hand and *social democracy*, not pure capitalism, on the other. In the social democracies of Scandinavia, for example, capitalists still retain private control of production and the exclusionary powers that go with it. However, the tensions generated between capitalists and workers can be largely "contained," though never eliminated, through state legislation and other means by which workers get enough usurpationary power that the bourgeoisie retains dominance, but just barely. The trick is to find a balancing point that leaves the capitalist class sufficient incentive to invest and accumulate surplus but that simultaneously reduces the exploitation of workers to the lowest possible level (1979:189). This containment of class struggle need not mean that Dahrendorf's complete legitimation or institutionalization of class conflict is achieved, only that workers and capitalists alike are able to decide how far they can or should go in usurping or excluding privilege.

It is interesting that this social-democratic solution to the problem of inequality returns us to certain basic assumptions about human nature and locates itself somewhere between Marx's belief in the potential selflessness of humanity and the conservative or structural-functionalist insistence on people's inherent motivation to acquire more power or rewards than others. Like Marx, the social-democratic philosophy suggests that all people can flourish under more egalitarian conditions and that, in the proper setting, people are capable of tying personal interest more closely to a concern for the collective good. Yet, as conservative thinkers have argued, no amount of structural change can totally eliminate the "small inner core of human individuality," with its self-interested motives and its belief in differential rewards for differential talent or effort (1979:189-190). From this perspective, some degree of inequality, restricted and reduced though it may be, is perhaps a natural, inevitable, or necessary outcome of social relationships.

Of course, in posing this alternative to state socialism, Parkin is well aware that social democracy has also run into snags when its principles are put into practice. For example, the record of social-democratic governments in western Europe and elsewhere has not been stellar in reducing material inequalities or the concentrated power of capital (1979:200). Yet even modest advances along these lines, when compared to the militarism, totalitarianism, and material shortages of socialist societies, would probably make some form of social democracy the preferred system for most of the working population.

Summary Observations

Parkin's neo-Weberian perspective on social inequality has been the subject in this section of the chapter. Overall, his approach represents a provocative and constructive attempt to reorient Weber's original power perspective by introducing into prominence the concept of social closure.

Parkin is able to sustain both Marx's and Weber's stress on class as the crux of social inequality, while also accounting for the other important forms of closure or power relations that regularly emerge and become established in social settings. While Parkin's approach thus contributes significantly to a truly general conception of social inequality, there are at least two points that would benefit from additional discussion or elaboration.

First, Parkin's main focus on the legal bases for power or closure, though justifiable, could be expanded to include more detailed discussion of the nonlegal bases for social domination arising from informal, but equally effective, rules established in traditional beliefs, customs, and habitual practices. Though Parkin is clearly aware of these forms of closure, and the manner in which they can exclude women or racial minorities from power in spite of their *legal* equality, it would be worthwhile to give them greater play, especially since this would be consistent with Weber's original analysis.

Second, Parkin's suggestion that the state has no power, except in such situations as the fusion of party and state under state socialism, seems open to some question. Given Parkin's neo-Weberian view, it stands to reason that he would follow Weber in noting the special power attached to state bureaucrats, power that is not reducible to the class, ethnicity, gender, party, or other external affiliations they possess but that inheres in their roles as bureaucratic administrators and decision makers internal to the state itself. In that sense, heads of state organizations have power in the same way that any other privileged factions do. In a similar vein, one could note that the unique coercive powers of the state's military and police branches also give them special, and in some cases ultimate, control in society.

Anthony Giddens
The Structuration of Class, Power, and Inequality

The last major approach to social inequality we shall examine is that found in the writings of Anthony Giddens. Giddens is recognized as one of the leading figures in contemporary social thought, both for his provocative analyses of Marx, Weber, Durkheim, and other classical theorists and for his more recent development of a general *theory of structuration* as an alternative perspective in sociology (e.g., Giddens, 1971, 1976, 1977, 1979). In the process of pursuing both these projects, Giddens has sought to rethink several topics of special relevance to the study of social inequality, especially past and present conceptions of class, power, and the capitalist state (1973, 1981a, 1981b).

It was noted at the beginning of this chapter that Giddens is often categorized as a neo-Weberian, particularly by Marxist critics of his views (Binns, 1977; Crompton and Gubbay, 1977; Wright, 1978, 1979). While there is some validity to this assessment at a very general level of discussion, it should be observed that, as Giddens himself argues, on some issues he owes rather more to Marx than to Weber. Moreover, in generating the finer points of his own perspective, Giddens frequently draws on and builds from a wide range of additional viewpoints that include structuralism and hermeneutics, among others.

These conditions should be kept in mind when noting Giddens' location between the Marxist and Weberian camps on our left-right continuum in Figure 5.1. This position reflects his joint sympathies with basic elements of both Marx and Weber, who, as we have seen, have more in common than many analysts realize. However, Giddens' position on the continuum also signifies his felt need to supplement and modify the views of these classical thinkers. Giddens concurs with Weber's initial attempt to deal with certain points left undeveloped in Marx, especially the pluralist nature of class and power, the importance of bureaucracy in modern systems of domination, and the role of the state as the focus of legal and repressive power in advanced societies. In turn, Giddens has stressed the need to correct and elaborate the manner in which Weber has dealt with these and other issues (1981a:296-300; cf. 1973:100-102).

The culmination of Giddens' efforts to expand and redirect existing perspectives is his own structuration approach to the analysis of social processes. It is beyond our purposes to explore all the intricacies of this general orientation; nevertheless, its specific application to the problem of social inequality is crucial to consider because, in many respects, it offers the most promising basis for a comprehensive analysis of this area. As with the other perspectives we have examined, the discussion in this section centers on four main issues: the concept of class or class structure, the significance of power in systems of social inequality, the role of the state, and the prospects for inequality in future society.

Class Structure in Advanced Societies

The beginnings of Giddens' overall structuration perspective can be found in his initial analysis of the class structure in advanced societies (1973). Rather like Wright after him, Giddens argues that the two-class system envisioned by Marx, involving bourgeoisie and proletariat, is acceptable primarily as an "abstract" or "pure" model of the capitalist class structure, one that omits certain residual class locations in real societies (1973:27-28). Giddens holds with all Marxists and most Weberians that the crucial factor generating this class system is "ownership or exclusion from ownership of property in the means of production" (1973:100, 271-272). In the end, however, his links to Weber on this issue seem clearer, for he adopts the original Weberian position that classes are largely products of differences in power among groups within the capitalist market. In the economic setting, capitalists enjoy greater power than workers because they retain rights over productive property, while workers have only the right to sell their labor in exchange for a living wage paid by capitalists. Where Giddens reveals his central tie to Weber, and his basic divergence from Marx, is in his contention that there is a third important category of rights that underlies the different economic power, or "market capacity", of people under capitalism. This third factor is the "possession of recognized skills" and "educational qualifications" (1973:101-103).

Using this mixture of Marxian and Weberian precepts, Giddens argues that the three rights, powers, or capacities — property, education or skills, and manual labor — are fundamental to a corresponding "threefold class structure" that is "generic to capitalist society." It is primarily because these three bases of power predominate in the economic sphere that social relationships arise among an "upper" class of those who control most productive property, a "middle" class of those without appreciable property who nonetheless have special education or skills to exchange in the market, and a "lower" or "working" class who have only their manual labor to sell.

Of course, if this three-class scheme is taken too literally, it is subject to the same criticisms as Marx's two-class model, since there are many exceptions that do not fit easily into any of the categories. Giddens himself notes that one cannot draw absolutely clear boundaries between classes, as if they were "lines on a map." This is because some groupings, such as the old petty bourgeoisie or independently employed doctors and other educated professionals, tend to straddle class lines in that they have partial access to more than one of the three types of rights. Using terminology similar to Parkin, Giddens suggests, then, that the degree of "closure" or "exclusion" produced by these rights is not always complete. Besides, the amount that such mixed positions actually blur class lines will vary across different societies, and even different regions within the same society, so that no single model can capture precisely all the detailed differences in class structure that arise in this range of situations.

It is here that Giddens introduces the idea of structuration, primarily as an aid in dealing with these anomalies in real class systems. Rather than speak of classes as if they were discrete groups, explicitly delineated and separated in all instances, Giddens recommends that class structure be construed as a *variable* phenomenon that is generally anchored in a three-class system but that differs in its *degree* of structuration, in the extent to which classes are generated and reproduced over time and place as identifiable, distinct social clusters. In this sense, one can argue that property, educational qualifications, and labor power do act as the major powers or rights that interconnect, or *mediate* between, the economy and the classes arising from it. The three resulting classes will be more clearly defined or structurated in those societies or situations where these three mediate factors tend not to be mixed together in the same occupations or positions.

In addition, at an immediate, day-to-day, or *proximate* level, Giddens suggests three other factors that can either blur or reinforce the three-class model he outlines. The first proximate factor is the way in which labor is divided in the work setting itself. In some societies, for example, manual laborers are physically separated from specially trained or educated nonmanual workers and invariably perform different tasks. In these cases, the split between middle and working classes is reinforced still further, thus increasing class structuration in such societies.

Similarly, a second proximate factor is the manner in which authority relations are structured in the work setting. Sometimes there is no real difference in the decision making or supervisory powers of manual workers and specially trained personnel, while in other situations special personnel have authority prerogatives that divide them from manual workers in the same way that their greater education or training does. In the former case there would be some blurring of the boundary between middle and working class, at least on this basis, while in the latter instance the boundary would be enhanced.

The final proximate factor in class structuration is the pattern of *distributive groupings*, by which Giddens means primarily the amount of clustering that occurs because of distinct life styles or material consumption habits. The best illustration of this factor is the purchase of housing and the physical segregation or mixing of class clusters that can result. In societies where upper, middle, and working classes invariably live in clearly designated areas that do not overlap, their pattern of consumption of housing would obviously reinforce the underlying three-class system and make it more readily discernible as a social *reality*. On the other hand, if the predominant pattern in a society or region is a heterogeneous mixing of people in the same neighborhood, regardless of their market capacities in the economic sphere, then class structuration would be less pronounced and class lines would be more blurred than otherwise (1973:107-110).

What Giddens offers, then, is a basic three-class model that differs from Marx's dichotomous view in two key ways: in its designation of a heterogeneous middle class of educated and skilled personnel, who tend to differ from both capitalists and manual workers; and in its incorporation of a variable element in the conception of class structure, which allows for the possibility that classes in different settings can be more or less distinctly delineated or "structurated," depending on the extent to which six particular factors act in unison, or against one another, in promoting clear class cleavages. Though there are significant differences in both terminology and focus, Giddens thus shares with many recent theorists a concern with complications that, in contrast to Marx's pure model of classes, are still present in existing capitalist societies.

Perhaps the most telling aspect of Giddens' analysis is his conclusion that these complexities do not negate the truths in Marx, but are more significant for understanding capitalist class systems than current Marxists believe. Hence, the middle class is likely to be a persistent reality in advanced capitalism, not some transient fraction or secondary set of contradictory locations. In addition, class affiliations will continue to be elaborate at times, not only because of the variable mix of mediate and proximate divisions, but also because factors such as gender and ethnicity interact with class structuration (1981a:304-307). These views underscore the pluralist image of class and inequality that, more than anything else perhaps, separates Giddens from Marxism (1973:273-274). This pluralism in Giddens carries over into his pivotal analysis of power.

Power and Domination

Giddens' most recent theoretical concerns have centered on refining the concept of power and incorporating it into his more general theory of structuration (1979, 1981b). Here, in characteristic fashion, Giddens notes Weber's advances over Marx (who never attempted a complete analysis of power), while at the same time claiming that Weber's view of power is itself in need of elaboration and revision (1981b:4-5).

We shall avoid a detailed review of Giddens' treatment of power since it involves subtler distinctions and more complex terminology than are appropriate for our discussion. However, in more simplified form, Giddens' formulation is useful here because it connects rather closely with the Weberian view that still prevails on this issue but also adds to Weber's conception in certain important respects.

Giddens asserts that power differences are not the only factors linking people together in society, but they do form one such link and are basic to *all* social interaction. Power is defined as any "relations of autonomy and dependence between actors in which these actors draw upon and reproduce structural properties of *domination*" (1981b:28-29). Giddens' use of the term domination to define power shows the close connection that he perceives between these two ideas. It is interesting that Weber also ties power and domination together, as we saw in Chapter 3. The interpretation offered there was that power refers to any capacity of an actor (or faction) to exercise his or her will relative to other actors, while domination denotes the regular patterns or structured relations between actors that arise as such power differences are established, routinized, and regenerated over time.

Now, while there are undeniable divergences between Giddens and Weber on other points, they share a rough correspondence in this distinction between power as human capacity and domination as a structural manifestation of power. Thus, Giddens sees domination as "structured asymmetries of resources drawn upon and reconstituted in such power relations" (1981b:50; cf. 1979:91-93). What Giddens adds to Weber here is a much more explicit and sophisticated elucidation of this two-sided sense of power, something that is implicit in Weber but must be eked out of his discussion. In fact, Giddens devotes considerable effort to demonstrating that power is "doubled-edged" in a variety of other ways as well: it typically combines some amount of both repression from above and legitimate compliance from below, it can be used to coerce and constrain but also to liberate and transform, it can operate through formal rules and laws or informal customs and traditions, it can involve acts of commission by superiors but also acts of omission or passive resistance by subordinates, and so on (1979:88-94; 1981b:49-51). Of course, as we have seen, some of the same points can be found in Weber's writings and also in the more recent analyses of Lenski and Parkin, among others. But Giddens is perhaps most notable for his systematic treatment of this duality in power systems and for his recognition that power exists both as a capacity of persons and as a pattern of relations, sustained or reproduced over time and space.

It is this same reproductive process, whereby people interact in patterned relations so as to structure (or else change) those relations, that is the essence of what Giddens means by structuration. We have already seen one illustration of this process, in the case of class structuration. Class distinctions tend to be solidified or reinforced when people's interactions are determined by their economic capacities (the three mediate factors in capitalism) and by immediate social circumstances related to those capacities (the three proximate factors). The more clearly these bases for interaction separate out clusters of actors from one another, the greater class structuration there is.

The class system also provides the foremost example of how power differences and structures of domination develop in social systems. However, in Giddens' view, capitalist class relations are not the only important case of domination or exploitation in society: "Certain fundamental forms of exploitation do not originate with capitalism, or with class divisions more generally" and "not all forms of exploitation can be explained in terms of class domination." Domination and exploitation also occur in other asymmetrical relations, including those between nation-states — between colonies and imperialistic countries, for example — between ethnic groups, and between the sexes (1981b:25, 60, 242).

Thus, Giddens leaves no doubt that there is some degree of pluralism in his conception of power or domination. This pluralism is also evident in his overall conception of societal institutions. Although Giddens is highly critical of structural functionalism, and even argues that the term function be banned from sociological discourse, he nonetheless contends that the functionalist perspective is correct to recognize the major institutions of society and their embodiment in large-scale social structures (1981b:16;1979:97). As was discussed in Chapter 4, structural functionalists conceive of institutions as systems of persistent rules, norms, and values that people tend to live by, or keep in mind, in their interactions with others. These institutions give rise to concrete social structures that roughly correspond to the institutions. An illustration is the formal establishment of a religious structure, or church, in accordance with a particular set of religious values and beliefs.

In a similar fashion, Giddens delineates four basic types of institutions, and connects them to a range of concrete social structures. *Political* institutions operate primarily in the political structures of the state and are concerned with "authorization" or the domination of *people*. *Economic* institutions operate mainly in the economic structure and involve "allocation" or the domination of *material phenomena*. Here Giddens suggests that command over people and command over material things are the two key means for establishing power or domination in society. Giddens' third category includes *symbolic* institutions, those embodied in religion, education, and the communications media, for example, or in what Poulantzas and Wright would call ideological apparatuses. In his final category, Giddens chooses to distinguish *legal/repressive* institutions from the other three types, although their obvious connections to the legal, military, and police branches of the state suggest they could be included more simply under the political category (1981b:47).

In any case, Giddens' discussion of institutions and structures provides further confirmation of his pluralist view of power and society. This is most obvious, perhaps, in his distinction between political power and economic power, between domination of people and domination of things. In addition, however, the correspondence between institutions and structures is not a simple one-to-one relationship, so that both types of domination operate, at least in secondary form, in the religious and other structures of society as well. It is in this sense that Giddens sees power as a dispersed phenomenon, an integral element of all social life (1981b:28, 49). This does not mean that power can never be disproportionately concentrated in certain structures or factions. On the contrary, it is clear that those who control the economic and political systems are the principal players in the overall power struggle. But it is also the case that any conception that traces power solely to one class, group, or structure is likely to give us an incomplete understanding of the total system of domination in advanced societies.

The Role of the State

Giddens' dualistic view of power as both a human and a structural quality is roughly paralleled in his analysis of the state in advanced societies. In Giddens' opinion, Poulantzas and others are partly correct to represent the state as a structure or framework within which power is exercised by classes (or other interests) external to it. However, this does not negate the fact that these structured relations between positions within the state are also occupied by real people as well, by state leaders, bureaucrats, and lesser officials who retain special capacities or powers of their own (1981b:218-220).

Probably the most important sense in which the state is largely a structure for channeling the power of others is in its connections with the economy under capitalism. Giddens accepts the view most closely identified with Offe, but roughly similar to that found in other Marxists such as Poulantzas and Wright, which sees the state as dependent upon the activities of private capitalists for its revenue (cf. Offe, 1974; Offe and Ronge, 1975). For this reason, the state structure to some extent is organized by state leaders to facilitate the economic goals of the bourgeoisie. In part, the state personnel are said to be caretakers or managers who, where possible, direct and augment the flow of capitalist economic power in order to aid and maintain both the bourgeoisie's surplus accumulation and the state's tax base. This is seen as the prime reason for the state's growth and its increased intrusion into economic affairs under advanced capitalism (1981b:165, 211; Giddens and Held, 1982:192).

According to Giddens, the state in capitalist society also channels power in a somewhat different sense, by "insulating" political power from economic power so that these two means of control seem to the working class to be unrelated. Rather than rally the proletariat to achieve progressive economic change, perhaps even revolution, through political action, the prevailing political parties instituted within most capitalist states keep these issues separate. For the most part, economic struggles are fought as labor-management disputes over wages in the industrial sphere and pose no fundamental threat to the capitalist system itself. Thus, although workers have formal political equality with all other citizens in capitalist democracies, little thought is given to using politics to attain economic equality as well (1981b:127-128).

Nevertheless, in acknowledging these ways in which the state is a structural conduit or framework for the power of external, especially capitalist, interests, Giddens asserts that the state is also a collection of social actors, of leaders and officials with considerable power in their own right. Here Giddens seems to follow Weber to some degree, in that he stresses two bases for domination that are the state's special preserve. First is the monopoly of organized violence inherent in the state's repressive (police and military) branches. Second is the capacity of these branches, as well as various legal and bureaucratic state organizations, to store information and strategic knowledge for surveillance purposes. These two means for dominating and controlling the populace give those who run the state certain powers that are not subject to the will of the bourgeoisie or any other outside group. Moreover, these state powers are evident in virtually all modern societies, capitalist, socialist, or otherwise. Giddens finds it odd that few contemporary analysts, particularly in the structural-functionalist and Marxist camps, have paid much attention to these bases for state power. Clearly, there is ample evidence of their importance and their use in this century by totalitarian regimes on both the left and the right (1981b:94, 175-177, 244). The threat posed by these powers of repression and surveillance is one central element in Giddens' assessment of the prospects for future societies.

The Future of Inequality

Giddens' comments concerning the future of social inequality once again reveal his characteristic blend of Marxian and Weberian viewpoints. Like Weber, Giddens is highly critical of current brands of state socialism and extremely doubtful that they can achieve the true transcendence of capitalism they allegedly seek. Nevertheless, like Marx, Giddens retains a personal desire to see a successful transformation of the present exploitation and injustice of capitalist society and harbors some optimism that the possibilities for democratic or "libertarian" socialism do exist (1981b:175).

Giddens sees serious flaws in the modern versions of both capitalism and socialism, although like Parkin he apparently finds capitalism, at least the social-democratic variety common in western Europe, to be less objectionable than the state-directed system prevalent in today's socialist countries. Advanced capitalism has been successful on certain counts, most notably the greater political freedoms and material affluence it has provided compared to socialist and other nations. Unfortunately, modern capitalism also fosters fundamental forms of injustice or exploitation that have yet to be alleviated. The relative affluence of people living under capitalism, including workers, has often come at the expense of people in undeveloped countries elsewhere, as part of the global activity of modern capitalism and the international exploitation of nation-state by nation-state. In addition, within capitalist countries, ethnic and sexual forms of exploitation continue to be significant bases for discrimination and injustice. Finally, of course, advanced capitalism shares with all such systems that it is premised on the exploitation of one class by another.

Thus, despite providing some measure of material security to workers, capitalism remains a highly unequal form of economic organization, one in which workers have little control over production and in which their labor is itself "commodified" and dehumanized. The political rights and freedoms capitalism offers have failed to compensate for or eliminate these inequities, for capitalism's basic contradiction still remains: it is a system that is impossible without the social or collective production of surplus, and yet it also demands that a select few derive private and disproportionate benefit from that surplus. While this arrangement is not in imminent danger of collapse, in Giddens' view, it is subject to chronic pressures. To Giddens, whether these pressures can be contained, as Parkin and others have argued, depends primarily on the ability of the state to mediate capitalism's basic contradiction, to maintain social conditions that are at least acceptable to the general population without undermining bourgeois domination (1981a:317-319; 1981b:238-239, 250-251).

One of the main reasons why capitalism is not immediately threatened by revolution is the general failure of socialism to fulfill its promises. In Giddens' view, current examples of state socialism are at best clumsy prototypes that cannot transcend the capitalist system until they come to grips with their own contradiction. Socialism's contradiction is that it seeks mass equality and participation in social policies and decisions and yet requires a centralized system of production and administration that focuses power in the state. As we have already noted, the concentration of state power, especially through control of surveillance and repression, is a serious threat to equality and freedom that is at least as likely under socialism as under capitalism. Similarly, the bureaucratic domination, sexism, racism, and colonialism common to capitalist systems are also prevalent in current state-socialist regimes.

The crucial lession here for Marxists is that the abolition of class exploitation by socialist revolution is not enough by itself to bring a just society, since other bases for exploitation still persist. The inability of many Marxists to perceive this stems from their singular concern with class and their consequent failure to note that class relations, though pivotal, are but one manifestation of power differences. Giddens concludes that it is power, conceived along the line he suggests, that has "universal applicability" to the study of exploitation and inequality. If equality and democracy are to be realized, through socialism or otherwise, it is essential that the use of power in all its forms be examined and understood (1981a:319-320; 1981b:201, 244-248). The unique situation of the modern era, with its trend toward a capitalist "world economy" and its prospect of total nuclear destruction, makes this understanding even more imperative (1981b:196-198,250).

Summary Observations

The purpose of this segment of the chapter has been to outline and assess Giddens' conception of social inequality, with special reference to his structuration approach to class, power, and other related issues. Of the recent perspectives we have examined, Giddens' seems to offer the most comprehensive and inclusive strategy for thinking about social systems and the inequalities that inhere within them. In addition to retaining Marx's classical concern with class and Weber's pluralist revisions and modifications of Marx, Giddens attempts to incorporate what he believes is the central strength of structural functionalism as well: the delineation of major institutions and their attendant concrete structures in advanced societies. The economic, political, religious, and other structures that are identified in this way can all, in varying degrees, be conceived as systems of power, in which patterned relations of domination are established and reproduced over time and space, based on differential control of material ("allocative") and human ("authoritative") resources.

Although there are also clear differences in approach, Giddens' recognition of these distinct structures of domination roughly parallels the separation of economic, political, and ideological apparatuses suggested by Poulantzas, Wright, and other neo-Marxists. The advantage Giddens has over these conceptions stems mainly from his more general concern with analyzing all power relations arising within these structures, as opposed to focusing exclusively on class relations.

Giddens' stress on the universal role of power in generating all forms of inequality has vague affinities with Dahrendorf, closer connections with Lenski, and even greater similarities with Parkin's social-closure conception. There is a pleasing clarity in Parkin's viewpoint that contrasts with Giddens' rather complex formulation and with Giddens' propensity, as Parkin notes, "to drive conceptual wedges between empirically inseparable things" (Parkin, 1980:892; see also Giddens, 1980). Nevertheless, the complicated nature of Giddens' analysis is also a tribute to its completeness. It would appear that Giddens, more than Parkin, offers us a perspective on inequality that acknowledges the full range of social situations in which power is exercised and inequality established. Giddens also combines Parkin's astute awareness of power as a property of real people with the neo-Marxist (and functionalist) sense of structural arrangements as repositories and channels for power that exist, in a way, apart from the persons that staff them.

For these reasons, then, it could be argued that Giddens' overall approach provides the most fully developed guide for thinking about and analyzing social inequality that presently exists in social theory. Inevitably, of course, there are specific points raised by Giddens, and by the other theorists for that matter, that remain open to debate, and that are unlikely to be reconciled to the satisfaction of every theoretical camp. Nevertheless, it should be evident by now that the writers we have examined are concerned with many of the same issues and, in different ways, have all contributed to a more complete appreciation of what social inequality is and how it should be conceived. In the closing chapter, we shall briefly summarize and reassess these contributions, in an effort to outline the general direction that current thought seems to be moving us in the analysis of social inequality.

CHAPTER SIX

Theories of Social Inequality a Summary Evaluation

Now that we have covered the major theoretical ground in the study of social inequality, some recapitulation of the most crucial points is in order. This review will be a selective one, intended to underscore certain special contributions from each writer rather than to repeat in detail all the issues that have been considered in previous chapters. This will enable us to offer some concluding speculation on what elements should be included in a summary overview of social inequality in modern societies.

The Major Perspectives:
A Selective Review

It should be clear at this stage that Marx's ideas, with which we began our analysis, still stand at the absolute center of any complete discussion of structured social inequality. Despite the many criticisms leveled against Marx by friend and foe alike, it seems certain that his understanding of the origins of class relations in the sphere of production, and his grasp of the internal workings and contradictions of capitalism, will continue to be unique and lasting contributions to modern social thought. Marx's work is incomplete as a general perspective on social inequality, in part because the development of such a perspective was not his purpose. Nevertheless, in examining the mechanisms for the revolutionary overthrow of capitalism, the task that required most of his intellectual efforts, Marx also succeeded in identifying the principal cleavage, the great divide in all systems of social inequality: between those who own or control the means of material production and those who survive through their labor power. This essential truth is the point of reference and departure for all the writers who follow.

The second great figure in the study of social inequality is Max Weber. Although several important differences exist between Weber and Marx, there are also fundamental similarities in their thought, especially on the question of class and its pivotal role in the structure of modern society. Those who stress the disagreements in the ideas of Marx and Weber often seem to overlook the affinities between them, as well as Weber's self-professed wish to provide a positive, rather than a destructive, critique of Marxist thought. Weber's major contributions center on this constructive effort to amplify or modify Marx, especially through Weber's recognition in the class system of positions that are neither bourgeois nor proletarian but tend somehow to persist in a middle range between the two main classes; his perception that class relations are best understood as the key type among a more general or plural set of power relations, involving sectional interests and multiple struggles; his delineation of the numerous forms of domination in social structures, including not only legitimate power or authority but also the domination that derives from tradition, habit or custom, fear of repression, and so on; his identification of bureaucratic organizations as the predominant mechanisms for domination in the political, economic, and other spheres of modern life; and his early awareness of the increasing role played by the state in the overall power structure, through its monopoly of repressive force and its connections to the economic system. All these points add immeasurably to the subsequent assessments of social inequality in recent times.

The third classical theorist we considered was Durkheim. The inclusion of Durkheim in an analysis of inequality is perhaps surprising to some, since he is not conventionally seen as a central figure in the field. However, Durkheim's thought offers us an important link between certain basic ideas in Marx and Weber and more recent structural-functionalist formulations. In particular, Durkheim reveals an awareness of such problems as class struggle and alienation under capitalism that is similar to Marx. At the same time, such Weberian concerns as the state and the role of power in society receive more than passing attention. Like Weber, Durkheim sees power, and the social constraints that go with it, arising out of a growing set of legal rules that nonetheless are supplemented at all times by the influence of informal traditions, conventions, habits or customs, and occasionally by coercion. Durkheim also anticipates more recent thinkers in a sense, for he too notes the two-sided nature of power, that power can be a positive as well as a limiting force in society, and that rules not only establish power but also prevent its abuse. What separates Durkheim from Marx and Weber, and provides his otherwise tenuous connection to structural functionalism, is his greater stress on the positive, not the negative, consequences of power differences and inequality, specifically within the division of labor.

After Durkheim, we then examined the structural-functionalist school. Here the predominant strategy is to emphasize Durkheim's sense of the integrative benefits of inequality and to ignore, for the most part, his awareness of the exploitation and injustice that also tend to exist in social hierarchies. This narrow reading of Durkheim is compounded by a peculiar interpretation of Weber, in which any inequalities and power relations that are not based on legitimate authority or consensus go largely unrecognized. The deficiencies in the structural-functionalist approach, which occur because of these omissions, have been discussed earlier. However, in spite of these and other weaknesses, there are at least two elements in structural-functionalist analyses that seem to have a sustained influence in the study of social inequality. First, as Giddens notes, structural functionalism has contributed greatly to the identification of major social institutions and the concrete economic, political, and other structures to which they are tied. Although structural functionalists rarely view them in this way, these structures are a step toward the delineation of a general set of structures of domination in society.

Second, the contention by structural functionalists that there is something inevitable or natural about social inequality is a view that a majority of the population advocates, especially when inequality refers to things like differential rewards for differences in talent or effort (cf. Jasso and Rossi, 1977; Robinson and Bell, 1978; Della Fave, 1980). Of course, popular acceptance of inequality is not a guarantee that it is a natural or inevitable phenomenon. Moreover, as noted in Chapter 1, that social inequality exists in virtually all known societies is not a proof that it must persist in the future. Still, it is difficult to concur with those who simply explain away inequality as some doomed remnant of bourgeois consciousness, a false or distorted form of human relationship that will end with the demise of capitalism. The ready evidence in modern socialist systems of unequal rights, opportunities, rewards, and privileges is sufficient in itself to cast doubt on such claims (e.g., Yanowitch, 1977; Lane, 1982; Giddens and Held, 1982). Hence, until we can achieve some universal shift to an altruistic consciousness among people, there would seem to be at least a kernel of truth in the structural-functionalist view of this question. Even subsequent critics of structural functionalism often appear to agree that such traits as effort, motivation, talent, or training are at least partly responsible for inequality and that, *within certain limits*, most people will perceive this situation as both inescapable and, to some extent, justifiable.

Having conceded this aspect of the structural-functionalist viewpoint, it is worth noting that such *individual* inputs seem to be only a minor factor in the determination of most social inequalities, at least in comparison to the *structural* differences in power or class that exist in society. In addition, as many neo-Marxists contend, whatever mobility occurs within these structures because of personal "worth" or effort does little or nothing to change the structures themselves. The point to stress is that established structures do define the prospects and life chances of people in most instances but that the roles of individual capacity and human agency should not be overlooked.

After structural functionalism, the first of the more recent theorists we considered was Dahrendorf. Dahrendorf's contributions to the study of inequality mainly involve his rejection of some of the more extreme structural-functionalist accounts. He is most notable for questioning the assumption that all forms of inequality are somehow based on consensus, for calling attention to the inherent conflict in social hierarchies, and for attempting to draw a conceptual connection between class and power (or more precisely, authority). Unfortunately, as we have seen, the third aspect of Dahrendorf's work confuses matters by treating all authority differences as class differences.

The next writer to be assessed, Lenski, fosters a similar confusion of class and power. Nevertheless, he compensates for this with his identification of the multiple bases for power that typically arise in modern societies, and with his suggestion that power in its various forms is primarily responsible for the unequal distribution of material privilege and prestige to groups and individuals. In this manner, Lenski directs us to a more global conception of what social inequality is. In doing so, he also moves us back toward Weber, Marx, and the last theoretical exchange we examined: the current debate between neo-Weberian and neo-Marxist views.

A basic conclusion of this book is that the most promising ground for conceiving of social inequality is presently to be found in the disputes involving the Marxist class analyses of Poulantzas and Wright on the one hand and the power perspectives of Parkin and Giddens on the other. It is also evident from previous discussion that the overall thrust of our review generally favors the broadly Weberian views of the latter two writers. The reasons for this choice center mainly on the greater generalizability of the power concept over the class concept, and on the plural inequalities that this allows us to recognize. The existence of some degree of pluralism, and of distinct bases for power in addition to class power, is *explicitly* denied by Poulantzas and other Marxists; yet, as we have seen, these elements are *implicitly* acknowledged in the Marxist delineation of fractions or contradictory locations in the class system and of the economic, political, and ideological apparatuses in capitalist society. The reluctance to give express recognition to this pluralism, or to see any conceptual equivalence in the fact that class, gender, race, and other bases for inequality all involve power relations, may stem from a fear that class would thereby be diminished in importance as a concept in this area. Such a fear, however, seems unwarranted. It is possible to arrive at a conception of social inequality that maintains the primacy of class analysis but that also appreciates the complex nature of both class relations and the other power relations that are at work in shaping social structures. In varying ways, this is what Parkin and especially Giddens have done.

This is not to say that the recent Marxist contributions to the analysis of inequality should be discounted. On the contrary, Wright's work in particular has been valuable for clarifying and redirecting issues first raised by Poulantzas and others. In addition, Wright's conception of the capitalist class structure, as outlined in Figures 5.2 and 5.3, appears at present to be the most systematic scheme for portraying class relations and their existence across the various economic, political, and ideological structures of society. For this to be a more complete picture, however, it also requires that Giddens' duality of social arrangements be incorporated, that this skeleton of class positions be invested with the human content that both Giddens and Parkin favor when discussing classes. In that event, we can accept that relations of productive control form the underpinnings of the class system, but we can also affirm that clusters of real people will coalesce around the different bases for interaction or closure that are inherent to these relations.

Such a dual sense of classes as structures and classes as people is useful for avoiding fruitless debates that insist classes must be only one or the other. Similarly empty controversies, over whether power is a capacity of persons or a relation beween them and whether the state has power or not, could also be eased if it were seen that both actors and the patterns of interaction between social positions are involved in all these things. Although various writers reveal some awareness of this dual nature of class and power, Giddens has been most successful in incorporating it into his overall perspective on inequality in social systems. His treatment of power is particularly valuable for its assimilation of elements from several other analyses. Included here are his revitalized version of Weber's conception of domination; his use of institutional or structural elaborations similar to those in functionalism and recent Marxism; and his awareness, like Parkin, of the multiple forms of closure and exploitation in society.

Social Inequality: A Summary Portrait

Having highlighted the crucial themes in classical and contemporary theories of inequality, we come again to the fundamental questions raised in the opening chapter. We are now in a better position to answer such questions about what social inequality is and how it should be conceived; however, it is also clear that no single set of answers will be universally acceptable, since no single perspective can subsume the others or resolve all the disagreements among theorists. For these reasons, no grand synthesis of viewpoints is either likely or advisable. Nevertheless, there are some views that many, if not most, of the writers do share, at least at a general level of discussion. There should be no surprise in this; given the erudition of the thinkers involved, the surprising outcome would be if they did *not* agree on certain basic points. It can be argued that the broad similarities found in many of the perspectives may at least move us toward some "common vocabulary," as Parkin calls it, for discussing social inequality (Parkin, 1979:42).

As a provisional step in this direction, Figure 6.1 offers a summary picture, or composite drawing, of how social inequality in modern societies might be perceived. This is an abstract representation of the major means for establishing power relations in social settings, the resulting structures of domination that emerge and are reproduced, and the principal bases for social inequality that typically operate within and across these structures.

Power and Domination

First, it is apparent that the concept of power is pivotal in this portrait. Power is defined here as a differential capacity to command resources, which gives rise to structured, asymmetric relations of domination and subordination between social actors. There are three key means by which power is normally generated in social systems: control of material resources, of people, and of ideas. The first two means of power correspond roughly to Giddens' concepts of allocation and authorization, and to a broadly similar delineation of "human and non-human resources" found in Goldthorpe (1974:218; cf. Grabb, 1982). The third designation of power through ideas is an extension of the twofold scheme. It is reminiscent of Francis Bacon's famous remark that "knowledge is power," that ideas and information can serve as the means (or the medium) of power in the same way that money or people can. The recognition of this third type of power is generally compatible with previous writers we have examined, virtually all of whom, in varying degrees, note the importance of controlling special knowledge and information or the influence that beliefs and ideas can have on social life. In addition, by combining this category of *ideological* power with the other two types, we arrive at a classification that corresponds with the three-way division of social structures (economic, political, and ideological) that most theorists seem to advocate.

Thus, below the three means of power shown in Figure 6.1 are three attendant structures: the economic, the political, and the ideological.

Figure 6.1

The Major Means of Power, Structures of Domination, and Bases for Social Inequality

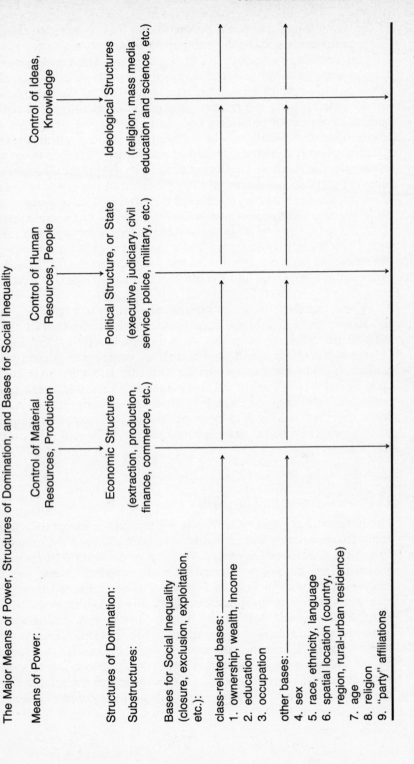

Means of Power:

Control of Material Resources, Production	Control of Human Resources, People	Control of Ideas, Knowledge

Structures of Domination:

Substructures:

Economic Structure	Political Structure, or State	Ideological Structures
(extraction, production, finance, commerce, etc.)	(executive, judiciary, civil service, police, military, etc.)	(religion, mass media education and science, etc.)

Bases for Social Inequality
(closure, exclusion, exploitation, etc.):

class-related bases:
1. ownership, wealth, income
2. education
3. occupation

other bases:
4. sex
5. race, ethnicity, language
6. spatial location (country, region, rural-urban residence)
7. age
8. religion
9. "party" affiliations

These social structures could be analyzed in many ways, but because of our specific interest in power and patterned relations of inequality, they are presented here as structures of *domination*. The connections in the diagram are oversimplified in that they imply a simple one-to-one linkage between each type of power and each structure. In fact, the downward arrows indicate only the *primary* linkage, since each form of power can operate in at least a secondary fashion in any of the structures. For example, control of people may be the principal activity within the political structure, but it is also evidenced in the control imposed by owners on workers in the economic structure. Similarly, the political structures that form the state do not derive all their power from the capacity to legislate or coerce human behavior, for they also control material resources through tax revenues, government ownership of some business enterprises, and so on. As for control of ideas or knowledge, this is most clearly identified with the ideological structures, but it is also a means for retaining power elsewhere, as illustrated by the access to special technical knowledge in the economic structure and the information-gathering powers within the state.

In this manner, then, the vertical dimension in Figure 6.1 signifies the structures (and internal substructures) of domination in the social systems that society comprises. At a more concrete level of discussion, these structures are manifested mainly as bureaucratic or corporate organizations. These organizations are patterned according to formal rules, laws, or rights of office but are also guided by a mix of informal practices, traditions, customs, or habits. It is these formal and informal rules that, taken together, largely determine the nature and extent of inequality in society, what the social bases for inequality will be and how much they will matter.

The Social Bases for Inequality

The horizontal dimension in Figure 6.1 provides a list of individual and group characteristics that typically have been used as the major bases for inequality in advanced societies. We have noted several times before the dualistic view of power fostered by various writers, most particularly Giddens. One way to look at Figure 6.1 is to think of the vertical dimension as the *structural* part of this duality and to treat the horizontal plane as the second part of the duality, the *human content* of power relations. Along this side of the diagram are the personal attributes and affiliations that inject the structures of domination with their social and human elements. It is the combination of these two aspects of power systems, in which people are processed and located within and across the structures, that in total forms the multifaceted system of inequality in society.

Class-Related Bases for Inequality

The personal traits and capacities that are listed can be divided into two main categories. First are three class-related factors: ownership (which also subsumes possession of wealth or income), education, and occupation. Ownership corresponds loosely with the various forms of property ownership that both Marxists and Weberians consider the key mode of economic control or closure in society. Education parallels the credentials basis for inequality that Parkin, Giddens, and others have stressed. Occupation is almost a residual category here, in that it subsumes such traits as skill level, manual versus nonmanual labor, and so on that are not captured in the other two class-related bases for inequality. These three factors operate within and across all the structures of domination shown in the vertical dimension. In conjunction, they push capitalist societies toward a class system that is highly complex, that varies in specific details from country to country, but that has at its core three major categories: an upper class composed mainly of the bourgeoisie, large-scale owners and controllers of material production, along with a smaller number of leaders from other spheres, who control political and ideological production and also tend to have sizeable personal fortunes or business holdings; a heterogeneous central category of people who may have limited powers of ownership, such as owners of small business, but who are distinguished primarily by their access to special education, training, recognized skills, or other credentials; and a lower or working class whose members are largely without property or special credentials and rely almost completely on labor power for their material existence.

Although this image of the class structure seems closest to that of Weber or Giddens, it is also broadly similar to that posed by neo-Marxists such as Wright. The one contentious issue is whether the central category represents a separate middle class all its own or a set of contradictory locations apart from the two main classes. In fact, the choice of terms here is, in a sense, less important than the simple truth that there is something else in addition to the capital-versus-wage-labor distinction that exists in reality and requires explanation or study. That both Marxists and non-Marxists now tend to agree on this third category, if not on how to label it, seems sufficient grounds for including it here.

Other Social Bases for Inequality

The second set of human attributes shown in the horizontal dimension of Figure 6.1 is a variable list of bases for inequality that are not inherent to class formation, although they are normally correlated with class inequalities in most cases. Whether and to what degree these bases for inequality actually operate will clearly differ from society to society. It should also be noted that this list is not necessarily exhaustive. There are other more subtle or less obvious human traits that may affect patterns of inequality, including physical beauty, for instance. On the whole, though, these social characteristics are the major factors operating within modern systems of structured inequality.

Most of these bases have been noted by several of the writers we have reviewed. Such attributes as sex, ethnicity (including also race and language grouping), religion, and age have been cited by Lenski, Parkin, and others. Spatial location, however, is not commonly seen as a basis for social inequality. Giddens appears to be the one writer among those we have considered who makes explicit reference to the ways in which geographic location can affect patterned relations of power or inequality. Giddens' key example is the exploitation of one nation-state or country by another. This form of inequality concerns the processes by which developed nations systematically keep underdeveloped nations in situations of subordination in the world economy (cf. Frank, 1969; Wallerstein, 1974). In addition, however, the inequalities that arise *within* countries can also be delineated, especially between people of different regions or between those who live in rural versus urban settings. These spatial bases for inequality are infrequently noted by sociologists but are implicit in the tradition of "core-periphery" or "metropolis-hinterland" studies in Canada and elsewhere (e.g., Innis, 1956; Creighton, 1956; Davis, 1971). The final basis for inequality listed in Figure 6.1 concerns access to or exclusion from the power that people experience through their party affiliations. Following Weber, this refers not just to formal political parties. It also serves as a residual term that subsumes all the other political groupings, broadly defined, that people become involved with in order to gain advantages, or redress disadvantages, relative to others: trade unions, professional associations, and pressure groups of various kinds.

It is all these elements in combination — the means of power, the structures of domination, and the individual or group bases we have outlined — that are the basic components in any summary overview of social inequality. Taken together, they form the framework for the creation and reproduction of inequality in modern societies.

With this brief sketch, our review of the major theoretical works in the field of social inequality is now complete. Of course, any such analysis is never really complete, since it is always subject to the revisions or elaborations that become necessary as new conceptual developments emerge and ultimately refine or replace existing ideas. For now, our most reasonable hope is that, in this analysis, the key insights of classical and contemporary theory have been made clear and that the broad brushstrokes of a general portrait of social inequality have been painted a little more boldly.

REFERENCES

Aberle, D.F., A.K. Cohen, A.K. Davis, M.J. Levy, Jr., and F.X. Sutton
    1950   "The functional prerequisites of society." Ethics 60 (January): 100-111.

Althusser, Louis
    1969   For Marx. New York: Pantheon.
    1976   Essays in Self-Criticism. London: New Left Books.

Althusser, Louis, and Etienne Balibar
    1970   Reading Capital. London: New Left Books.

Aron, Raymond
    1970   Main Currents in Sociological Thought, Vol. 2. Garden City: Anchor Books.

Avineri, Shlomo
    1968   The Social and Political Thought of Karl Marx. Cambridge: Cambridge University Press.

Balkwell, J.W., F.L. Bates, and A.P. Garbin
    1982   "Does the degree of consensus on occupational status evaluations differ by socioeconomic stratum? Response to Guppy." Social Forces 60 (June): 1183-1189.

Baran, Paul, and Paul Sweezy
    1966   Monopoly Capital. New York: Monthly Review Press.

Barber, Bernard
    1957   Social Stratification. New York: Harcourt, Brace and World.

Bell, Daniel
    1960   The End of Ideology. New York: The Free Press.

Bell, Wendell, and Robert V. Robinson
    1980   "Cognitive maps of class and racial inequalities in England and the United States." American Journal of Sociology 86 (September): 320-349.

Bendix, Reinhard
    1962   Max Weber: An Intellectual Portrait. Garden City: Anchor Books.

Benson, Leslie
    1978   Proletarians and Parties. London: Methuen.

Berlin, Isaiah
    1963   Karl Marx: His Life and Environment. Oxford: Oxford University Press.

Binns, David
    1977   Beyond the Sociology of Conflict. London: Macmillan.

Blau, Peter
    1964   Exchange and Power in Social Life. New York: Wiley.
    1977   Inequality and Heterogeneity. New York: The Free Press.
Blau, Peter, and Otis Dudley Duncan
    1967   The American Occupational Structure. New York: Wiley.
Blishen, Bernard
    1967   "A socioeconomic index for occupations in Canada."
            Canadian Review of Sociology and Anthropology 4:41-53.
Blishen, Bernard and Hugh McRoberts
    1976   "A revised socioeconomic index for occupations." Cana-
            dian Review of Sociology and Anthropology 13 (February):
            71-79.
Braverman, Harry
    1974   Labor and Monopoly Capital. New York: Monthly Review
            Press.
Carchedi, Guglielmo
    1977   On the Economic Identification of Social Classes. London:
            Routledge.
Coleman, Richard P., and Lee Rainwater
    1978   Social Standing in America: New Dimensions of Class.
            New York: Basic Books.
Collins, Randall
    1979   The Credential Society. New York: Academic Press.
    1982   Sociological Insight: An Introduction to Non-Obvious
            Sociology. New York: Oxford University Press.
Connell, R.W.
    1979   "A critique of the Althusserian approach to class." Theory
            and Society 8(3):321-345.
Coser, Lewis A.
    1977   Masters of Sociological Thought. New York: Harcourt,
            Brace, Jovanovich.
Coxon, A., and C. Jones
    1978   The Images of Occupational Prestige. London: Macmillan.
Creighton, Donald
    1956   The Commercial Empire of the St. Lawrence. Toronto:
            Macmillan.
Crompton, R., and J. Gubbay
    1977   Economy and Class Structure. London: Macmillan.
Curtis, James E., and William G. Scott (eds.)
    1979   Social Stratification: Canada (second edition). Scarbor-
            ough: Prentice-Hall of Canada.

Dahrendorf, Ralf
    1958   "Out of Utopia: toward a reorientation of sociological analysis." American Journal of Sociology 64 (September): 115-127.
    1959   Class and Class Conflict in Industrial Society. Stanford: Stanford University Press.
    1968   Essays in the Theory of Society. London: Routledge and Kegan Paul.
    1969   "On the origin of inequality among men." Pp. 16-44 in A. Beteille (ed.), Social Inequality. Middlesex: Penguin.
    1979   Life Chances. London: Weidenfeld and Nicolson.

Davis, A.K.
    1971   "Canadian society and history as hinterland versus metropolis." Pp. 6-32 in R.J. Ossenberg (ed.), Canadian Society: Pluralism, Change, and Conflict. Scarborough: Prentice-Hall of Canada.

Davis, Kingsley
    1949   Human Society. New York: Macmillan.
    1953   "Reply to Tumin." American Sociological Review 18 (August):394-397.
    1959   "The myth of functional analysis as a special method in sociology and anthropology." American Sociological Review 24 (December):757-772.

Davis, Kingsley, and Wilbert E.Moore
    1945   "Some principles of stratification." American Sociological Review 10 (April):242-249.

Della Fave, L. Richard
    1980   "The meek shall not inherit the earth: self-evaluation and the legitimacy of stratification." American Sociological Review 45 (December):955-971.

Demerath, N.J., and Richard A. Peterson (eds.)
    1967   System, Change, and Conflict. New York: The Free Press.

Durkheim, Emile
    1893   The Division of Labor in Society (first edition). New York:
    [1964]   The Free Press.
    1895   The Rules of Sociological Method. New York: The Free
    [1964]   Press.
    1896   Socialism and Saint-Simon. Yellow Springs, Ohio: Antioch
    [1958]   Press.
    1902   The Division of Labor in Society. Preface to the Second
    [1964]   Edition: Some Notes on Occupational Groups. New York: The Free Press.

Engels, Friedrich
    1872   "On authority." Pp. 730-733 in R.C. Tucker (ed.), The Marx-
    [1978]   Engels Reader (second edition). New York: Norton.
    1882   Letter from Engels to Bernstein. In Marx Engels Werke,
    [1967]   Vol. 35. Berlin: Dietz Verlag. Institut für Marxismus-
              Leninismus Beim ZK Der Sed.
    1890a   Letter from Engels to Conrad Schmidt. Pp. 488-495 in Marx
    [1967]   Engels Werke, Vol. 37. Berlin: Dietz Verlag. Institut für
              Marxismus-Leninismus Beim ZK Der Sed.
    1890b   Letter from Engels to J. Bloch. Pp. 462-465 in Marx Engels
    [1967]   Werke, Vol. 37. Berlin: Dietz Verlag. Institut für Marxis-
              mus-Leninismus Beim ZK Der Sed.
Fallding, Harold
    1968   The Sociological Task. Englewood Cliffs: Prentice-Hall.
    1972   "Only one sociology." British Journal of Sociology 23
              (March):93-101.
Frank, André Gunder
    1969   Capitalism and Underdevelopment in Latin America. New
              York: Monthly Review Press.
Gagliani, Giorgio
    1981   "How many working classes?" American Journal of So-
              ciology 87 (September):259-285.
Gerth, Hans, and C. Wright Mills (eds.)
    1967   From Max Weber: Essays in Sociology. Oxford: Oxford
              University Press.
Giddens, Anthony
    1971   Capitalism and Modern Social Theory. Cambridge: Cam-
              bridge University Press.
    1972   Politics and Sociology in the Thought of Max Weber. Lon-
              don: Macmillan.
    1973   The Class Structure of the Advanced Societies. London:
              Hutchinson and Company.
    1976   New Rules of Sociological Method. London: Hutchinson.
    1977   Studies in Social and Political Theory. London: Hutchin-
              son.
    1979   Central Problems in Social Theory. Berkeley: University
              of California Press.
    1980   "Classes, capitalism, and the state." Theory and Society
              9 (November):877-890.
    1981a   "Postscript (1979)." Pp. 295-320 in The Class Structure of
              the Advanced Societies (second edition). London: Hutch-
              inson.
    1981b   A Contemporary Critique of Historical Materialism, Vol.
              1: Power, Property, and the State. London: Macmillan.

Giddens, Anthony, and David Held (eds.)
1982   Classes, Power, and Conflict. Berkeley: University of California Press.

Goldthorpe, John H.
1972   "Class, status, and party in modern Britain." European Journal of Sociology 13:342-372.
1974   "Social inequality and social integration in modern Britain." Pp. 217-238 in D. Wedderburn (ed.), Poverty, Inequality, and Class Structure. London: Cambridge University Press.

Goldthorpe, John H., and Keith Hope
1974   The Social Grading of Occupations: A New Approach and Scale. Oxford: Clarendon Press.

Grabb, Edward G.
1982   "Social stratification." Pp. 121-157 in J.J. Teevan (ed.), Introduction to Sociology: A Canadian Focus. Scarborough: Prentice-Hall of Canada.

Grabb, Edward G., and Ronald D. Lambert
1982   "The subjective meanings of social class among Canadians." Canadian Journal of Sociology 7(3):297-307.

Guppy, L. Neil
1981   "Occupational prestige and conscience collective: the consensus debate reassessed." Unpublished doctoral dissertation, Sociology Department, University of Waterloo.
1982   "On intersubjectivity and collective conscience in occupational prestige research: a comment on Balkwell-Bates-Garbin and Kraus-Schild-Hodge." Social Forces 60 (June):1178-1182.

Habermas, Jürgen
1975   Legitimation Crisis. Boston: Beacon Press.

Hindess, B., and P.Q. Hirst
1975   Pre-Capitalist Modes of Production. London: Routledge.
1977   Modes of Production and Social Formation. London: Macmillan.

Hodge, Robert W., V. Kraus, and E.O. Schild
1982   "Consensus in occupational prestige research: response to Guppy." Social Forces 60 (June):1190-1196.

Hodge, Robert W., Paul M. Siegel, and Peter H. Rossi
1964   "Occupational prestige in the United States: 1925-1963." American Journal of Sociology 70 (November):286-302.

Hodge, Robert W., Donald J. Treiman, and Peter H. Rossi
1966   "A comparative study of occupational prestige." Pp. 309-321 in R. Bendix and S.M. Lipset (eds.), Class, Status, and Power (second edition). New York: The Free Press.

Hunter, Alfred A.
    1981   Class Tells: On Social Inequality in Canada. Toronto: But-
            terworths.
Inkeles, Alex, and Peter Rossi
    1956   "National comparison of occupational prestige." Ameri-
            can Journal of Sociology 61 (January):329-339.
Innis, Harold A.
    1956   The Fur Trade in Canada. Toronto: University of Toronto
            Press.
Jasso, G., and P.H. Rossi
    1977   "Distributive justice and earned income." American So-
            ciological Review 42 (August):639-651.
Jeffries, Vincent, and H. Edward Ransford
    1980   Social Stratification: A Multiple Hierarchy Approach. Bos-
            ton: Allyn and Bacon.
Johnson, Harry M.
    1960   Sociology: A Systematic Introduction. New York: Har-
            court, Brace and World.
Johnson, Leo
    1979   "Income disparity and the structure of earnings in Canada,
            1946-74." Pp. 141-157 in J.E. Curtis and W.G. Scott (eds.),
            Social Stratification: Canada (second edition). Scarbor-
            ough: Prentice-Hall of Canada.
Kallen, Horace M.
    1931   "Functionalism." Pp. 523-526 in E. Seligman (ed.), Ency-
            clopedia of the Social Sciences, Vol. 6. New York: Mac-
            millan and the Free Press.
Kolko, Gabriel
    1962   Wealth and Power in America. New York: Praeger.
Lane, David
    1982   The End of Social Inequality? Class, Status, and Power
            under State Socialism. Winchester, Mass.: Allen and Unwin.
Lenin, V.I.
    1917   The State and Revolution. In Selected Works. London:
    [1969] Lawrence and Wishart.
Lenski, Gerhard E.
    1966   Power and Privilege: A Theory of Social Stratification. New
            York: McGraw-Hill.
Lévi-Strauss, Claude
    1968   Structural Anthropology. London: Allen Lane.
Levy, Marion J., Jr.
    1968   "Structural-functional analysis." Pp. 21-29 in D.L. Sills (ed.),
            International Encyclopedia of the Social Sciences, Vol. 6.
            New York: Macmillan and The Free Press.

Lipset, S.M., and Reinhard Bendix
    1963   Social Mobility in Industrial Society. Berkeley: University of California Press.

Lockwood, David
    1956   "Some remarks on 'The Social System.' " British Journal of Sociology 7 (June):134-146.

Lukes, S.M.
    1974   Power: A Radical View. London: Macmillan.
    1978   "Power and authority." Pp. 633-676 in T. Bottomore and R. Nisbet (eds.), A History of Sociological Analysis. New York: Basic Books.

Malinowski, Bronislaw
    1926   Crime and Custom in Savage Society. London: Routledge.
    1929   The Sexual Life of Savages in Northwest Melanesia. London: Routledge.

Marcuse, Herbert
    1971   "Industrialization and capitalism." Pp. 133-151 in O. Stammer (ed.), Max Weber and Sociology Today. New York: Harper and Row.

Marx, Karl
    1843   Contribution to the Critique of Hegel's Philosophy of Law.
    [1975]   In Marx Engels Collected Works, Vol. 3. New York: International Publishers.
    1844   Economic and Philosophic Manuscripts of 1844. In Marx
    [1975]   Engels Collected Works, Vol. 3. New York: International Publishers.
    1847   The Poverty of Philosophy. In Marx Engels Collected Works,
    [1976]   Vol. 6. New York: International Publishers.
    1858   Grundrisse. Foundations of the Critique of Political Econ-
    [1973]   omy. Harmondsworth: Penguin.
    1859   A Contribution to the Critique of Political Economy. Excerpt
    [1970]   in H. Selsam, D. Goldway, and H. Martel, (eds.), Dynamics of Social Change. New York: International Publishers.
    1862   Theories of Surplus Value, Vol. 2. Moscow: Progress Pub-
    [1968]   lishers.
    1867   Capital, Vol. 1. New York: International Publishers.
    [1967]
    1875   Critique of the Gotha Program. New York: International
    [1938]   Publishers.
    1894   Capital, Vol. 3. New York: International Publishers.
    [1967]

Marx, Karl, and Friedrich Engels
    1846   The German Ideology. In Marx Engels Collected Works,
    [1976]   Vol. 5. New York: International Publishers.

1848   The Communist Manifesto. New York: Washington Square
[1970]   Press.

McLellan, David
1971   The Thought of Karl Marx. New York: Harper and Row.
1973   Karl Marx: His Life and Thought. London: Macmillan.

Michels, Robert
1915   Political Parties. A Sociological Study of the Oligarchical
[1962]   Tendencies of Modern Democracy. New York: The Free
          Press.

Miliband, Ralph
1969   The State in Capitalist Society. London: Weidenfeld and
          Nicolson.

Mills, C. Wright
1951   White Collar. New York: Oxford University Press.
1956   The Power Elite. New York: Oxford University Press.
1959   The Sociological Imagination. New York: Oxford Univer-
          sity Press.

Münch, Richard
1982   "Talcott Parsons and the theory of action. II. The conti-
          nuity of the development." American Journal of Sociology
          87 (January):771-826.

Nisbet, Robert A.
1959   "The decline and fall of social class." Pacific Sociological
          Review 2 (Spring):11-17.

North, Cecil C., and Paul K. Hatt
1947   "Jobs and occupations: a popular evaluation." Opinion News
          (September).

Nosanchuk, T.A.
1972   "A note on the use of the correlation coefficient for as-
          sessing the similarity of occupational rankings." Canadian
          Review of Sociology and Anthropology 9 (November):357-
          365.

Offe, Claus
1974   "Structural problems of the capitalist state." German Po-
          litical Studies 1.

Offe, Claus, and Volker Ronge
1975   "Theses on the theory of the state." New German Critique
          6:139-147.

Parkin, Frank
1972   Class Inequality and Political Order. London: Paladin.
1978   "Social stratification." Pp. 599-632 in T. Bottomore and
          R. Nisbet (eds.), A History of Sociological Analysis. New
          York: Basic Books.

1979   Marxism and Class Theory: A Bourgeois Critique. London: Tavistock.

1980   "Reply to Giddens." Theory and Society 9 (November):891-894.

Parsons, Talcott

1937   The Structure of Social Action, Vol. 1. New York: The Free Press.

1940   "An analytical approach to the theory of social stratifi-
[1964]   cation." Pp. 69-88 in T. Parsons, Essays in Sociological Theory. New York: The Free Press.

1947   Max Weber: The Theory of Social and Economic Organization. New York: The Free Press.

1951   The Social System. New York: The Free Press.

1953   "A revised analytical approach to the theory of social strat-
[1964]   ification." Pp. 386-439 in T. Parsons, Essays in Sociological Theory. New York: The Free Press.

1966   "On the concept of political power." Pp. 240-265 in R. Bendix and S.M. Lipset (eds.), Class, Status, and Power (second edition). New York: The Free Press.

Pineo, Peter, John Porter, and Hugh McRoberts

1977   "The 1971 census and the socioeconomic classification of occupations." Canadian Review of Sociology and Anthropology 14 (February):91-102.

Poulantzas, Nicos

1973a   Political Power and Social Classes. London: New Left Books.

1973b   "On social classes." New Left Review 78:27-54.

1975   Classes in Contemporary Capitalism. London: New Left Books.

1978   State, Power, Socialism. London: New Left Books.

Radcliffe-Brown, A.R.

1922   The Andaman Islanders. Cambridge: Cambridge University Press.

1935   "On the concept of function in social science." American Anthropologist 37 (July-September):395-402.

1948   A Natural Science of Society. New York: The Free Press.

1952   Structure and Function in Primitive Society: Essays and Addresses. London: Cohen and West.

Riesman, David, N. Glazer, and R. Denney

1953   The Lonely Crowd. New York: Doubleday.

Robinson, Robert V., and Wendell Bell

1978   "Equality, success, and social justice in England and the United States." American Sociological Review 43 (April):125-143.

Runciman, W.G. (ed.)
    1978   Max Weber: Selections in Translation. Cambridge: Cambridge University Press.

Salomon, Albert
    1945   "German sociology." In Georges Gurvitch and Wilbert E. Moore (eds.), Twentieth Century Sociology. New York: Philosophical Library.

Schacht, Richard
    1970   Alienation. Garden City: Doubleday.

Selsam, Howard, David Goldway, and Harry Martel (eds.)
    1970   Dynamics of Social Change. New York: International Publishers.

Shils, Edward, and Henry Finch (eds.)
    1949   The Methodology of the Social Sciences. Max Weber. New York: The Free Press.

Singer, Peter
    1980   Marx. Oxford: Oxford University Press.

Sorokin, Pitirim A.
    1927   Social Mobility. New York: Harper and Row.
    1947   Society, Culture, and Personality. New York: Harper and Row.

Stehr, Nico
    1974   "Consensus and dissensus in occupational prestige." British Journal of Sociology 25 (December):410-427.

Stolzman, James, and Herbert Gamberg
    1974   "Marxist class analysis versus stratification analysis as general approaches to social inequality." Berkeley Journal of Sociology 18:105-125.

Treiman, Donald J.
    1977   Occupational Prestige in Comparative Perspective. New York: Academic Press.

Tumin, Melvin M.
    1953   "Some principles of stratification: a critical analysis." American Sociological Review 18 (August):387-393.

Wallerstein, Immanuel
    1974   The Modern World-System. New York: Academic Press.

Weber, Max
    1905   The Protestant Ethic and the Spirit of Capitalism. New
    [1958]   York: Charles Scribner's Sons.
    1922   Economy and Society, Vol. 1-3. New York: Bedminster
    [1968]   Press.

Weiss, Donald D.
    1976   "Marx versus Smith on the division of labor." Pp. 104-118 in Technology, the Labor Process, and the Working Class. New York: Monthly Review Press.

Wesolowski, W.
    1966   "Some notes on the functional theory of stratification." Pp. 64-69 in R. Bendix and S.M. Lipset (eds.), Class, Status, and Power (second edition). New York: The Free Press.

Williams, Robin M., Jr.
    1960   American Society. A Sociological Interpretation. New York: Knopf.

Wright, Erik Olin
    1978   Class, Crisis, and the State. London: New Left Books.
    1979   Class Structure and Income Determination. New York: Academic Press.
    1980   "Class and occupation." Theory and Society 9 (January):177-214.

Wright, Erik Olin, C. Costello, D. Hachen, and J. Sprague
    1982   "The American class structure." American Sociological Review 47 (December):709-726.

Wright, Erik Olin, and Luca Perrone
    1977   "Marxist class categories and income inequality." American Sociological Review 42 (February):32-55.

Wright, Erik Olin, and Joachim Singelmann
    1982   "Proletarianization in the changing American class structure." American Journal of Sociology 88 (Supplement):S176-S209.

Wrong, Dennis
    1959   "The functional theory of stratification: some neglected considerations." American Sociological Review 24 (December):772-782.
    1961   "The over-socialized conception of man in modern sociology." American Sociological Review 26 (April):183-193.
    1979   Power: Its Forms, Bases and Uses. New York: Harper and Row.

Yanowitch, Murray
    1977   Social and Economic Inequality in the Soviet Union. London: Martin Robertson.

Zeitlin, Irving M.
    1968   Ideology and the Development of Sociological Theory. Englewood Cliffs: Prentice-Hall.

INDEX